D1548316

THE GOD RELATIONSHIP

In this book, Paul K. Moser proposes a new approach to inquiry about God, including a new discipline of the ethics for inquiry about God. It is an ethics for human attitudes and relationships as well as actions in inquiry, and it includes human responsibility for seeking evidence that involves a moral priority for humans. Such ethics includes an ongoing test, a trial, for human receptivity to goodness, including morally good relationships, as a priority in human inquiry and life. Moser also defends an approach to the evidence for God that makes sense of the elusiveness and occasional absence of God in human experience. His book will be of interest to those interested in inquiry about God, with special relevance to scholars and advanced students in religious studies, philosophy, theology, and Biblical studies.

Paul K. Moser is Professor of Philosophy at Loyola University Chicago. He is the author of *The Elusive God* (winner of a national book award from the Jesuit Honor Society); *The Evidence for God; The Severity of God; Knowledge and Evidence* (all Cambridge University Press), and *Philosophy after Objectivity*, co-author of *Theory of Knowledge*, editor of *Jesus and Philosophy* (Cambridge University Press) and *The Oxford Handbook of Epistemology* (Oxford University Press); co-editor of *The Cambridge Companion to the Problem of Evil*, and *The Wisdom of the Christian Faith* (both from Cambridge University Press). He is the co-editor of the book series, *Cambridge Studies in Religion, Philosophy, and Society.*

The God Relationship

The Ethics for Inquiry about the Divine

PAUL K. MOSER
Loyola University Chicago

CAMBRIDGE
UNIVERSITY PRESS

CAMBRIDGE
UNIVERSITY PRESS

University Printing House, Cambridge CB2 8BS, United Kingdom

One Liberty Plaza, 20th Floor, New York, NY 10006, USA

477 Williamstown Road, Port Melbourne, VIC 3207, Australia

314-321, 3rd Floor, Plot 3, Splendor Forum, Jasola District Centre, New Delhi - 110025, India

79 Anson Road, #06-04/06, Singapore 079906

Cambridge University Press is part of the University of Cambridge.

It furthers the University's mission by disseminating knowledge in the pursuit of education, learning and research at the highest international levels of excellence.

www.cambridge.org
Information on this title: www.cambridge.org/9781316646809
DOI: 10.1017/9781108164009

First published 2017

A catalogue record for this publication is available from the British Library

Library of Congress Cataloging in Publication data
Names: Moser, Paul K., 1957– author.
Title: The God relationship: the ethics for inquiry about the divine /
Paul Moser, Loyola University in Chicago.
Description: New York: Cambridge University Press, 2017. |
Includes bibliographical references and index.
Identifiers: LCCN 2017002773 | ISBN 9781107195349 (hardback: alk. paper)
Subjects: LCSH: Spirituality – Christianity. | God (Christianity) |
Philosophical theology.
Classification: LCC BV4501.3.M6748 2017 | DDC 212/.6–dc23
LC record available at https://lccn.loc.gov/2017002773

ISBN 978-1-107-19534-9 Hardback
ISBN 978-1-316-64680-9 Paperback

The God relationship of the individual human being is the main point.
– Søren Kierkegaard as Johannes Climacus (1846)

Contents

Preface   *page* ix

1. The God Relationship: Basics and Plans   1

    1. Modes of Inquiry   3
    2. Empowerment and Ethics in Inquiry   15
    3. Caring and *Agapē* in Inquiry   21
    4. Trial for Compassion   27
    5. Curative Relationships and Knowledge   33
    6. Probing and Defending   40
    7. Plans   47

2. The God Relationship and Faith   56

    1. Aspects of Overwhelming   57
    2. From Creation-Enhancing to Overwhelming   62
    3. From Overwhelming to Faith and *Agapē*   68
    4. Gethsemane, Dereliction, and Inquiry   85
    5. Sympathetic Faith   92
    6. Fragility for Faith   105
    7. Conclusion   113

3. The God Relationship and Evidence   116

    1. Whose Existence?   117
    2. Argumentism about God   120
    3. A Self-Authenticating God   129
    4. Whither Arguments?   137
    5. Intellectualist Underpinnings and Shortcomings   145
    6. Motives for Intellectualism   156
    7. Divine Self-Hiding and Sacrifice   161

      8. Self-Sacrifice in Evidence for God   176
      9. Whither Hiddenness?   185
      10. Conclusion   190

4. The God Relationship, Wisdom, and Meaning   193
      1. Wisdom: Evaluative, Practical, and Philosophical   195
      2. God's Wisdom and Revelation   200
      3. Participation and Speculation   215
      4. Meaning, Purpose, and Will   230
      5. Experiencing God's Will   239
      6. Faith and Felt Meaning   244
      7. Meaning in Death   250
      8. Conclusion   254

5. The God Relationship, *Koinonia*, and Defense   256
      1. Virtues and Volitions   256
      2. Redemptive *Koinonia*   260
      3. *Koinonia* in Divine *Agapē*   265
      4. Obstacles and Responses   274
      5. Some Biblical Data on Witness   284
      6. Divine Witness to Filial *Agapē*   289
      7. Abiding in *Agapē*   301
      8. I–Thou Defense of Faith in God   308
      9. Conclusion   330

References   332
Index   339

Preface

Many religious people talk about their *relationship* with God, but few people have explored the consequences of such talk for human inquiry about God. (Søren Kierkegaard is a rare and an important exception.) This book explores those consequences by introducing and developing a topic almost universally neglected by inquirers about God: *the ethics for inquiry* about God for humans. It combines this topic with an equally neglected position: the view that humans can choose either to empower or to block God with regard to the option of God's self-manifesting in their salient, or definite, evidence. This human capability would arise not from a divine inadequacy, but from God's valuing what is good in a human relationship with God, including one's freedom either to approve or to disapprove of having salient evidence of God in one's experience. Humans thus would be in a position to give God approval to intervene in their salient evidence, even if some ambiguous or indefinite evidence of God can come to them without their approval.

A perfectly good God would not stalk humans coercively with salient divine evidence, but would seek to have humans, in self-avowed need, *freely make themselves* available and receptive to any salient evidence of God. In addition, this God would not want to be trivialized by becoming just an object of experience, feeling, or thought for humans. Instead, this God would seek a good *cooperative relationship* with humans, rather than just humans having experiences, thoughts, feelings, or actions regarding God. The corresponding salient evidence of God's reality would follow suit, as would faith, knowledge, wisdom, and meaning stemming from God. That is, they would be suitably appropriated by humans in, and only in, a cooperative relationship with God. Without such an interpersonal relationship, various goods easily become prideful idols for a person, complete with harmful self-righteousness.

The role of a cooperative relationship is important, because it does not require one to have a *constant* experience, feeling, or thought of God for well-founded commitment to God. However elusive or subtle, experience of God is crucial, but it need not be constant or available on demand. In focusing on experiences, thoughts, feelings, and actions regarding God, philosophers and theologians have neglected the importance of a cooperative relationship with God, to the detriment of a case for theism. This book corrects for this neglect in connection with the following topics: basics of the God relationship (Chapter 1), faith's trial with God (Chapter 2), seeking hidden evidence of God (Chapter 3), wisdom and meaning from God for human life (Chapter 4), *koinonia* and defending faith in God (Chapter 5).

Inquiry is an active, intentional pursuit, and the ethics for inquiry about God is an ethics for responsibly pursuing what would be true, well-grounded, and morally good in a divine–human relationship. Such ethics requires inquirers actively to pursue evidence for God's reality and to be open to assessment by a standard of intending (or not intending) to care morally as God cares, including for others in inquiry. Inquirers' intending (or not intending) in this regard would make them available (or unavailable) for uncoerced personal transformation toward the moral character of the God who would value freedom in human commitment to God. Such intending would make them personally available to God's own moral domain. As perfectly good, God would not relinquish the moral domain for something less good, just as God would not relinquish truth in inquiry.

The relevant ethics for inquiry about God has *standards* for putting oneself in a responsible position to receive what is good as a priority in inquiry. It does not entail, however, one's earning or meriting what is good. It is an ethics for human attitudes and relationships as well as actions in inquiry, and it includes human responsibility for seeking evidence that involves a moral priority for humans. It will be ethics in relation to a perfectly good moral character, if it is actually directed toward a God worthy of worship. Such ethics will include an ongoing test, a trial, for human receptivity to goodness, including morally good relationships, as a priority in human inquiry and life. The trial can take humans to their own limits for being good, thus indicating a need for outside help in the trial. Bearing on inquiry in general regarding God, the ethics in question, we shall see, exceeds what some philosophers call "the ethics of belief."

The book does not simply assume that the claim that God exists is true or even justified. It thus speaks at times of what God *would be* or *would do* (if God exists). It identifies what expectations of God we should have *if* the claim that God exists is true or justified. Each person, however, will need to discern if the expectations in question are satisfied in his or her own experience. This is part of the irreducibly existential, person-oriented nature of faith in God. The outstanding question is whether we humans are willing to engage in the existential challenge on offer, at the cost of who we are, how we live, and how we relate to others, including our enemies. A key issue is whether we are willing to empower, rather than to obstruct, God in the option of God's self-manifesting in our experience. The book explores the importance of this issue, and asks whether a distinctive kind of personal transformation, including a reordering of one's priorities, in cooperative relationship with God is a clue to the veracity of the story on offer.

I thank the following people for helpful discussions or written comments on my work: Scott Aikin, Dave Bukenhofer, Tom Carson, Blake Dutton, Kristen Irwin, Linda Moser, Ben Nasmith, Clinton Neptune, Randy Newman, Greg Wolcott, Tom Wren, Matthew Yaw, students in my graduate philosophy seminars at Loyola University Chicago, and anonymous referees for Cambridge University Press and for various journals. For help at Cambridge University Press, I thank Beatrice Rehl for her excellent work as Senior Editor and Mary Bongiovi for her fine work as Content Manager. I also thank Gail Welsh at Out of House Publishing for her effective work as Project Manager and Dr. Lawrence Osborn at Osborn Editorial Services for his careful copy-editing.

Some parts of the book make use of revised materials from some of my previous essays: "God and Evidence," *European Journal for the Philosophy of Religion* 5 (2013), 91–105; "God without Argument," in *Is Faith in God Reasonable?*, eds. Corey Miller and Paul Gould (Routledge, 2014), pp. 69–83; "The Virtue of Friendship with God," in *Religious Faith and Intellectual Virtue*, eds. Timothy O'Connor and Laura Callahan (Oxford University Press, 2014), pp. 140–155; "Divine Hiddenness and Self-Sacrifice," in *Hidden Divinity and Religious Belief*, eds. Eleonore Stump and Adam Green (Cambridge University Press, 2016), pp. 71–88; "Affective Gethsemane Meaning for Life," in *God and Meaning*, eds. Stewart Goetz and Joshua Seachris (Bloomsbury, 2016), pp. 167–84; "The Conformation Model," in *Four Views on Christianity and Philosophy*, eds. Paul Gould and Richard Davis (Harper, 2016), pp. 175–200; "Inner Witness of the Spirit," in the *Oxford Handbook of the Epistemology of Theology*, eds. William Abraham and Fred Aquino (Oxford University Press, 2017).

P.K.M. Chicago, Illinois

∾

The God Relationship: Basics and Plans

We humans ask questions, if we do anything. Our questions seem to know no bounds, ranging from the trivial to the familiar to the profound. Some of our questions arise self-consciously, and others persist subconsciously, at times with some torment for us. In either case, however, we humans engage in inquiry, even when answers are elusive or unavailable. Our questions can reveal our true priorities, regardless of whether we are aware of our motives for inquiry. Our motives are, in part, reality-seeking and thus truth-seeking, or at least answer-seeking, because answers can serve various theoretical and practical purposes for us. An answer to a biological question, for instance, can bring us important truth about biological reality, and an answer to a scheduling question can enhance the realization of our meeting plans.

We shall see that some long-standing questions about God take on new significance when we attend to what is *fitting* for our inquiry about God, relative to what would be God's unique *moral* character and purposes for humans. The book thus introduces and develops the *ethics for* inquiry about God, and identifies the results for some long-standing questions about God. Such ethics will not be ethics as usual if it is ethics for inquiry about a being who has a morally perfect character. In that case, it will need to be suitably attentive to the unique moral character under inquiry, and it will have significant implications for the intentions and conduct of the people undertaking the inquiry.

The relevant ethics for inquiry will be an ethics for actively pursuing what would be not only true or justified but also good in inquiry about God. It will be an ethics for *responsible* inquiry regarding God's reality and goodness, and the responsibility will be defined by the nature of what the inquiry concerns, that is, the nature of the subject-matter of the inquiry. It would be question-begging now to define "responsibility" in terms of responsiveness *to God* (as, for instance, in H. Richard Niebuhr 1963), because a key part of the inquiry is *whether* God exists. I aim to avoid begging key questions against agnostics about God, because that practice would gain nothing now.

We may think of responsible inquiry about God as one's *doing the best one can* in the process and not just the result (such as a true object) of the inquiry, in a manner respectful of its subject-matter. So, an inquirer about God would not be responsible in introducing requirements that exclude God's existence at the start (assuming that the relevant notion of God is internally coherent). Introducing such requirements would make for defective, irresponsible inquiry, when one could do better. For instance, we should not exclude at the start the prospect that God is inherently redemptive toward interpersonal relationships with humans. So, responsible inquiry should allow that God seeks, above all, interpersonal relationships of sympathetic cooperation from humans, and supports faith, evidence, knowledge, wisdom, and meaning regarding God in the context of such cooperative relationships.

The ethics for inquiry about God will bear on whether an inquirer has put himself or herself in a responsible position to receive salient evidence, and perhaps other benefits, from the morally perfect God in question. (Chapter 2 offers some ethical principles for inquiry about God.) We may proceed with the following meaning of "salient" from the *Oxford English Dictionary*, second edition: "standing out or prominent in consciousness." One's salient evidence, then, is definite in a way that avoids the kind of ambiguity or vagueness requiring one to withhold judgment about what the evidence indicates. A key goal of responsible inquiry about God is to test for such evidence in a manner that amounts to one's best effort. So, the position of the inquirer, including the inquirer's intentions and actions, can be directly relevant, because that position can bear on one's receptivity (or the lack thereof) to pertinent evidence of divine reality. For instance, whether one receives salient evidence of God's self-manifested reality could depend on whether God makes that evidence salient to one, and whether God makes it salient to one could depend on what one intends to value (or not value) regarding God's reality and perfect goodness.

The book's main questions include: Is God real? If so, *which* God? Would God, if perfectly good, seek an ongoing *personal relationship* with a human, and not just discrete experiences, thoughts, feelings, or actions in a human? If so, what would that relationship include, and what would be its benefits for a human? In addition, if God does seek an ongoing personal relationship, what would the corresponding salient evidence of God's reality look like, and how could a human appropriate it? Why, in any case, is God's reality obscure at best to many people? Is there any way to remove this obscurity, or at least to accommodate it given the problem of evil facing God's existence and goodness? How *should* one inquire about God, in keeping with God's perfectly good moral character, if one aims to have true and justified belief regarding God's reality and goodness? Does the relevant inquiry about God, furthermore, bear on the value or purpose of human life? An ethics for inquiry about God will emerge from our investigation, despite the widespread neglect of such ethics by inquirers.

1. MODES OF INQUIRY

We use different *modes of inquiry* in our quest to find answers to our questions, if unknowingly at times. A mode of inquiry is, put broadly, a way of seeking a correct or a justified answer to a question. Such a mode can be – to name just three options – mathematical, scientific, or interpersonal. A mode of inquiry needs to be suited to identifying the kind of content or subject-matter involved in a question. Otherwise, it will be a questionable, if not irresponsible, way of approaching the question. For instance, we cannot rely solely on mathematical derivation to answer scientific questions in organic or inorganic chemistry. As a result, mathematics does not supersede inquiry in organic or inorganic chemistry, even when it accompanies and organizes such chemistry.

A mathematics teacher might raise a question about the relation between the lengths of the sides of a right triangle by using part of the Pythagorean equation: $a^2 + b^2 = ?$ ("a" and "b" representing the sides other than the hypotenuse). A mode of inquiry in this case could be *purely mathematical*, consisting only of thinking about and organizing the (conceptual and propositional) mathematical content needed to derive the Pythagorean Theorem, in equation form: $a^2 + b^2 = c^2$. In that case, the mode of inquiry would be non-empirical, or *a priori*. This mathematical mode of inquiry would not require one to be engaged beyond one's handling relevant mathematical content, and this makes the mode purely mathematical, even if one draws logical inferences in one's mathematical thinking. (I thus use "mathematical" broadly to allow for the inclusion of logical inferences.)

A mode of inquiry can entertain sensory content, such as qualitative content from perception. In that case, the mode of inquiry would be empirical, at least in part, and not purely *a priori*. For instance, a chemistry teacher might raise a question about the (degree of) solubility of sodium chloride in water. In that case, a typical mode of inquiry would mix sodium chloride with water under conditions of stirring, and then measure the result as a ratio of dissolved sodium to added water. This would be an *empirical* mode of inquiry that attends to sensory content in the inquirer's perceptual experience. It also would be *scientific* in virtue of following an experimental procedure characteristic of one of the natural sciences, in this case, chemistry. (This point does not depend on a controversial claim that all science is experimental; it allows that parts of astrophysics and cosmology, for instance, may not be. We also should allow that an empirical mode of inquiry need not be strictly scientific.) The relevant procedure in chemistry would attend to sensory content and corresponding content-relations, but it would not attend at all to a personal agent (as a personal agent) in its content or subject-matter. This is typical of a scientific mode of inquiry in the natural sciences.

In contrast with a purely mathematical or scientific mode, an *interpersonal* mode of inquiry requires interaction with a personal agent, an agent with a *will* and its corresponding *intentions*. Neither the objects of mathematics nor the objects of chemistry require interpersonal interaction in inquiry. They do not include a personal will or its intentions represented in their content or subject-matter. So, they do not provide in their content an opportunity for volitional cooperation with their objects in human inquiry.

Someone, in search of a correct answer, might ask me: Are you my companion? In response, I would do well not to turn to mathematics or chemistry to find a correct answer. Instead, I would need to attend to interpersonal interaction whereby I come (or came) to *know the person* asking the question. I may need to discern how that person aims to live her life, and then to relate this finding to how I intend to live my life. An important question for me would be whether our life-plans allow for something needed for companionship: *interpersonal cooperation*. Neither mathematics nor chemistry would settle that question for me. I would need to inquire via interpersonal interaction and attention to an opportunity for interpersonal cooperation.

For the sake of acquiring true belief and justified belief, inquiry about God should begin with an acknowledgment of the variability in modes of inquiry. It thereby will avoid any misleading assumption that reduces all inquiry to a mathematical mode or a scientific mode, for instance. Otherwise, we will risk obstructing our acquiring relevant evidence in our inquiry. If God is a personal agent with definite purposes in supplying evidence of divine reality to humans, these purposes will bear on the fittingness of a mode of inquiry about God's reality. We should consider that God, if real, would be perfectly good, by a moral standard, and thus would seek what is best (all things considered) for humans. In that case, we may suppose that God would not settle for isolated or episodic human experiences, thoughts, feelings, or actions regarding God. Instead, God would seek an enduring personal relationship with humans for their benefit; otherwise, God would be morally deficient in neglecting something good in interpersonal matters. We may call this *the God relationship* with humans and ask how it would bear on our inquiry about God.

The God relationship would be an enduring dispositional state irreducible to discrete experiences, thoughts, feelings, or actions. So, a person could be in such a state while asleep, without any acting or thinking. For instance, one could be in a relationship of faith in God while not thinking of God at all, even if a discrete episode of trust launched one's state of faith in God. The God relationship does require a kind of commitment, as we shall see, but the commitment does not require constant experience, thought, or feeling regarding God. This is important because it allows for reasonable, well-founded commitment to God in the absence of a present experience, thought, or feeling regarding God. So, one's not having a present experience, thought, or feeling regarding God will not undermine a well-founded God relationship.

A key question concerns what the God relationship (if real) would include. If God would be perfectly good, in being worthy of worship, then God would be perfectly loving toward all other agents, including God's enemies.

God's being thus loving would require that God seek what is best (all things considered) for all people. This would require that God seek what enables humans to flourish together in community, given that humans depend on each other for many vital benefits. The kind of love in question would be unselfish, other-regarding, and good-seeking, and thus may be called *agapē*, in keeping with a New Testament Greek term for "love." It requires caring without moral deficiency for (the overall good of) others, in contrast with selfishness toward other people.

The divine goal would be to have mutual *agapē* relationships between God and every human and between all humans who interact, for the benefit of all concerned. Let's call such *agapē*-centered relationships *koinonia* relationships. The ancient Greek term *koinonia* connotes such morally significant interpersonal features as the following: cooperation, amity, harmony, peace, fellowship, sincere communication, kindness, mercy, empathy, and sympathy as compassion, in a good relationship. We thus will use this term to capture the heart of an *agapē* relationship. The ethics of inquiry about God would offer a human the prospect of an ethical struggle for *koinonia* with God's perfectly good moral character.

The divine goal, if God exists, would be for humans to imitate God's moral character in personal *koinonia* relationships. In Latin, this goal is known as *imitatio Dei*, and it emerges recurringly in Jewish and Christian monotheism. (Islam typically avoids talk of the *imitatio Dei*, to avoid undue human affinity to God, but it endorses human guidance by God's moral character, particularly by divine mercy.) The Jewish Bible includes the following command: "Speak to all the congregation of the people of Israel and say to them: You shall be holy, for I the Lord your God am holy" (Lev. 19:2; I use the NRSV here and in subsequent biblical translations, unless otherwise noted). Similarly: "I am the Lord who brought you up from the land of Egypt, to be your God; you shall be holy, for I am holy" (Lev. 11:45;

cf. Lev. 20:26). The holiness thus commanded includes at least moral righteousness, in contrast to the immoral practices, such as the sacrificing of children, found in some surrounding cultures. (I use biblical passages when they offer explanatory benefits, without assuming the infallibility, inerrancy, or authority of the Bible as a whole.)

The New Testament ascribes to Jesus a command to imitate God's moral character. In Luke's Gospel, Jesus teaches: "Love your enemies, do good, and lend, expecting nothing in return. Your reward will be great, and you will be children of the Most High; for he is kind to the ungrateful and the wicked. Be merciful, just as your Father is merciful" (Luke 6:35–36). Similarly, in Matthew's Gospel, Jesus announces: "I say to you, Love your enemies and pray for those who persecute you, so that you may be children of your Father in heaven; for he makes his sun rise on the evil and on the good, and sends rain on the righteous and on the unrighteous. . . . Be perfect, therefore, as your heavenly Father is perfect" (Matt. 5:44–45, 48; cf. Eph. 5:1, 1 Pet. 1:15–16, 1 John 4:11). The central idea here concerns *moral* perfection or completeness, given the emphasis on the love of one's enemies. God sets the moral standard, and humans are to follow suit, in direct imitation of God's moral character, particularly divine *agapē*.

Søren Kierkegaard speaks of the *imitatio Dei* in connection with the New Testament love commandment as "*the Christian like for like, eternity's like for like*" (1847, p. 376). This "like for like" is an important part of what he calls "the God relationship." He highlights that relationship through his pseudonym, Johannes Climacus: "The God relationship of the individual human being is the main point" (1846, p. 77). He also sets a standard for this relationship to be I–Thou in orientation, involving God in the second person relative to a human. He states: "God can never become a third party when he is a part of the religious; this is precisely the secret of the religious" (1846, p. 66). In becoming a "third party," God would be omitted from standing in an

I–Thou relationship with humans and thus would stand outside a directly interpersonal relationship.

Kierkegaard has in mind a relationship that can be morally and psychologically demanding. He remarks: "Worship is the maximum for a human being's relationship with God, and thereby for his likeness to God" (1846, p. 413). In Kierkegaard's perspective, God can, and does, maintain high standards, including high moral standards, for the God relationship: "God . . . is certainly one who is allowed to attach importance to his person, and therefore he is not constrained to reduce the price of the God relationship because of a religious slackness" (1846, p. 231). (For discussion of Kierkegaard on the God relationship, see Walsh 2009, Torrance 2016.)

Kierkegaard holds that our inquiry about God should attend to the God relationship available to us, in contrast with God's reality apart from us (1846, p. 199). He has Climacus state the following: "The relationship with God has only one evidence, the relationship with God itself; everything else is equivocal" (1846, p. 446). Given divine moral perfection, a person's relationship (or lack thereof) to God will be *morally* implicated in inquiry about God, if God exists, as that person is challenged to meet, personally and interpersonally, the moral expectations of God. This book will identify how we are morally implicated and challenged if the God relationship is indeed on offer to humans. We thus shall attend to how humans would have to appropriate relevant evidence of a morally perfect God, with special attention to responsible human inquiry about God.

We can appreciate a need for a distinctive mode of inquiry regarding God if we acknowledge the following: God would be *sui generis*, at least regarding moral character, and would want inquirers not just to know that something is true (about God), but to enter into a *koinonia* relationship with God that includes *imitatio Dei*. So, inquiry about God, if a morally perfect God exists, would become morally existential, because the "how," particularly the moral process, of getting the truth about God would matter crucially. Such existential inquiry would directly engage one's will and affections, not just one's thinking, because it would engage *how one loves* what or whom one loves.

If God is *sui generis*, at least regarding moral character, God may need to be *self-authenticating* toward humans, with *God* ultimately confirming God's reality. This could include God's supplying the ultimate epistemic standard for God's reality by personal example in self-manifestation (*de re*, in a sense to be clarified) of God's moral character to humans over time. It also could include a divine effort to replace among humans any epistemic standards that obscure the ultimate evidence of divine reality in God's self-manifested moral character.

In a case of my will's being engaged, I could have experiential content of feeling challenged, and even convicted, by another person to replace my selfish ways, including my selfish willing, with unselfish love toward others. The person offering the challenge might want to keep this challenge confidential, just between the two of us, perhaps in order to discourage my blaming others for my selfishness. So, this person might not display to others his challenge to me, and I need not be able to reproduce for others his challenge to me in its original form. The original challenge to me comes from another person, after all, and not from me, and it could be for the good of all concerned. I therefore could have experiential content regarding such a challenge to me, such as felt uncoercive pressure on my will toward unselfish love, even if that content would not be agreed upon by persons other than me and the source of the challenge. Responsible inquiry about God should be sensitive to a consideration of this kind, because it suggests a potential need for an interpersonal mode of inquiry different from a mathematical or scientific mode of inquiry. The intended analogy includes God's aiming to have one willingly convicted in conscience by God's self-manifested moral character. We shall see how this figures in distinctive evidence of God's reality and moral character. (See Chapter 5.)

A person's faith in God would be irreducible to a belief *that* God exists, because such faith would include *trust in God*. Even so, it could be based on undefeated evidence had by a person, and that evidence could have a *de re* component irreducible to a concept, proposition, or judgment. Being *de re*, this component would concern a *thing*, broadly speaking, and not (inherently) a proposition or judgment that something is the case. The evidence could include the person's having a *de re* acquaintance relation of direct encounter with God. This relation would include the direct acquaintance or encounter of a human will with God's moral character and will, courtesy of the uncoercive pressure of a divine will on a human will. That pressure could stem from a divine intention to have a person willingly be convicted to conform to, and to cooperate with, God's moral character.

Divine volitional pressure toward willingly being convicted could create volitional dissonance in a person, and it could be morally transformative in a cooperative person. Given that people can have mistaken beliefs about their experiences, we shall ask what best explains one's having an experience of such pressure and dissonance, relative to the whole range of one's experience and evidence. Such an inquiry can identify whether God's reality actually figures in a best available explanation of one's experience for one and thereby gains rational credibility for one. (Chapter 5 returns to this topic; see also Moser 2008, chap. 2.)

Part of God's will, if God is worthy of worship, would include unselfish love for others, and direct acquaintance with such love would be *de re*. More accurately, it would be *de te*, because (objectively speaking) it would be an I–*Thou* relation of direct encounter between a human and God (in the second person). It would not be enough for this relation if one experienced just *any* good thing, because God, being an intentional agent, would not be just *any* good thing. One would have to experience uncoercive volitional pressure from God's moral character as one is *intentionally* challenged and perhaps willingly convicted (other than by oneself or one's peers) to conform to a good will, particularly in unselfish love toward others.

De re direct acquaintance of the relevant kind would not *include*, in the acquaintance relation, a person's conceptualizing God *as God* or forming a belief that certain features apply *to God*. We need not digress to the issue of whether minimal conceptual factors, such as merely demonstrative or ostensive factors, always contingently accompany *de re* direct acquaintance. Conceptual and propositional factors regarding God would leave one with a *de dicto* relation that goes beyond *de re* direct acquaintance as direct attention-attraction by a thing or person. (With influence from Kierkegaard 1846, a number of writers have identified the importance of an I–Thou relation in faith in God; see, for instance, Buber 1923, Heim 1936, Brunner 1964, and Farmer 1942.)

Most, if not all, readers are familiar with direct attention-*attraction* by a thing or a person. It includes one's being apprehended in attention, or awareness, by a thing or a person, without one's *selective* use of attention that includes conceptualizing or judging regarding the content (at least in any way that goes beyond mere ostension). God could attract one's attention in that way, even if one fails to conceptualize the event as involving God. So, one's experience of God could lack one's being aware *that* God is its source. Even so, the God relationship for humans sought by God would not be just an event or episode of love given or experienced; it would be an enduring relationship of love. We will explore the importance of this consideration for the ethics of inquiry about God.

If God is worthy of worship, and hence morally perfect self-sufficiently, then God is in a distinctive category relative to our familiar world. Specifically, if monotheism is true, its God is *sui generis*, and the same is true of God's moral character. If God self-manifested aspects of this moral character, such as divine love, to some humans, then this self-manifestation would be irreducible to a concept, proposition, or judgment. It also would supply unique evidence of God's reality to some humans, specifically to those who have cooperatively received the self-manifestation (in a manner to be clarified). In addition, the self-manifestation could occur over time (and hence be diachronic rather than synchronic), and it could be spontaneous in a manner that challenges some of one's own tendencies in thought or action and thus give no indication of being created by oneself. The latter considerations, we shall see, could figure in what best explains one's overall experience for one.

God would not be required to self-manifest to all humans by any particular time in earthly life. Some humans may not be prepared by that time to receive the self-manifestation in agreement with God's purpose for it. God thus could hide or at least keep divine self-manifestation from some people, at least for a time. (Chapter 3 returns to this topic.) So, we should not require that the evidence of God's reality be had or agreed upon by all inquirers about God. Even so, God could supply self-authentication of divine reality via self-manifestation for humans who are suitably receptive. This position does not entail that a subjective religious experience or a religious document is self-authenticating, because *God*, who could be self-authenticating, would not be a religious experience or a religious document.

If God desires human inquiry about God to include, at least as a goal, a *koinonia* relationship between God and humans, and not just the acquisition of truth, our asking about God's reality and goodness should take on a new focus. To that end, God would want human inquiry about God to include not just a third-person perspective, but an I–Thou component with God in the second person. Part of the desired answer to the inquiry would be an ongoing lived relationship, in keeping with God's moral character,

and not just a solution to a problem or an explanation of
a datum. If God is morally perfect, the suitable mode of
interpersonal inquiry will be *ethically* relevant to fit God's
moral character. It thus will involve not just one's mind,
but also one's intentional self, including one's will and purposes in action. Thinking, then, will not exhaust this mode
of inquiry. One's intentions in inquiry will be subject to ethical assessment from the standard of what would be God's
morally perfect character.

We should consider that the ethical assessment in question may go beyond humans inquiring about God to *God's*
inquiring about humans. An analogue to this divine inquiry
of humans is suggested by John's Gospel, in the following
exchange between Jesus and the apostle Peter.

When they had finished breakfast, Jesus said to Simon Peter,
"Simon son of John, do you love [*agapas*] me more than these?"
He said to him, "Yes, Lord; you know that I love you." Jesus
said to him, "Feed my lambs." A second time he said to him,
"Simon son of John, do you love me?" He said to him, "Yes,
Lord; you know that I love you." Jesus said to him, "Tend my
sheep." He said to him the third time, "Simon son of John, do
you love me?" Peter felt hurt because he said to him the third
time, "Do you love me?" And he said to him, "Lord, you know
everything; you know that I love you." Jesus said to him,
"Feed my sheep. . . . After this he said to him, "Follow me."
(John 21:15–17, 19; cf. Mark 10:51)

If the question from Jesus to Peter represents God's question for human inquirers, regardless of whether they have
betrayed God, we can see the ethical relevance of human
inquiry about God. Part of the ethical relevance would
include a role for *agapē* in such inquiry.

Generalizing the approach of Jesus, we may suggest that
a question will emerge about whether an inquirer loves
God, or at least would love God if God exists. A question
about how one loves (for instance, selfishly or unselfishly),

including what one's love is directed toward, will be central to responsible inquiry relative to God's moral character. The question of Jesus to Peter does not call for a mathematical or scientific mode of inquiry, but it does call for interpersonal interaction with the source of the question. Corresponding inquiry about God, if God exists, likewise should fit with its personal subject-matter, and hence be ethically sensitive. It also should be open to a response that includes *imitatio Dei*, such as that suggested by the injunction, "Follow me." So, truth-seeking regarding God, if God exists, may turn out to be ethically robust, and not just reflective or intellectual. God may value truth-seeking *and* goodness-appropriating in proper inquiry about God, even if one can draw a conceptual distinction between the two in the abstract.

Two areas of ethical assessment arise for an interpersonal mode of inquiry about God, if God exists: the ethics of *attentiveness* toward God's will and the ethics of *cooperation* with God's will. Attentiveness matters, because our not paying attention for (potential) volitional pressure from God, toward our being willingly convicted by God, can leave us without apprehending direct salient evidence of God and thus with being unteachable directly by God. We shall see how our response to intended conviction in conscience can play an important role in this regard. Cooperation matters too, because God, being perfectly good, would seek human cooperation with the perfect divine will, for the relational good of humans. Such cooperation is central to human faith in God and to a *koinonia* relationship with God that includes *imitatio Dei*. We shall explore the significant consequences of this lesson for the ethics of inquiry about God.

2. EMPOWERMENT AND ETHICS IN INQUIRY

If God seeks an uncoercive relationship of *koinonia* with humans, we face a striking result indicated by the following statement from Mark's Gospel: "[Jesus] could do [*edunato*] no deed of power there; . . . he was amazed at their unbelief" (Mark 6:5–6). Could it be that God enables *humans* to empower God to self-reveal to them so as to be suitably apprehended by them? Given a key role for free human agency, this book supports an affirmative answer, even though inquirers have overlooked the question almost universally. In this area, we misunderstand God to our own detriment, as we neglect the kind of empowerment God would enable in, and expect from, humans. On the positive side, if we acknowledge the empowerment in question, we can identify a morally significant cooperative role for humans in enabling salient evidence of God for themselves.

We can feel the strangeness of Mark's comment that Jesus "*could* do no deed of power there," in connection with human "unbelief" as indifference or opposition to God. We need to face this strangeness to see if it yields some illumination of the human empowerment of God for self-manifestation. We shall see that it has profound importance for human inquiry about God, particularly in signaling a neglected kind of moral empowerment humans have toward God. Such empowerment would emerge from the divine support of human freedom and responsibility in relation to the salient evidence of God available to humans. It thus would come from God's own power, a kind of divine self-restraint, and would not be any kind of deficiency in God. It also would come from God's perfect moral goodness, as God would value what is morally good for humans, as genuine agents, in divine self-manifestation to them. God still could limit the *use* of human freedom, but it would not be a live option for God to remove the *capacity* for such freedom in certain cases, such as cases where God seeks *koinonia*. That capacity would be central to *interpersonal* relationships of the sort God would value as a perfectly loving agent.

The apostle Paul speaks of humans who "do not approve to have God in their knowledge," including in their evidence

(Rom. 1:28, my trans.). Similarly, he speaks of God's "giving them over to the desires of their hearts" (Rom. 1:24, my trans.), and we may apply this to the desires of some humans not to have God in their evidence. The latter application has been widely neglected by theologians, philosophers, and others, but it fits well with the recurring biblical theme of God's occasional hiding from humans. The latter theme includes the blunt announcement of Isaiah: "Truly you are a God who hides himself" (Isa. 45:15). Even if God provides some initial, ambiguous evidence to humans in divine self-manifestation, this evidence would not have to be salient, and God could withdraw any self-manifestation from human experience and evidence if humans handle it improperly.

Allowing human approval for salient divine evidence would be the price God pays to enable humans to direct their lives without divine opposition in their evidence. It would include the powerful human freedom to omit any indication of God from one's experience and salient evidence. Supporting human free agency in divine–human relationships, God typically would minimize or withhold self-manifestation in cases where humans prefer to exclude God from their evidence. Contrary to some portraits, then, God would not be a stalker of humans in forcing salient divine evidence on them. Just as the human stalking of others with undesired evidence would be morally oppressive and defective, we should consider that the same would apply to a God who stalked humans with salient divine evidence.

As an alternative to stalking, a perfectly good God would seek interpersonal relationships of cooperative mutuality or reciprocity, including relationships of freely given *agapē*, between God and humans. In that case, God would expect humans, in their self-avowed need, freely to *make themselves available* to receive evidence of God, in a way that includes their being willing to cooperate with it. God would value this as a relational good in their receiving evidence, because it would conform to the good divine intention of the evidence, that is, the intention in giving the evidence. God thus could give humans the freedom to realize, if painfully, the actual consequences of "the desires of their hearts" in this morally important area. In that case, the stakes for inquiry about God would be high, with the nature of human lives at risk. (It is an open question whether God could be coercive at times toward persons *after* their free reception of God; see Hick 1964.)

A perfectly good God would enable human freedom not simply for one's refraining from honoring God, as Paul suggests in Romans 1:21, but also for one's avoiding the experiencing of God's presence or power in one's salient evidence. Extending to the content of one's salient evidence, such freedom would go beyond any option not to believe that God exists. Experiencing God in one's salient evidence could oppose one's preferred direction for living, and this opposition could amount to being stalked by God. In this respect, experiencing a perfectly good God in one's salient evidence can contrast with one's experiencing, for instance, a familiar household object.

Experiencing God in a salient, or definite, manner would have a directional weight different in kind from the influence of a household object. The salient presence of God in human experience could have a kind of power that interferes with one's preferred mode and direction for life. So, a perfectly good God would be sensitive to human approval, even if implicit, of divine presence or power in salient human evidence, in order to give human agents over to "the desires of their hearts." This kind of freedom would enable humans to learn what life without God's salient presence involves. It thus could lead to a moral wake-up call for receptive humans, and even to eventual receptivity toward God.

The role of human approval, even if implicit, in having salient evidence of God's reality calls for a discipline of *ethics* for human inquiry about God. Philosophers, theologians, and other inquirers have failed to explore such ethics for inquiry, but this book corrects the deficiency. We shall see that there is such a discipline, a special ethics of responsibility for inquiry about God. Applying to attitudes as well as actions, it demands responsibility toward the distinctive subject-matter of inquiry, and, if God exists, toward God's perfectly good moral character and the moral demands arising from that character. We thus shall introduce a new discipline of inquiry to accommodate and to promote the distinctive ethics for theological inquiry. (Chapter 2 identifies some key principles.)

The word "discipline" applies here, because it connotes practical as well as informational features in human inquiry about God. The practical features include ingredients of human action, including human intention, which is irreducible to human experiencing, thinking, or feeling. The needed ethics for inquiry, we shall see, exceeds what philosophers, in the wake of W.K. Clifford and William James, have called "the ethics of belief." The latter area, concerning belief, is narrower in scope than the ethics of *inquiry* for God.

The new discipline takes theological inquiry beyond merely intellectual considerations to the *morally relevant intentions* of inquirers. Such inquiry, we shall see, looks very different in this new perspective. It comes alive in ways that are existential, practical, and ethical. If God is a perfectly good object of inquiry, with perfectly good expectations for inquirers, we might expect theological inquiry to call for a special discipline of ethics. On reflection, it seems naïve if not presumptuous to suppose that suitable human inquiry about God, if a morally perfect God exists and seeks good interpersonal relationships, would be free of moral assessment, challenge, and intended conviction by God.

If inquirers need a moral challenge, for their own good, God would relate to them accordingly. At a minimum, a perfectly good God would not support or cooperate with bad or harmful inquiry about God, but would encourage morally good and responsible inquiry. In addition, if people are not ready for a moral challenge from divine self-manifestation, God would have the patience to wait (as suggested, for instance, in John 16:12–13).

Many inquirers assume that human inquiry about God should be purely or largely intellectual, a matter just or primarily of reflecting carefully on pertinent evidence from experience and thought. Typical inquiry about God by philosophers, for instance, illustrates this intellectualist approach. We shall see, however, that a problem arises. Inquirers may need to put themselves in a suitable position, including an intention to cooperate, to receive salient evidence of God and God's reality. In that case, inquirers may need to *act* in certain ways to acquire salient evidence of God, and these ways would not be limited to intellectual reflection. If these ways are guided by considerations of responsibility in intention and action, it would be fitting to acknowledge the ethics for inquiry about God. It also would be fitting to ask about the moral relevance of one's intentions in inquiry, at least regarding how they relate to what is responsible in inquiry about a morally perfect God.

Perhaps God has vital news to reveal to humans, but we have difficulty in apprehending and receiving it. We thus could neglect the news from God, even if it is important for our lives. Our difficulty in apprehending it could stem from an inadequate use of our imagination, and our difficulty in receiving it could arise from some human attitudes and tendencies in conflict with it. This book aims to identify the news in question, while proposing a way to ease the human difficulty in apprehending and receiving it. This news differs from many stories about God in circulation, because it invites a distinctive kind of human cooperation with it in empowering God to self-reveal to humans. In addition, it acknowledges a subtle but active role for God that offers a constructive challenge and promise to all interested humans. We shall see what it is to be suitably "interested," in terms of responsible inquiry about God and of what one cares about, or what one loves, in relation to others.

3. CARING AND *AGAPĒ* IN INQUIRY

Some people assume that God would have no real concern for how we, as responsible persons with intentions, should relate morally to God and others in inquiry. They presume that God would be neutral about our morally relevant attitudes as inquirers, as if God were a morally indifferent object of knowledge. Perhaps, however, God's caring about inquirers runs deeper by extending to our moral attitudes, including our intentions to care or not to care about others in connection with our inquiry. God may seek to have us intend to care morally toward others as God cares, even in how we proceed with inquiry about God. In that case, human moral resolve, or the lack thereof, toward others would bear importantly on inquiry about God and God's reality. So, what we intend to care about would matter significantly in such inquiry, if a morally perfect God exists.

We may think, in general, of our *caring* about something as our positively valuing that thing. Such valuing entails our intending to benefit or to commend the thing valued in some way under certain circumstances. So, we are not indifferent to what we care about. We may think, in general, of our *intending* to do something as our settling on doing it under certain circumstances. Such intending goes beyond desire and belief to a commitment, or a resolve, to do something under relevant circumstances. Intending to care, therefore, is no mere experience, thought, or feeling, not even an experience, thought, or feeling of God's caring for oneself. It involves a person as an agent with intentional attitudes that underlie action, thus resisting any reduction to merely experiential, intellectual, or sentimental features of a person. Our intending to care morally as God cares, then, would not be accomplished simply by our thinking or believing about God and evidence of God's reality. Such intending, we shall see, would figure in empowering God to self-reveal to humans, owing to the goodness (valued by God) of free human agency in this area.

If perfectly good, God would want humans freely to intend, or to will, to be caring and compassionate toward other agents as God is caring and compassionate, because this would be in their shared best interest. In that case, we would need to conduct our inquiry about God to fit with God's caring about humans. This would not require that we match God's moral character, as if that were possible for morally imperfect humans on their own. Instead, it would demand that we have an intentional attitude of moral resolve that seeks conformity with God's moral character, if God exists, that is, an intention for *imitatio Dei*. It would be a moral defect of indifference for God not to have such a demand of humans, and such a defect would undermine the status of being a perfectly good God who is worthy of worship. We shall see what this entails in connection with a discipline of ethics for inquiry about God. It entails at least a divine expectation of an inquirer to make oneself available to, and ideally cooperative toward, God's moral domain of caring in interpersonal relationships, which God would not sacrifice for a lesser good. We shall consider whether humans are responsible for seeking, and not just reflecting on, the reality of that moral domain. (Chapters 2 and 3 offer an affirmative response.)

Various questions about our intentions bear on human inquiry about a perfectly good God. A key question is: Do I intend to cooperate with any demands or expectations of God regarding my relating to God and others? More generally: What do I intend to do with my inquiry about God and its results, particularly in relationship to others? Do I intend to be caring and compassionate toward others with the process and its results, in the way a perfectly good

God would be? Such issues would matter to a God who cares about others, even though we typically ignore them in inquiry about God. In ignoring them, we may block or obscure evidence of God's self-manifestation to us, if the human reception of that manifestation is to include a central role for caring toward others. God may want to discourage the moral trivializing of human inquiry about God, and thereby may typically withhold salient evidence of self-manifestation when inquirers neglect the kind of caring God expects. This book draws out the significant implications of this prospect for the ethics of inquiry about God.

Our inquiry about God has three main options regarding other people. First, we could be indifferent about the process and the results of our inquiry for the benefit of others. We might aim to secure truth and avoid error in our inquiry, but value nothing in meeting divine expectations for our relating morally to others. Such inquiry, we may say, would be *morally indifferent* or *purely cognitive*, focusing exclusively on the ingredients for a kind of factual knowledge (that something is the case) regarding God's reality. This kind of inquiry seems common among educated people from various fields, but it is not our only option for responsible inquiry.

Second, we could intend to use the process and the results of our inquiry about God to belittle or to exclude others in a harmful way. We often see this kind of *morally negative* intention in strident religious disputes about God or God's reality, and it is rarely, if ever, fruitful in inquiry. In fact, it runs afoul of the moral character of a perfectly good God.

Third, we could intend to use the process and the results of our inquiry to benefit others, to bring good to them in a compassionate manner. We typically do not see this intention expressed in inquiry about God, but it would be *morally positive* and thus morally commendable. This intention would fit with the character of a morally perfect God who cares about all other persons, even in connection with their inquiring about God. We should acknowledge, nonetheless, that a person could care about certain things in common with God's caring but not know or believe that God exists. We shall see the significance of this in cases of religious diversity.

A perfectly good God would want more from human inquiry about God than factual knowledge that God exists. If God seeks human faith, or trust, in God, we should consider that God wants faith that goes beyond intellectual factors. We should consider that God would want what Paul calls "faith operating through love (*agapē*)" (Gal. 5:6, my trans.). We can understand such faith to be motivated, or empowered, by unselfish love. It thus would be more than faith that merely expresses love, because love would be in its *motivational* base. This kind of faith, as we shall explore, may be central to apprehending divine evidence aright. If, however, faith is to be empowered by unselfish love, we can ask where that love originates. We shall ask, and we shall see that the relevant love includes self-sacrifice for others. We thus shall identify the importance of Paul's injunction to "abide in kindness" (Rom. 11:22, my trans.), that is, kindness fitting to God's moral character. In this perspective, inquiry about God, if God exists, is morally robust in being sensitive to how one loves what one loves, and it can either empower or block God regarding divine self-manifestation to a person.

The present theme regarding *agapē* fits with the following remark in 1 John 4:8: "Whoever does not love does not know God, for God is love [*agapē*]." A refusal to intend to care morally as God cares for others could obstruct one's knowing God by failing to empower God to self-manifest, in accordance with God's purpose in self-manifestation. On the positive side, God would care for others, and one's intending to care in the same way (even if one does not believe that God exists) would contribute to one's being in a responsible position to know God at God's preferred time, if God exists. It would enable one to transcend mundane reality, including selfishness, and perhaps, in due course, to recognize an agent-source of love beyond oneself. This fits with the following remark from Albert Schweitzer: "All living knowledge of God rests upon this foundation: that we experience [God] in our lives as Will-to-Love" (1933, p. 277).

If "God is love," one's intending to care morally for others as God does would prepare one to meet God in the moral domain of the divine: that of *agapē* (best understood as self-sacrificial love for something good). In this regard, (intending to care morally for others as God cares could be a source of recognizing extra-mundane personal reality, or at least a way of testing for its existence] We should consider that God would prefer to self-reveal to humans through their intention to care about, to love, others as God does, in order to encourage human cooperation with God's moral character and will. We shall ask, then, whether humans can become aware of God through *agapē* and an intention for *agapē* that would be fitting in relation to a perfectly good God.

Without uncritically assuming the authority of the Bible, we do well to consider the following advice from 1 John 4:1: "Do not believe every spirit, but test the spirits to see whether they are from God; for many false prophets have gone out into the world." We need some way to distinguish between any claims from God and claims merely alleged to be from God. How are we to do this? This question calls for an answer to another question: How would God make God available to be known by us, or at least to have God's reality known by us? The test cannot require our having a full explanation, or a complete theodicy, of God's ways, particularly regarding the permitting of evil. The book of Job illustrates that we are in no such position, if only because we lack an explanation of much human suffering. We shall consider the more plausible view that the test requires a priority for *agapē* of a special sort, in interpersonal relationships, even when it seems absent on the surface of our circumstances. (Chapters 2 and 3 return to this matter.)

Many people believe that God exists, and, in addition, some people have faith or trust in God. How are we to explain this, if an explanation is available? It would be a mistake to assume that faith in God is simply guesswork, because it often has support from experience of some kind. Two pressing questions concern what such experience is and how it supports faith in God. Put generally, the issue is how some humans proceed, and reasonably may proceed, from their experience to their faith in God. We want to know whether their experience adequately grounds their faith in God, and thus saves them from irrational faith. Faith with no adequate ground will be no better than mere guesswork, and such guesswork has little to offer humans with serious needs and desires, including a need for wisdom and meaning for life (on which see Chapter 4).

This book offers a distinctive approach to the kind of experience in question and relates it to grounded faith in God. The relevant experience includes an experienced trial or test of a distinctive sort, namely, a trial that applies to God as well as to humans, who must approve, if implicitly, of receiving salient divine evidence in the trial. The idea of a trial for God, and not just for humans, has found little representation in the past. This book corrects that inadequacy and identifies the significant implications for human inquiry about God. Such inquiry will have new depth from this perspective, and will offer a neglected story about God for humans.

Memorably, W.V.O. Quine quipped that logic chases truth up the tree of grammar. In a related vein, we might say that religion, properly understood, follows God down the valley of trial for compassion in interpersonal relationships. We shall consider whether a distinctive personal transformation toward relational *agapē* in the trial can provide salient evidence of God's reality, and thereby move the account on offer beyond mere speculation. The trial in question would take humans to their own limits for being good and offer a way beyond those limits. It will raise the issue of whether one is willingly being convicted by God toward increasing *agapē* for others. As perfectly good, God would seek such willing conviction in humans, without coercion.

We will have to face the following simple but perennial question: Does God exist? If that is a question for the ages, it is a question for us too, here and now. As some recent work in psychology shows, we need to avoid cognitive bias in how we frame the question. Our larger context for our interpretation matters. We need to give due attention to a *notion* of God that allows for a viable God, particularly a God at least as subtle, resilient, and caring as good humans. (This notion is not to be confused with a belief or an affirmation that God exists.) A holdover from ancient Greek philosophy portrays God as immutable and aloof, beyond sympathetic care for humans. A similarly tenuous God inhabits later deism, and leaves corresponding human attitudes toward God abstract and largely theoretical. We can do better, with better framing in relation to what would be God's perfectly good moral character and its role in inquiry about God and in a trial with humans for compassionate relationships of *agapē*.

4. TRIAL FOR COMPASSION

If God would be at least as caring as good humans toward others, we face the prospect of a God of *redemptive sympathy* toward humans. Seeking an alternative to the immutable gods of Parmenides and Plato, Abraham Heschel (1962) introduced the important idea of the *pathos* of God, that is, the active caring of God toward humans in history. He thus aimed to characterize the redemptive God of the Jewish Bible as undertaking actions for the good of humans. Going beyond Heschel, I suggest that divine caring for humans would not be merely behavioral, but would include a distinctive kind of *felt sympathy* toward them. The God in question would be altogether compassionate toward other

persons, for their good, and thus would be willing to suffer
for and with them. This kind of compassionate God would
not be limited to a life of thought or to "thought thinking itself," contrary to a famous suggestion of Aristotle.
Morally robust actions and relationships from God in the
lives of humans would be part of the divine goal, as we
shall see.

The plot thickens if God is not only compassionate
toward other persons, but also consciously supportive of
disseminating compassion for their good in interpersonal
relationships. In that case, we shall see, God would be a
God of trial with humans and not just trial for humans.
We may think of trial, in the language of the *Oxford English
Dictionary*, second edition, as "the action of testing or putting to the [test] the fitness, truth, strength, or other quality of anything," including "the fact or condition of being
tried by suffering." This need not be a trial in a court of
law, but it would be a genuine trial nonetheless, in human
life and not just in thought. It could be a challenging test
that reveals, in the interpersonal conduct of life, who God
really is and who a human really is, regarding what they
ultimately care about and how they care. It thus could be
an important means of self-disclosure for all concerned.

We shall consider the prospect of a God who undertakes
a twofold trial: a trial for humans and a self-imposed trial
for God. We shall consider that God is present in the trial
for humans as a *subject* of the trial, and thus humans face
a trial *with* God. The trial is *for* God in that it tests something important about God, specifically about God's moral
character and about what God ultimately cares about and
how God cares. Some theological writers, including Martin
Luther and Søren Kierkegaard, have discussed the topic
of humans tested by God, but the novelty here is *God's*
being tested too, in the trial of humans with God. God and
humans thus would be in the trial together, being tested
for their moral character in the face of difficult challenges.
In this perspective, it is a mistake to hold that only humans

are tested by God. God, too, is in the mix of the trial, intentionally, and God allows humans either to empower or to block salient evidence from God for themselves regarding divine reality.

We arrive at the following issue: What is the trial of God and humans *for*? In other words, what is its main purpose? The best short answer: It is testing for the reality of what God would value most in moral agents, including in God: their freely having enduring, faithful compassion toward other people for the sake of good, *agapē*-oriented relationships between those people, even when circumstances are difficult. In brief, the trial is for the presence of the redemptive compassion of *agapē* in God and humans toward other persons, including human *agapē* toward God (see Deut. 13:3).

God could undergo a self-imposed trial, particularly in relation to humans, in order (a) to practice compassion under challenge, as something inherently good, (b) to reveal to others the compassionate character of God, and (c) to explore the effectiveness of this trial in encouraging others toward a life of redemptive compassion in interpersonal relationships. If God is praiseworthy, as many people hold, then God would make praiseworthy choices about divine conduct, and would not follow an inexorable course. God would deserve credit for *choosing* to be perfectly good, and this credit would acknowledge God's free choice in favor of what is good in action. God, then, would differ from our computers, for instance, which are not praiseworthy even if good.

The Bible portrays God as being under self-imposed trial in various contexts. A quick sample will serve for now. At one point, God commands Israel to test God, regarding divine blessings for Israel's faithfulness in giving to others (Mal. 3:10). We also have stories of God's giving signs to show divine faithfulness to humans (Judg. 6:17, Isa. 7:10–12). At another point, however, God commands Israel not to put God to the test in a certain way: namely, in a way that shows distrust toward God despite God's past faithfulness (Deut. 6:16; see also Matt. 4:7).

The difference is between a test sensitive to God's moral character of faithfulness and a test enabling humans to sit in misplaced judgment over God while neglecting God's faithfulness. For instance, a test demanding that God satisfy my selfish desires, say for a large deposit in my personal bank account, would be unsuitable. So, there are suitable tests of God, and there are unsuitable tests. The suitable tests, given proper human motives, could put one in a responsible position where God's faithful character is revealed to one, and thus where one's faith in God is not just wishful thinking or a leap in the dark.

Suitable tests of God's reality aim to assess God's reality regarding perfect goodness in God's moral character, purposes, and promises. An agent who is just somewhat good or just largely good will not meet the perfectionist standard for being God. If God is to be worthy of worship, and hence worthy of unqualified commitment, God must be perfectly good in the moral domain. God thus must be above moral reproach in all areas. Otherwise, God would not be worthy of unqualified commitment or worship. At least, many of us use the title "God" in a perfectionist way, and this use itself seems to be above reproach. This use enables one to distinguish a test by God and a temptation to do evil. A perfectly good God would not offer such a temptation but could offer a test for goodness, including interpersonal goodness, in moral agents. (For some harmful effects of settling for a less robust conception of God, see Buckley 1987.)

If God is to be perfectly good, God must be perfectly loving and hence perfectly compassionate toward others, even toward resolute enemies. Being just somewhat compassionate, just largely compassionate, or selectively compassionate toward others will not make the grade for being God. Being perfectly compassionate, however, would give God perfectly unselfish sympathy for others, even for people opposed or indifferent to God. In that respect, we would not face an "us vs. them" divide regarding people for whom God has compassion. Even though a perfectly compassionate God could be self-interested, God could not be *selfish* toward any people and remain perfectly good. Divine unselfishness would exclude not self-interest but self-advancement at the expense of what is good for other persons. God thus would not use people for selfish divine ends, and this feature would be part of a moral character worthy of worship. This consideration fits with the teaching of Jesus that God is compassionate and should be imitated with human compassion toward others (see Luke 6:36).

Tests, or trials, regarding God's reality for humans come in two broad kinds: *merely intellectual* tests and *morally lived* tests. A merely intellectual test would engage one's thinking, but it need not threaten to alter the direction of one's moral life. In contrast, a morally lived test would engage one's thinking but extend beyond it to bear on one's moral identity, including how one intends to live, particularly in relation to others. It would engage the larger moral life of a person, including one's attitude, feeling, conduct, and relationship toward other people. One's intentions toward others thus would receive assessment. So, an inquirer's test for God's reality could include a test for the moral status of the inquirer, if only to assess whether the inquirer's intentions are in a cooperative moral position to receive salient evidence from God. This would be a result of God's moral concern for inquirers, including for their intentions in handling evidence of God.

A morally lived test for God's reality and character would require that one entertain the moral character of perfect compassion. It also would require that one be sincerely open and prepared to be conformed to that character, in thought, attitude, feeling, action, and relationship, under certain circumstances. One such circumstance would include God's self-presenting divine compassion to a person and thereby witnessing to its (and God's) reality in that person's life. This book gives special attention to the importance of God's self-presenting of divine compassion and its role in a morally lived trial with God. We shall see that a perfectly good God would have no need to offer a merely intellectual test to humans. This lesson will bear negatively on purely intellectual or philosophical approaches to God's reality. It also will lead to a more experiential, volitional, and relational alternative to those approaches.

Human persons would have a crucial voluntary role in a morally lived test regarding God's reality. They would need to dare to undertake such a test for perfect compassion, and this would call for resolve, courage, and sympathy toward the bringing about of such compassion, if it is available. Such resolve, courage, and sympathy would risk the moral decentering for a person, away from self-indulgence and toward unselfish compassion for others. Even so, such decentering can be self-interested without being selfish, because it can be in one's interest without one's exalting oneself over others, at the expense of others. This kind of decentering can have uneasy consequences, personally and socially. It can lead to one's being at odds, practically and socially, with one's peers, and this can result in a difficult challenge to complete the test. Quitting the test can be easy under stress, and much could be lost. Even if one is invited to undertake the test, and to endure in a struggle for compassion, one can freely reject or ignore the test on offer. In a case of quitting, lived compassion will not be at the center of one's lived morality. Something else then will, and not for the morally better.

A morally lived test for compassion in a human life would be diachronic rather than synchronic. It would range over a period of time, perhaps even over a whole life, rather than occur at an instant. After all, as a test for a *life* of compassion, it would not be a test just for a moment or an event of compassion. It also could give different episodic results at different times, because compassion in a human life need not be constant. It can ebb and flow, under various circumstances and challenges. So, no single moment in a human life will tell the full story of a person's trial for a life of compassion. That story will be holistic, ranging over a whole life, and it will manifest the frailty and the inconstancy of humans.

A big challenge in a trial with God would arise from the *priority* of compassion demanded in God and humans. A God worthy of worship would be inherently and perfectly compassionate toward others; compassion for others would be a top priority, and not just one value among other values. God thus would require compassion in how one relates to others, including one's enemies, in all cases, and not just in selected cases. In this regard, the test would require compassion for others to function at the center of one's life, and not just at the periphery. This is a tall order, by any standard, and we shall ask whether the order is too tall for morally imperfect humans. Even if the ideal is perfectionist, its implementation among humans rarely is. Even so, this is no strike against the ideal itself. The goal of the trial still can be perfectionist, in keeping with the moral character of a God worthy of worship.

5. CURATIVE RELATIONSHIPS AND KNOWLEDGE

The story to be offered will identify a central role for interpersonal grace in testing for compassion. The main New Testament Greek term for grace is *charis*. Divine grace includes a humanly unearned *gift* of a reconciled divine–human relationship intentionally offered by God to humans. In that relationship, cooperative humans would receive the power of divine compassion to feel and to practice redemptive sympathy toward others, including their enemies. This book explores the ways in which this kind of cooperative relationship would bear on inquiry about God and would be relationally, or interpersonally, curative for humans as a source of compassion toward others. (We shall clarify the relevant sense of "curative" immediately below.)

 " healing

In receiving, valuing, and abiding in the God relationship, humans could move from a notion of perfect compassion to an experience of perfect personal compassion, that is, an experience of a *personal, intentional agent* who has such compassion for them. A felt trial for intended and lived compassion, accompanied by volitional pressure aimed at one's willingly being convicted toward God's moral character, is, we shall see, a central part of the latter experience. Such a trial could be one's only opportunity to test for God's reality. In that case, one would have no shortcut to God, outside a trial regarding one's response and moral character in relation to divine compassion involving *koinonia*. This consideration will figure in the ethics for inquiry about God.

Because the compassion in question is compassion for others, the trial is inherently social, and not simply individual. It bears irreducibly on a person's attitude, feeling, conduct, and relationship *toward others*, and is social in that respect. The biblical command to love God, in this perspective, is inextricably bound up with the accompanying biblical command to love other humans. Specifically, one cannot have suitable love toward God without having love toward the humans in one's life, including one's enemies. In addition, people typically will face the trial for compassion together, in relationships with others who can offer support. It is thus a social test, at least ordinarily. This would result from God's wanting social well-being, the *koinonia* of community, among humans, including their having interpersonal compassion reflective of God's compassion toward others.

Being perfectly compassionate, God's purposes in self-manifesting to humans would be sympathetic toward humans. They would include God's sharing in human suffering and calling for cooperative sympathy in the *felt* understanding of those purposes by humans. Without such sympathy, one might have an intellectual glimpse of divine purpose, but one will not enter into a felt, experienced understanding that is crucial to sharing in divine compassion. In that case, one's intellectual understanding would fall short of what God would seek from humans: a sympathetic cooperative relationship for the sake of receiving and being conformed to divine compassion in relationships. This kind of relationship would include a person in a good relationship with God by that person's participating in God's redemptive life, including God's feelings and purposes. It would underwrite a compassionate life with God, the heart of human redemption as reconciliation to God (on reconciliation, see Martin 1981).

A key feature of divine compassion would be God's *self-identifying* with humans in their plight needing redemption. It would aim at relational, interpersonal reconciliation between God and humans, in order to overcome the alienation of humans from (a good relationship with) God. This self-identifying would be for the sake of humans who, in turn, would be expected to self-identify with God in the divine redemptive effort. The reciprocity here includes the provision of divine power to humans, in their weakness, to enable them to cooperate with God in the divine redemptive effort. Paul finds this process exemplified by God in Christ, including by the self-emptying of Christ for God on behalf of humans (see, for instance, Phil. 2:5–11, Rom. 5:8–10, 2 Cor. 5:18–20), and he finds it at work in his own life (Phil. 3:7–11). This process, in Paul's thought, is part of what enables Christ and other humans to represent God to humans for the sake of their reconciliation to God.

The responsive self-identifying by humans must be sympathetic because it must be compassionate, including the human sharing in the feelings and purposes of God. It thus is participatory and lived, and not simply intellectual or reflective. It therefore enables one to be open to live in a future with God, where new developments and challenges in relationships occur. Such a future calls for human hope in God, beyond beliefs regarding God, and this hope eventually would call for a decision about the trustworthiness of God for the future as well as the present. In this regard, at least, human hope in God is not fully realized now. We shall see, in Chapter 4, how this lesson bears on the meaning or purpose of human life, including when such meaning or purpose is subtle and elusive for humans. We also shall see how a divine–human relationship having such meaning can be relationally curative for humans, and how a trial with God would aim to be curative in that way. The ethics for inquiry about God will have to acknowledge such a trial for humans, if a perfectly good God exists.

 A relevant definition of "curative" in the *Oxford English Dictionary*, second edition, is: "having the tendency or power to cure . . .; promoting cure." The *OED* also offers a pertinent definition that includes the term "corrective." So, a relationally curative God would have the power, the tendency, and the aim to cure others by bringing corrective power as well-being to them in a cooperative relationship with God. A human candidate for the relational cure would have a voluntary decision to make in cooperating or not cooperating, and thus would not be purely passive. One's cooperative decision would empower God, at least morally, to bring divine power into one's salient evidence.

The well-being in question could be bodily in part, but it need not be. It could be psychological or spiritual, such as when a person is moved from abject despair to hope in God and even to communion with God, owing to a cooperative relationship with God. In addition, the well-being on offer could arise over time rather than at an instant, roughly in the manner of one's recovering over time from a bad habit (say, from smoking, over-eating, or under-eating). (Chapter 5 returns to the pertinent notion of communion with God.)

A relationally curative God would have a distinctive purpose: to bring well-being to others in a cooperative and sympathetic relationship of *koinonia* with God and others. A human trial with God could test for the realization of this purpose in human lives. The purpose in question would honor the free agency of humans, because a perfectly good God would not be coercive in suppressing human freedom to choose against God. So, humans freely could reject not only the relational cure God offers, but also God's presence in their salient evidence. In self-restraint, God would allow for this rejection in order to sustain genuine human agency in relating or not relating to God, particularly if such agency is needed for human relationships of love and cooperation toward God and others.]This book explores a twofold question: In what sense would God be relationally curative toward wayward humans, and how would this sense of "being relationally curative" bear on how God relates to humans in their salient evidence and fragile lives and on how humans should relate to God? Our reflection on this question will shed considerable light on human inquiry about God, including on salient evidence of God's reality and the ethics for inquiry about God.

Much human inquiry about God overlooks what would be the distinctive features of a relationally curative God, perhaps owing to an undue focus on *non-relational* goods for humans. In doing so, it neglects some important features we should expect in the evidence of God's reality. Two such features are noteworthy here. The first feature, as suggested, is that a relationally curative God would seek to self-manifest to humans in ways that self-identify with them in their various situations, including their most difficult and fragile conditions. So, Christian theology represents God in Christ as identifying with people in their fragile humanity, including in their suffering, dying, and death. This is offered as part of divine compassion for others.

As God's unique representative, in the Christian perspective, Christ becomes human and undergoes not only testing and (moral) maturation, but also persecution, shame, and death at the hands of humans. He also feels abandoned by God at the time of his death by crucifixion and cries out to God in apparent despair (see Mark 15:34, Matt. 27:46). In doing so, he identifies with humans who undergo testing, maturation, suffering, persecution, despair, felt abandonment by God, and death. We might say that Jesus thereby learned how to relate compassionately, in self-manifesting action, to other humans in their trials and tribulations. He felt something of what they feel, and thus came to appreciate their fragile predicament by way of sharing in it. This is redemptive compassion in action, whatever else is involved. (Chapter 2 returns to this theme.)

Why would God bother with self-identification with humans, especially given its required sharing in human grief, suffering, shame, despair, and death? What is to be gained in such a self-giving process? A partial answer is that God would seek for humans a special kind of knowledge of God: *relationally curative knowledge* that goes beyond knowledge that God exists and includes a good, reconciled relationship with God. Such curative knowledge would include human reconciliation to God, at least with some degree of human acquaintance, cooperation, and communion with God, and therefore would be redemptive for humans to some extent. Paul thinks of such knowledge as involving one's "being renewed in knowledge according to the image of [one's] creator" (Col. 3:10). This image would include the self-manifested character of God in compassion for others, and it would be irreducible to divine verbal testimony, even if God would sometimes offer self-interpretation of a divine self-manifestation.

Relationally curative knowledge would figure in God's aim to remove shame, distrust, hate, and selfish fear among humans in relation to God. That is, it would counter human alienation from (a good relationship with) God. It therefore would contribute to the reduction of experiential, psychological, and existential conflict and distance between humans and God. In addition, it would require that humans self-identify with God in relationally curative ways toward others. People often neglect the latter requirement for the divine redemption of humans, and this distorts the cooperative and reciprocal human role in divine redemption.

This book explores the significance of relationally curative knowledge in human knowledge of God and in the divine redemption of humans. It offers sympathetic cooperation from humans as central to participation in this redemption and in the corresponding human knowledge of God. A human trial with God would call for such cooperation, in connection with the ethics for inquiry about God.

The second feature of a relationally curative God includes the following: If God aims to cure self-exalting human pride, God may need to be subtle, elusive, and hidden at times in divine self-manifesting to humans, in order to avoid encouraging or affirming human pride. Self-exalting pride about having evidence of God's reality can hinder oneself and others from God's redemptive endeavor, because it can turn people away from considering God as a truly good, non-competitive agent. So, a relationally curative God may intentionally offer subtle and elusive evidence of divine reality that does not feed selfish human pride and perhaps even challenges it. God's aim would be to cure such a relational "sickness" among humans, and the evidence of God's reality would follow suit and hence be in intention redemptive for humans.

Blaise Pascal suggests in his *Pensées* (1662) that God would be subtle and elusive in self-manifestation, but the idea has been lost on many philosophers and other inquirers. It is especially neglected in natural theology where supposedly transparent arguments for God's reality are offered, sometimes as if God would be pleased with mere rational belief that God exists. A redemptive God, however, would be after something more profound in humans than mere rational belief that God exists: something relationally curative and transformative in human character, in cooperative relationship with God. Any quick and easy route to mere rational belief that God exists could interfere with what God primarily seeks, owing to people coming to hold that they have "arrived" at pleasing God when they have not. In that case, many people would suffer from misplaced confidence relative to God's redemptive expectations for humans. If God is worthy of worship and hence morally perfect, redemptive expectations would not be optional for God. They would be characteristic and even obligatory. So, there may be no quick way around a human trial with God in humans knowing God.

6. PROBING AND DEFENDING

We shall ask whether a relationally curative God, in being elusive, would allow for *decisive* human inquiry about God, that is, inquiry admitting of a well-founded decision about divine reality. In other words, can humans probe the question of God's existence in a manner that yields an evidentially well-founded answer? The English term "probe" comes from the Latin term "*probare*," which means "to test" or "to prove." In English, we use the term to mean, among other things, (a) to test, examine, or investigate or (b) to prove, verify, or justify. In the present context, it can connote testing for who God is (or is not), including for God's distinctive traits.

Not all people share a single standard of evidential adequacy. Even so, we can proceed with the rough idea of salient, or definite, evidence had by a person (but not necessarily by all persons) that is undefeated by opposing evidence. My having salient evidence does not require everyone else's having it too, as my evidence for my toothache, for instance, illustrates. Evidence is a *truth-indicator* for a person, and it can be fallible, subject to defeat by other evidence, and variable among persons. Truth itself is a different story, being factual or reality-based in a way that need not depend on a human experiential or belief perspective. A denial of the factuality of truth will itself entail a claim to factuality, and hence risk self-referential inconsistency. So, for the sake of consistency, we should not go there, despite the mistake of many critics of objective truth. (For details on the nature of evidence and truth, see Moser 1989, 1993.)

Talk of "probing God" can be ambiguous, because "probing" can be either a verb or an adjective. One question, then, concerns *who* would do the initial probing: A human or God? Both could probe, but one or the other would initiate the process. God could prompt humans to probe God, regarding who God is, as a result of God's probing them. Even if God probes first in human lives, God would seek mutual probing for the good of humans, and this fits with the idea of a human trial with God. In their sincere probing of God, humans could become attentive to some important character traits of God and perhaps even cooperate with God in various relationally curative endeavors. A number of biblical writers enjoin humans to "seek" God and God's kingdom and to "taste and see" what God is like (see Isa. 55:6, Matt. 6:33, Ps. 34:8). This suggests that probing with the mind does not exhaust the human probing of God. One could probe with one's will, too, or with what some biblical writers call "the heart." This would be in keeping with Paul's remark that "one believes with the heart" (Rom. 9:10). Similarly, one could probe with obedient action toward God. (Chapter 3 will return to this important theme in connection with the available evidence of God's reality.)

God's probing of humans could include God's "proving" God's own reality to humans, perhaps by a direct self-manifestation to them. The word "proving," however, is potentially misleading here, because its main well-defined use occurs in logic and mathematics, and not in matters about God. We have a possible wrinkle, in addition, if God has certain relationally curative purposes toward humans. Suppose that God wants people not merely to believe, even rationally, that God exists, but to yield to God in a cooperative relationship of faithful and sympathetic obedience, for their own benefit. In that case, the probing of God or by God could depend on some considerations regarding the volitional state of a person, particularly that person's *willingness* to yield to God in sympathetic cooperation and communion. This would go beyond merely intellectual probing, and it would include, as suggested, a role for humans to empower God in divine self-manifestation to them.

God could withhold divine probing if a person is not ready for such probing or is unwilling to take it seriously. One's taking it "seriously" would include one's being willing to yield to God as supremely authoritative if one acquires salient evidence of divine reality and goodness. This kind of seriousness would go beyond one's being a mere spectator regarding the question of God's reality. It would give one a lived-engagement, and not just speculation, regarding that question in relation to God. We shall explore the importance of such lived-engagement. It would involve the whole person before God, and not just intellectual reflection. It also would yield, as we shall see, a robust if elusive source of meaning or purpose for human life (see Chapter 4).

The reality of a perfectly good God would bear on the priority and even the singularity of a certain value for humans, particularly the value that God would expect to be primary for humans in relationships. Disturbingly, Jesus suggests that only "one thing" is necessary for humans (Luke 10:38–42), and Paul offers a similar view (Phil. 3:7–8). The "one thing," in keeping with the "first" commandment prescribed by Jesus (Mark 12:28–30), concerns a person's supreme unselfish love (agapē) toward God, in contrast with a person's many other, lesser loves. A person's supreme love is that person's primary love; it does not depend on, or owe its reality to, the person's other, lesser loves. On the contrary, the lesser loves should fit in with the supreme love, for the sake of coherence in what one loves. Otherwise, lesser loves can steal the special place of what should be one's primary love, given one's actual commitment to love.

When a perfectly good God is the object of one's supreme love, one's love of God should be "wholehearted," that is, pure or unmitigated relative to any conflicting loves. This kind of wholehearted love allows for lesser loves, such as love toward other humans, but it does not allow for loves that detract from one's love toward God. In seeking God's kingdom "first," one makes it part of one's supreme love, and, according to Matthew's Jesus, God's kingdom focuses on God's *will*. As his memorable prayer goes: "Thy kingdom come. Thy will be done." So, in this perspective, God's will has the priority in one's supreme love of God. If we disagree with Jesus here, we may find God to be not relationally curative, but grudging, untrustworthy, and unworthy of worship. We may focus on a lesser love (say, for control, health, wealth, or fame) that, when frustrated, appears to make God less than good. Such a misplaced focus figures in many interpretations of the problem of evil regarding God. (Chapter 2 will clarify this lesson in connection with faith and the fragility of human life.)

Satisfying a morally perfectionist title "God," a God worthy of worship would aim to be relationally curative in probing toward humans. From the standpoint of moral perfection and hence of worthiness of worship, God would be defective in lacking a relationally curative aim and practice toward humans. It would not be enough, however, for God to promote specific human beliefs about God, because such beliefs are compatible with a harmful, anti-God moral character, practice, and life. God would need to care about, and to seek to challenge, convict, and correct where needed, one's motivational attitudes, such as desires and intentions, and one's feelings and actions that accompany belief that God exists. God would seek, through various means of challenge, to bring humans into a cooperative relationship of communion with God that guides humans in conforming sympathetically to God's moral character and actions. Such communion, in receiving divine power and guidance, would be relationally curative for humans relative to God and perfect goodness.

In a minimal form, the communion in question could be free of belief that God exists, while preserving volitional interaction between God and humans and even cooperation of humans with God. Beliefs about God do matter, but they would not be exhaustive of or crucial to such communion or to a human's moral standing relative to a God worthy of worship. Mature humans are moral agents and decision-makers, and not just bearers of beliefs about God. They can cooperate with challenges and intrusions in their lives even when their beliefs are thin regarding the sources of those challenges and intrusions.

As suggested, the divine probing or testing of human moral agents would not coerce human decisions regarding God, pro or con, because coercion would extinguish genuine human agency in deciding about God, and hence would undermine vital interpersonal relations between God and humans. Humans then would lack the genuine agency to participate fully in interpersonal relations with God and other agents. A perfectly good God would seek human cooperation with God that includes freely willed cooperation and even companionship as *koinonia* with God. This God would be very different, then, from the god of deism, who would be aloof, casual, and perhaps inactive regarding the probing for a relationship of sympathetic cooperation with humans. (Chapter 5 returns to the relevant notion of companionship or *koinonia* with God.)

Writers from various disciplines have commented extensively on God's role (or the lack thereof) in physical cures and, more generally, in the redemption of humans. Even so, the topic of God as *relationally* curative in the context of a trial with God where humans empower God to self-manifest has not received adequate attention among theologians, biblical scholars, philosophers of religion, religious studies theorists, or sociologists of religion. The bearing of this topic on inquiry, evidence, knowledge, and faith regarding God has not enjoyed adequate treatment in the literature. This book corrects that neglect and explains the importance of doing so in connection with the ethics of inquiry about God.

A neglected part of the story, we shall see, is a kind of reciprocity or mutuality in the relationally curative process.

The evidence of the reality of a relationally curative God would require more than God's emerging and announcing a relational cure on offer for humans, although some critics of theistic belief seem to assume otherwise. Taking a hint from the Gospel of Mark, we have suggested that God would await human willingness to cooperate with what God morally cares about, in order to avoid forcing salient divine evidence on a person. The absence of such human willingness could impede the divine offer of salient evidence and the corresponding aims of a relationally curative God. This absence of willingness, one may argue, would omit the apprehending of the evidence *for what it is*: something intended to convict one toward, and thereby draw one into, a *koinonia* relationship with God.

The fitting way to apprehend the divine evidence and the corresponding *koinonia* relationship for what they are – *koinonia*-seeking, we might say – would be to enter in to the *koinonia* sought. The entering in would include a sympathetic *commitment* to the desired *koinonia* and not just experiences, thoughts, feelings, or actions regarding it. So, human intentions and decisions would loom large in this context. They could either open or close a person to receiving not only salient evidence from God but also a divine–human curative relationship of *koinonia*.

We may think of the needed human willingness as enabling the cooperative mutuality or reciprocity that a relationally curative God would seek. This mutuality would include personal interaction that would be initiated by God but actively received and sympathetically welcomed by a willing human. The active, welcoming reception includes the kind of positive response that various biblical writers call "faith" in God. This book will illuminate the kind of faith in question, and highlight the kind of mutuality and underlying experience it involves (see Chapter 2). We shall see that the widespread neglect of the mutuality and experience in question obscures the character of a relationally curative God and the conditions for adequately grounded faith in such a God. We also shall see how the experience of a trial with God can invite and support faith in God.

Inquirers about God will want to know whether, and if so how, faith in God can have a rational defense of its veracity or evidential groundedness (regarding actual divine intervention), that is, an "apologetics." A distinctive approach emerges from this book's perspective. We may call it "I–Thou apologetics," because it aims to move a person either from a lack of salient evidence of God's reality or from abstract, impersonal evidence to an experiential acquaintance with God. If God is perfectly good and hence aims to be relationally curative for humans, God would seek direct acquaintance with cooperative humans. Such acquaintance could bring a person into an I–Thou relationship with God as an experienced reality for that person, rather than as a mere concept. This could anchor a cooperative dispositional relationship between the person and God that transforms the person to share in the moral character of God. In thus being related to God, the person could cooperatively receive, firsthand, salient evidence of God's reality and moral character. The needed defense of faith would be firsthand and first person as a result. I–Thou apologetics would promote the value and the reality of such a defense (see Chapter 5).

My perspective on apologetics agrees with the aforementioned suggestion from Kierkegaard that God would seek to be known by humans in the second person (as a "Thou"), and not just the third person, even for humans who do not believe that God exists. This would be part of God's effort to uphold God's unique value for humans. We shall extend this suggestion to outline an apologetics that makes an I–Thou relationship primary in a defense of faith in God. A person receives the defense in the first person, as an "I" in relationship to a second person, "Thou." The primary defense is in the I–Thou relationship itself, for the human in that relationship. Any third-person defense, outside of an I–Thou relationship, would be secondary at best in that it ultimately would depend on a second-person relationship. We shall see how this dependence works in human experience. In addition, we shall see how an I–Thou apologetics invites people to put themselves in a position to receive firsthand salient evidence of God. The result will clarify the role of a human in empowering God to support a primary defense of faith in God. It also will extend our understanding of the ethics for inquiry about God and of the importance of such ethics.

7. PLANS

This book explains how, in a human trial with God, God would seek to be known by, and relationally curative toward, people willing to make themselves available to God and thereby to be cooperative toward God upon receiving salient evidence of God. In doing so, it illuminates the notion of a God who is subtle, elusive, and hidden at times in a trial intended to be relationally curative, that is, curative of interpersonal relationships between God and humans. It also contends that God would be self-manifesting, and in intent convicting, toward humans in an effort to offer salient evidence of God's reality and character directly to cooperative humans in a trial. This lesson, we shall see, has important consequences for the salient evidence of God's reality available to humans and hence for inquiry about God. The chapters identify this unique evidence and argue that it meets the standard for good evidence for some people, even if not for all people.

A person will have to decide for himself or herself whether the expectations for divine evidence are met in his or her experience. In this regard, the relevant evidence calls for the existential engagement of an individual person in making a vital decision regarding God on the basis of evidence. A person willing to cooperate with God would empower God to self-manifest to that person. In contrast, one's refusal to cooperate in a trial with God could hinder one from receiving an offer of salient evidence of God's reality. The book explains why this is so, with help from the ethics for inquiry about God.

Chapter 2, "The God Relationship and Faith," examines the bearing of a relationally curative God on human faith in God, with attention to a model from the trial of Jesus in Gethsemane. If God's relational cure for humans includes redemption as a reconciled relationship in *koinonia* with God, then God may need to challenge a person's will to be redirected toward sympathetic cooperation with God's morally perfect will. This challenge could include a situation that *morally overwhelms* a person, that is, takes the person aback in prompting a reconsideration of his or her life's overall moral direction. The result would be serious reflection on the use of one's will in ordering one's life and its priorities, and a further result could be, without coercion, a decision to reorient oneself toward God as supremely authoritative for one's life.

The chapter examines how a relationally curative God would be morally overwhelming toward humans, and it draws out some consequences for responsible inquiry about God's reality and for a suitable human response to God. It acknowledges that a person may have to struggle and suffer to receive salient evidence from God that seeks a *koinonia* relationship with God. So, the relationally curative process may be agonistic and difficult for humans as they develop faith in God. Even so, human willingness to cooperate with God could empower God to self-manifest to humans in redemptive ways. This willingness would include willingness to cooperate sympathetically with a morally perfect agent, and hence would involve ethical considerations about a human inquirer. The distinctive subject-matter of inquiry about God suggests an important role for the ethics for inquiry about God, specifically the importance of responsible inquiry relative to that subject-matter. The chapter identifies

some normative principles for responsible inquiry about
a morally perfect God.

Chapter 3, "The God Relationship and Evidence," identifies how a relationally curative God would self-manifest
the divine character to humans in a manner attentive to
human seeking. It examines a widely accepted position
called "argumentism about God," which implies that one's
knowledge of God's existence requires one's having an
argument for God's existence. The chapter raises doubt
that a relationally curative God would give divine evidence in accordance with argumentism. One problem is
that arguments for God's reality tend not to be relationally
curative or even to contribute to what is thus curative in
the way God would be curative toward divine–human *koinonia* relationships. Another problem is that interpersonal
evidence between two agents does not depend on either
agent's having an argument. Such evidence, we shall see,
is more basic than an argument.

In addition, the chapter challenges "intellectualism"
about God, which implies that we can get an adequate
answer to the question of whether God exists simply by
thinking hard enough about our evidence. Intellectualism
neglects the crucial distinction between the evidence
one *has* and the evidence *available* to one. One's coming
to have definite evidence about God may require one's
seeking that evidence in a certain way. In that case, mere
thinking would not settle the question of God's existence
for one, because one would need to exercise one's will in
pursuing the relevant evidence. In supporting the latter
view, the chapter illuminates how humans would have a
role in empowering God to self-manifest in their salient
evidence. It identifies how one would be able to make
oneself available to God in a manner suitable to God's
redemptive character and purposes. Given that God's
character and purposes would be morally robust, this
process of making oneself available would be subject to
an ethics of inquiry about God. It would involve, at least,

a consideration of responsible inquiry about God relative to its subject-matter.

Chapter 3 examines how a perfectly good, redemptive God would be elusive, subtle, and even hidden at times toward humans for good, redemptive purposes. One lesson is that we should not expect a relationally curative God always to be transparently and conveniently present to humans in their experience. If God needs to challenge some anti-God human tendencies toward selfish pride, for instance, we should expect God to bob and weave in self-manifesting toward humans, in order to convict the humans in question and reorient them away from their harmful pride. One desired result would be the diminishing of selfish human pride in having salient evidence of God's reality.

The chapter considers that a relationally curative God may use self-sacrifice for humans to manifest God's own moral character (in sharp contrast with human selfishness) and thereby to attract their attention. It acknowledges that God, seeking full redemption for each human, would want humans themselves to decide, freely, to make themselves available to, and to participate in, the life of divine self-sacrifice. Just as God would self-identify with humans in self-sacrificial love, so also God would expect humans to follow suit, in identifying with God. This kind of reciprocity would be central to the aforementioned human trial with God.

The chapter contends that human knowledge of God (and faith in God) would be morally and existentially robust, and not merely intellectual or theoretical. Such knowledge would be relationally curative for humans in their *koinonia* relationships with God and others. This lesson will confirm the importance of the ethics for inquiry about God, owing to the role of responsible human intentions in the inquiry. It also will acknowledge room for humans either to empower or to obstruct God in self-manifestation to humans in their salient evidence.

Chapter 4, "The God Relationship, Wisdom, and Meaning," considers how a relationally curative God would value a certain kind of wisdom beyond factual knowledge that God exists. Such wisdom would include special knowledge enabling one to prioritize one's values and valued things and to guide one's plans and actions in ways that are, all things considered, good. Following a suggestion from the apostle Paul, the chapter distinguishes between divine wisdom and worldly, or human, wisdom, and it contrasts divine wisdom with speculative philosophical arguments regarding God. The latter arguments, according to the chapter, do not sit well with the biblical testimonies of how God intervenes and works among humans for redemptive purposes that are relationally curative. This may not be a decisive problem, but it is noteworthy, especially if some of those testimonies are plausible. The chapter explains why God would not need speculative philosophical arguments to be known by humans, and would be better served by an alternative mode of intervention among humans: the direct self-manifesting of the divine character to receptive humans in a manner inviting a divine–human relationship of *koinonia*. Speculative philosophical arguments do not supply any such mode of divine intervention.

Chapter 4 identifies a distinctive kind of interpersonal assurance or certitude (in contrast with logical certainty) to be expected of a personal God who at times self-manifests and self-interprets to humans for relationally curative purposes. In doing so, the chapter takes exception to the familiar use of the traditional arguments of natural theology to gain assurance or knowledge of God. It also identifies how the divine wisdom on offer fits with a divine aim for relationships of *koinonia* between God and humans and between humans. Such wisdom, we shall see, calls for the ethics for inquiry about God, owing to the moral character of divine wisdom. It recommends that we attend to responsible inquiry attentive to the nature of the subject-matter in question.

Divine wisdom for humans would include wisdom about the meaning of human life. The chapter explores the bearing of a relationally curative God on the meaning or purpose *of* human life, beyond any meaning *in* human life that results just from human intentions. If God is morally perfect, then God would be redemptive toward humans and hence purposive in a way that offers meaning for human life. Chapter 4 identifies how the wisdom and *koinonia* from God would contribute to the meaning of human life. It argues that a redemptive God would want humans to be sympathetically cooperative in sharing in God's redemptive meaning or purpose for human life, even if the purpose runs afoul of independent human purposes or goals. The relevant meaning would become *sympathetic meaning* for humans in virtue of their cooperating sympathetically with it. Gethsemane emerges again as a model for participating in the life's meaning that includes the divine redemption of humans. The divine expectation, however, now goes beyond what is volitional to what is a matter of *pathos* as lived, engaged compassion toward others.

As perfectly sympathetic, God would have profound compassion, including self-sacrifice, for humans, and would seek human sharing in this compassion, including in a trial for compassion. Chapter 4 argues that we should expect the kind of sympathetic meaning in question to call for careful human discernment, owing to its being subtle, elusive, and even hidden at times. In such discernment, humans could come to a felt understanding of God's purpose for human life, even if they could not adequately convey this purpose directly to others in a felt manner. This lesson fits well with the character of a redemptive God who is subtle, elusive, and hidden at times in relation to humans. In addition, it allows for the relevant meaning to depend on an "I–Thou" acquaintance and a cooperative relationship between a human and God whereby a human conscience is morally challenged toward willingly being convicted by God. We shall see how the ethics for inquiry about God bears on responsible inquiry about the meaning for human life.

Chapter 5, "The God Relationship, *Koinonia*, and Defense," proposes that a relationally curative God would seek a distinctive kind of interactive fellowship or companionship with humans that goes beyond matters of knowledge, wisdom, and even obedience. This feature of the God relationship would require more than human obedience to God, because it would seek the affectively sympathetic and volitionally agreeable reception of God and God's will by humans. It also would call for a kind of divine–human fellowship, companionship, or communion, previously referred to as *koinonia*. It thus would be more challenging for humans than friendship in any ordinary sense, which may have nothing to do with personal redemption or even moral improvement. Relationally curative *koinonia* from God would seek to have humans freely share in God's perfect moral character and purposes, for their own relational good. It thus would promote the *imitatio Dei* for humans.

If a relationally curative God would love all other agents, then humans in *koinonia* with God would have to learn to love similarly, even to love their resolute enemies. In this respect, humans face an ongoing trial of compassion with God in relation to other humans. Chapter 5 acknowledges that success in this trial needs special power for humans, including the power to love one's enemies, and that this power would have to come from God as humans cooperate with God. Human willingness to cooperate with God could empower God to manifest divine power in salient human evidence and in human lives. The chapter elucidates the key role of such willingness in *koinonia* and identifies its role in the ethics for inquiry about God. The willingness in question would be marked by responsible handling of considerations and experiences of a morally perfect character.

If God works in self-manifestation and *koinonia*, we should acknowledge certain consequences for a defense of faith in God. Chapter 5 examines how God as an incorporeal Spirit, including a Spirit in *action*, would play a role in witnessing to God's reality for humans and thereby would ground a potential defense of faith in God. It considers what some of the biblical writers think of as the *inner witness* of the Spirit of God, and it relates this to the inward divine work for humans, including assurance and a defense from a relationally curative God. For instance, God's Spirit could witness to God's moral character by presenting unselfish divine love (*agapē*) to a person, including in conscience as one is willingly convicted of selfishness. Such a witness would differ from a witness *that* God manifests love, because the former witness would be *de re* in virtue of presenting the reality in question, with no required human belief or judgment regarding God. God would seek a reciprocal interpersonal witness whereby God witnesses divine goodness to humans, and humans, in turn, witness (with their lives) such goodness to God and others.

Chapter 5 contends that a cooperative reception of God's Spirit is no merely subjective matter, because it yields one's becoming compassionate and forgiving, to a discernible degree, as God is compassionate and forgiving. Such a transformation would be discernible by anyone suitably attentive and open to the relationally curative power of God. Even so, people could freely resist the witness on offer, and they could do so with logical consistency if they have a logically consistent set of beliefs. Humans thereby could disable or disempower God's effort to witness to humans and to transform them in a curative relationship of *koinonia*.

The chapter clarifies how the inwardness in question agrees with the moral character of a relationally curative God and calls for human abiding as *koinonia* with God. It also identifies how humans themselves can become evidence of a relationally curative God, even though such evidence does not yield an argument persuasive to all people. The witness and the defense identified include an I–Thou relation that does not generalize to the experiences or perspectives of all humans. This lesson, we shall see, has important results for the scope of a defense, or an apologetics, of faith in God. The chapter portrays the available defense in keeping with a God who would aim salient divine evidence toward redemption and hence anchor it in an I–Thou relation central to the God relationship.

Overall, then, we shall consider whether God is perfectly redemptive with the following result: Suitable human appropriation of faith, evidence, knowledge, wisdom, and meaning regarding God requires willingly being convicted and participating in an interpersonal relationship – the God relationship – that calls for sympathetic cooperation with God's will and sets constraints for responsible inquiry about God. The perspective to emerge may be called *relationship theism*, for short.

2

~

The God Relationship and Faith

A perfectly good God, as Chapter 1 suggested, would seek to be relationally curative toward humans in a *koinonia* relationship for their benefit. Our clarification of what this relationship would involve must precede our subsequent inquiry about the evidence for its reality. We need to clarify what this curative relationship would involve in connection with human faith in God, given the significance that monotheism typically assigns to such faith. If human faith in God includes trust in God, God could value such faith as part of human cooperation with God. A faith relationship with God, in that case, could be an important component of the God relationship with humans. Conceptions of faith vary widely among theologians and philosophers, and therefore we shall clarify a conception that fits with the God relationship under scrutiny. We also shall identify some corresponding principles of the ethics for inquiry about God.

With influence from Kierkegaard's pseudonymous author Climacus, theologians from Buber to Barth to Bultmann have portrayed God as being "wholly other" (*totaliter aliter*) relative to humans. This portrayal is understandable as an effort to underwrite divine transcendence and to avoid pantheism, but it easily overreaches and complicates an understanding of God as relationally curative toward humans. So, we need some correction here.

We need to avoid a portrait of God that makes God at odds with what Chapter 1 identified as *imitatio Dei* in *koinonia* relationships between humans and God. If humans are "in the image" of God to some extent, as various theologies imply, it can be misleading to say that God is "wholly other" relative to humans, at least qualitatively. This chapter offers a conception of a relationally curative God that is a better, but neglected, alternative for an understanding of faith in God. A relationally curative God, we shall see, may be *overwhelmingly* other at times (in a moral manner to be specified) without being *wholly* other. The chapter develops this position in an effort to illuminate how a relationally curative God would challenge a human will in order to invite or to deepen faith in God.

1. ASPECTS OF OVERWHELMING

Faith in God is often, if not characteristically, a cooperative response to one's willingly being overwhelmed by God for the sake of redirection toward a *koinonia* relationship with God. Such a response contrasts with any kind of sheer guesswork, fabrication, or wishful thinking. So, it would be misleading to suggest that faith in God is typically a leap "in the dark," even if it includes a "leap" as a (possibly well-grounded) decision to trust God now and in the future.

Regarding a cooperative human response to God's will, we shall find human faith in God to be modeled by Jesus in Gethsemane. Such faith is inherently volitional and irreducible to knowledge that something is the case, even though it could be supported by evidence from divine self-manifesting to humans. It includes *entrusting oneself* cooperatively to God or God's will, upon one's willingly being convicted by God. The struggle of Gethsemane can illuminate how God would be not only morally overwhelming but also relationally curative toward humans who respond

with faith in God. The relationship of faith requiring volitional cooperation with a perfectly good God has, corresponding to God's moral character, a distinctive ethical
component that bears on human inquiry about God.

If God is "almighty" or, in language about God attrib-
uted to Jesus, "the Power" (Mark 14:62; cf. Matt. 26:64),
then we should expect God to have power that can surprise and even overwhelm people at times. In one of
the most difficult passages in the New Testament, Jesus
seems overwhelmed by God in his cry of forsakenness
from the cross: "At three o'clock Jesus cried out with a
loud voice, 'Eloi, Eloi, lema sabachthani?' which means,
'My God, my God, why have you forsaken me?'" (Mark
15:34; cf. Matt. 27:46). Aside from the distinction between
being forsaken by God and *merely feeling* forsaken by God,
many interpreters infer that Jesus was overwhelmed in
some way by God, and I would suggest that this was an
opportunity for deeper moral focus for him. His expectations of God had left him with troubling perplexity about
God, given his lack of a prompt felt response from God
to his being crucified.

Although Jesus is citing Psalm 22 in his abject cry, I doubt
that he had in mind the whole of Psalm 22, particularly its
upbeat parts, given his seemingly dire predicament. In any
case, the role of being overwhelmed by God in human faith
in God can contribute to a morally robust conception of a
relationally curative God, in sharp contrast with an idol, or
a false god. We shall explore the bearing of this lesson on
the God relationship that includes *koinonia* with humans.

Something *morally overwhelms* a person, let us say, when
that thing moves the person to be taken aback or overcome in a manner that prompts the person to reconsider
the overall moral direction or purpose of his or her life,
relative to *agapē* (unselfish love) in personal relationships.
A perfectly good God would need to be overwhelming, if
uncoercively, in this manner toward wayward people, in
order to avoid a kind of moral indifference toward them.

The moral overwhelming of a person can arise from unco-ercive pressure on the person's will, such as when someone prompts me to reconsider and willingly be convicted of my habitual selfishness toward others. It is, in any case, irre-ducible to the merely physical or the merely psychological overwhelming of a person.

Let us say that a person is *consciously* morally over-whelmed by something when that person consciously experiences that thing as moving herself to be taken aback or overcome in the manner suggested. One's being morally overwhelmed can include various results, such as one's being surprised, awed, elated, frightened, haunted, trou-bled, angered, distressed, subdued, defeated, perplexed, or displaced. Being morally overwhelmed, then, can have various positive and negative results. Its results are neither always bad nor always good.

Something's morally overwhelming one typically includes that thing's deeply affecting one in some way, even if one does not understand its full import. By way of response, if one acknowledges God's reality, one may spontaneously ask, "Why, God, did this happen (to me)?" Answers, however, are not always forthcoming, even in outline, and some overwhelming events may seem too harsh to fit with the reality of a good God. (The book of Job illustrates this, memorably and convincingly.) Whatever else they share, many humans seem to share being mor-ally overwhelmed by different things in different ways at different times. They do not share, however, an account either of what ultimately brings about their being morally overwhelmed or of whether there actually is a common purpose for many cases of being thus overwhelmed. Some people hold that at least many cases of being morally over-whelmed are ultimately meaningless, with no underlying purpose at all. So, they do not look for a deeper meaning for all cases of the moral overwhelming of humans.

Some sources of being morally overwhelmed are good; others definitely are not. In addition, as suggested, the results of being morally overwhelmed are neither intrinsically good nor always good. A good source and a good result are found in a case where one is consciously morally overwhelmed by the kindness or mercy of a stranger, and thereby, willingly being convicted, one renounces one's habitual selfishness or destructive vengeance. We sometimes see such a case arising from a stranger who reports that her unselfishly showing mercy to others reflects God's mercy shown to her. In any case, one's being morally overwhelmed can be for the better for one, even if it leaves one perplexed about the intervening goodness and displaced from an earlier position of comfort, perhaps comfort in selfishness. New parents sometimes testify to such goodness, upon the arrival of a new baby in their lives, complete with around-the-clock duties for them.

Many memorable cases of being morally overwhelmed in human life include something not altogether good. Consider the awful effects on humans from earthquakes, hurricanes, tornadoes, tsunamis, wildfires, and epidemics, among other things. In addition, for human sources of moral overwhelming, one thinks of cases of genocide, war, murder, torture, rape, slavery, molestation, bullying, and kidnapping, among other things. Such phenomena can morally overwhelm humans even when they are not experienced firsthand, thus making it difficult to reflect on them even at a distance. We might say that something's being morally overwhelming toward humans can have long legs in spreading distress among humans.

The distress of being morally overwhelmed can prompt people to fear, resist, or flee being thus overwhelmed, as they seek protection and safety. This is no surprise, given the real danger involved in many cases of being morally overwhelmed. Humans build various structures – houses, fortresses, towns, nations, jails, and so on – to reduce the risk of being overwhelmed in harmful ways. Some of the desired protection from harm is against the ravages of nature; other protection is against serious threats from other humans. In either case, [the harmful effects from the overwhelming of humans invite protective measures, and humans have formed defensive skills in this area, complete with elaborate and expensive insurance policies. Many of these skills are prudent and above reproach.]

We can identify a problem related to our distinguishing between good and bad resistance toward being morally overwhelmed. A case of bad resistance can come from one's resisting good moral overwhelming, such as when I resist a stranger's overwhelming show of unselfish kindness toward me. I may be wary of such kindness, suspecting that it comes from a desire to manipulate or exploit me. Perhaps my suspecting arises from a troubled history of experiencing such manipulation or exploitation by others. In any case, I could tend to group the good with the bad in this regard and thereby block a genuine opportunity to realize goodness in my life. This tendency would add insult to injury in my life, and it would call for a correction by me.

We can understand how suspicion and fear, based on past experience, can block my receiving good overwhelming in my life. Such understanding, however, would not recommend approval or commendation of my behavior obstructing goodness. Instead, I would need to learn discernment between good and bad overwhelming in my life. In addition, I would need to learn how to receive, rather than to resist, good overwhelming in my life, even when difficult and frightening. This is an important part of ethical maturing, but it need not come easily, if it comes at all. So, a receptive attitude toward good overwhelming in my life can bring struggle and pain in my life.

[Being morally overwhelmed can, and often does, nudge a person in either of two directions: toward despair or toward hope about one's life. When one faces severe, destructive overwhelming that seems endless, such as long-term torture during war, despair often emerges and endures. One sees no available good that will end the destruction, and, therefore, one's situation can appear to go only from bad to worse. No basis for hope as a counter to despair appears within reach, and faith in a God who somehow will rescue can lapse. Some people testify to such a lapse in faith, and they take it to be understandable and reasonable. They assume that a good God would not fail them in this way. We shall see, however, that the matter is complicated owing in part to the kind of overwhelming found in Jesus's cry of dereliction.

When one finds a suitable counterbalance to the bad overwhelming in one's life, despair can yield to hope, because good overwhelming can figure in one's life as an antidote to despair. Perhaps a good personal relationship can play this role, but humans seem not to acknowledge a universally shared antidote to despair. Some humans acknowledge different antidotes, and others acknowledge no antidote at all. So, any generalization about a shared basis for hope will face empirical difficulty among actual humans. Given the wide-ranging diversity in human beliefs, this is not surprising news. What, then, of theology, including a relationally curative God as a counter to despair from bad overwhelming in human life? Is there room for relationally curative overwhelming from God? If so, what is its bearing on faith in God?

2. FROM CREATION-ENHANCING TO OVERWHELMING

If the term "God" serves as a perfectionist title for one worthy of worship, as Chapter 1 recommends, then any titleholder for the term will be morally perfect and hence free of moral defect. Various advocates of traditional monotheism, in the Jewish, Christian, and Islamic traditions, hold such a view. We should identify its implications for a relationally curative God's being morally overwhelming toward humans. God could be morally overwhelming in various good ways at times without *always* being overwhelming. God could impart goodness to humans in some cases without doing so overwhelmingly, such as when God blesses humans with a good environment without morally overwhelming them. (On divine blessing as irreducible to a saving act, in the Jewish tradition, see Westermann 1979, pp. 32, 43–45.)

The highly diverse biblical writings, taken as a whole, do not reduce divine action to God's moral overwhelming of others. Even so, God's moral overwhelming of humans at times in the biblical portrait is salient and familiar. The biblical writings include extensive, diverse, and fallible human testimony to God's acting toward and interacting with creation, including with creatures of God, who in turn can act toward and interact with God. In addition, this diverse testimony includes cases of God's interacting with God, such as God's self-referentially expressing regret to God about certain decisions and plans. We may speak of "human testimony" here because all of the biblical writings come to us from some human (group) or other, regardless of a divine role in the process. A human testimony need not be *merely* a human testimony, but it is at least a human testimony. We distort the crucial role of humans in the formation of the biblical writings if we neglect this point. (For relevant discussion, see Dodd 1960, pp. 13–40, 264–74, and Barr 1981, pp. 226–33, 289–99.)

According to the biblical writings, taken as a whole, God's acting toward and interacting with creation include the following: creating (things and needs), sustaining, blessing, promising, encountering, self-manifesting, self-hiding, challenging, convicting, commanding, redirecting, judging, killing, destroying, forgiving, reconciling, and fulfilling (promises). These actions and interactions need not morally overwhelm anyone, although they could do so in certain contexts of human confrontation with God. In addition, these divine actions and interactions would not be abstract in the way the content of a thought can be. They would include specific events in rather definite contexts, even if one can formulate abstract content *about* the events and contexts. As a way to accommodate such events and contexts, Claus Westermann recommends using action verbs, and not just abstract content, to characterize God (1979, p. 29; cf. Wright 1952, pp. 59–86, Knight 1959, pp. 17–21).

Corresponding to God's acting and interacting, the biblical writings portray human acting toward and interacting with agents, including God, in various ways. They include: finding and expressing human needs, lamenting, complaining, protesting, blaming, disliking, hating, doubting, distrusting, disobeying, fleeing, hiding, ignoring, despairing, lying, truth-telling, hoping, coping, liking, loving, trusting, obeying, thanking, praising, and worshiping. The biblical writings portray God as prompting occasions for such human actions, even if God is not always directly present as a directly experienced object in human experience. The God relationship under consideration does not require God's being present in that way.

As an interpersonal *state*, rather than an event or episode, the God relationship can persist when a person has no current experiences, thoughts, feelings, or actions regarding God. Faith in God, being an interpersonal state, shares this feature. The considerable emphasis in philosophy of religion and theology on experiences, thoughts, and actions regarding God has obscured the potential importance of a cooperative relationship with God to inquiry about God. We shall offer a correction of this misplaced emphasis.

God could be present as a causal influence that prompts human actions, but be absent from the contents of direct human experience. In this regard, divine presence would not reduce to divine presence *consciously experienced* by humans. Likewise, God could be morally overwhelming toward humans without being consciously experienced as such by them. God could hide divine presence and divine moral overwhelming from human recognition while maintaining such presence and overwhelming among humans. Such hiding could save some humans from premature judgment about God as it enables them to become prepared for learning who God really is, in contrast with the lesser gods made in the image of humans. (Chapter 3 returns to this topic.)

Karl Rahner (1964) has suggested that God can hide in a human experience of silence and thus seem distant, even though God is actually near. Denying that God *is* the silence, he proposes that God can use the silence to distinguish God from the counterfeit gods in human lives. Rahner adds: "Distant from you is only a God who does not exist: a tangible God, a God of a human being's small thoughts and his cheap, timid feelings, a God of earthly security, a God whose concern is that the children don't cry and that philanthropy doesn't fall into disillusion, a very venerable – idol! That is what has become distant" (1964, p. 218; see also Rahner 1973, p. 212). Human despair over this false god does not require despair over the God who could be near in the silence and in the felt distance. It does not require despair over the God who would not actually forsake the crucified Jesus despite his having felt being forsaken. So, we have two contrasting portraits of God before us, and only one will endure as fitting for a God who is worthy of worship and hence morally perfect and relationally curative toward humans.

A common lament among humans concerns why hardship from God – including the painful silence, the felt distance, and the stressful overwhelming – looms so large in their experience. It seems at times to be disproportionate to what humans actually need for moral correction, as Job famously lamented. Could a perfectly good God offer any counter here, beyond a lesson about divine incomprehensibility for humans? We should not expect to have a theodicy as a full explanation of God's purposes for human hardship, as if we were in a good position to identify and understand those purposes fully. Our cognitive limitations relative to God's purposes advise due modesty here. Job learned this lesson the hard way, and sometimes his successors do too.

The biblical writings, again taken as a whole, suggest that God allows and even creates hardship and overwhelming for humans for various purposes, but always against a background of God's good purposes. So, God's creating hardship and overwhelming for humans does not entail God's doing evil. If God's purposes in allowing and creating human hardship (even with judgment at times) are consistently good rather than bad, then we may speak of them as being broadly *creation-enhancing* in intent. In that case, however, a creation-enhancing act intended for good need not be an act that brings, or even aims to bring, salvation or divine reconciliation to a person. Creation-enhancing goodness is broader than an act of salvation as divine–human reconciliation; so, such goodness cannot be reduced to the latter kind of act. Even if God seeks human salvation, it would not follow that God does *only* what will, or even aims to, bring about human salvation as reconciliation to God.

The biblical writings portray God as aimed at creation-enhancing, particularly toward humans, and not as set *just* on acts of human salvation. Part of this divine aim would be to manifest human creatureliness, including creaturely need, before God, often when humans ignore or resist their being creatures before God. A human experience or acknowledgment of creatureliness can be an avenue to reconciliation with God, but it does not automatically go in that salvific direction. (On a relevant notion of a "creature-feeling," see Otto 1923, pp. 8–11.) A human will can block reconciliation to God, even if God wreaks hardship among humans in order to manifest human creatureliness and thereby to be creation-enhancing. So, we do well not to try to domesticate God or to make God docile in casual "niceness" in relation to humans. Otherwise, we create an indifferent idol, a casual false god. We then risk characterizing God as suffering from a kind of moral indifference in relating to humans.

The God of the biblical writings does not reduce to any such distant god as Plato's Demiurge or Aristotle's Prime

Mover, the latter being characterized by "thought think-ing itself." Instead, this God seeks actively to enhance goodness, at least of a moral sort, in a troubled creation, even when the outcome is not human salvation. This kind of seeking must accompany the kind of moral perfection characteristic of worthiness of worship and hence of being God. Otherwise, we will have counterfeit moral perfection, something unworthy of the exalted category "God." In this regard, a relationally curative God must meet standards unmet by any god of deism.

In opportune cases, a perfectly good God could move beyond mere creation-enhancing toward humans to the moral overwhelming of humans, in order to manifest human inadequacy and a relationally curative need before God. Without *causing* bad overwhelming of humans, or any other evil, God could *use* such overwhelming to bring peo-ple to face their being dependent creatures and their moral inadequacy before God. In doing so, God could forgo the immediate rescue of humans from their hardship for the sake of (deepening) acknowledged need of God. So, a rela-tionally curative process from God could leave humans with real hardship that has no quick fix. We have, in any case, no reason to assume that such a relational process must be easy or fast for humans, even if God is perfectly good and redemptive toward humans.

Without causing the crucifixion of Jesus, God could use it to overwhelm many humans morally, including Jesus, who sought to identify with other humans in their feeling forsaken by God. God did not save Jesus from experiencing the physical abuses by the Roman soldiers, such as mock-ing, scourging, and death by crucifixion. Jesus received no divine protection from experiencing these abuses, although God could have performed a preemptive rescue. (Job also serves as a memorable example of one's undergoing suffer-ing without a quick rescue by God; likewise for Paul: see 2 Cor. 4:8–11.) If, for a relationally curative purpose, God wanted Jesus to represent and to identify with humans in their predicament of hardship, the lack of a fast rescue by God would be no surprise. Being morally overwhelmed by God, then, remains a live option for humans, even if the specific divine purpose is obscure. We turn to how the moral overwhelming of humans relates to faith in a relationally curative God.

3. FROM OVERWHELMING TO FAITH AND *AGAPĒ*

An oversimplified chain from being morally overwhelmed by God to faith in God takes the following form and order:

  a. moral overwhelming of a human by God
  b. perplexity of this human about the overwhelming
  c. self-displacement from presumed control over the situation by this human
  d. psychological room created for the salient self-manifesting of God's moral character, will, and purpose to this human while willingly being convicted by God's will
  e. opportunity for this human to receive God via faith in God as a sympathetic cooperative response to God's manifested will.

The human story of interaction and struggle with God is rarely, if ever, this straightforward, but steps a–e often emerge from human stories in different ways, typically under different descriptions. (For an illuminating treatment of human perplexity regarding God, in relation to divine incomprehensibility, see Rahner 1991; cf. Niebuhr 1949, Rahner 1978, pp. 403–409.)

Faith De Re *and* De Dicto

An enduring faith in God demands human resolve of the will to resist falling into despair while being morally overwhelmed by God. Such faith is irreducible to one's assenting to the intellectual content of statements, because it engages the human will to intend to cooperate with God's will. It also includes trust as cooperative self-entrustment to God, even during the moral overwhelming of a human.

A *theologically neutral* mode of faith in God will be faith *de re* and not require one to believe that one's intention to cooperate is related to *God*. In this *de re* mode, one's faith will be related directly to *God's will*, via trust as cooperative self-entrustment *de re*, rather than to a notion or a judgment *about* God's will. Such *de re* faith may include minimal demonstrative content, such as that *this* is good, but a conception of *God* would not be required. In contrast, a *theologically demanding* mode of faith in God will require *de dicto* content regarding God, and this typically involves believing *that* something is the case regarding God. It often includes one's believing that God will fulfill God's promises, even when the prospects seem dim. At any rate, it would be a mistake to assume that there is such a thing as *the* (singular) mode of faith in God.

A theologically neutral mode of faith in God serves an understanding of God as one who does not require *de dicto* content regarding God from all people cooperating with God's will. People can cooperate in ignorance and even conceptual absence regarding (a notion of) God. A theologically neutral mode would fit with God's allowing for faith in God among those who do not believe *that* God exists or do not even have a conception of God. It thus would accommodate extensive diversity in *de dicto* content among those cooperating with God's will.

We shall proceed with attention to a theologically neutral mode unless a particular conceptual context requires *de dicto* content regarding God. Attention to such a neutral mode allows one to hold that *ideally* people would have faith in God accompanied by *de dicto* content, such as the content that God is good and trustworthy. In any case, a person could be related to God's will in both a *de re* manner and a *de dicto* manner, and this option would be ideal for the redemptive aim of the God relationship.

A serious problem arises when one identifies faith with belief and then characterizes belief as belief that something is the case. In this intellectualist perspective, faith in God is the same as belief that God exists. This approach to faith is misguided, because it omits a role in faith in God for *trust in God*. One can believe that God exists without trusting in God at all. To trust in God is to *count on God* for something, but belief that God exists does not require one's counting on God for anything. So, the idea of faith in God cannot be reduced to the idea of belief that God exists.

Trusting in God is episodic in that it is something one *does*, that is, it is acting toward God in a certain way. It includes one's committing oneself to God with regard to something, typically God's goodness (of some kind) in one's life. Faith in God, in contrast, is not episodic in the way that trust in God is, even though it includes as a base trusting in God at some past or present time. Instead, faith in God is a disposition-oriented state rather than an action. It includes one's *tending* to trust in God under relevant circumstances as a result of one's trusting or having trusted in God. (It is no easy task to specify all of the relevant circumstances, and we need not digress to that matter.) So, I can have faith in God when I am asleep, doing nothing at all.

The trust required by faith in God is, for present purposes, *self-entrustment* to God whereby one commits oneself to God, fully in an ideal situation, and does not commit just one's experiences, thoughts, feelings, or actions. A God worthy of worship (and hence characterized by moral perfection) would require such full personal commitment for the good of the person who has faith in God. This truth is reflected in the "primary love command" identified by Jesus on the basis of the Jewish Bible: "You shall love the Lord your God with all your heart, and with all your soul, and with all your mind, and with all your strength" (Mark 12:30; cf. Deut. 6:5). (We shall return to the relation between faith and love, at the end of this section and in Chapter 5.)

Because faith in God includes trust in God as self-entrustment to God, we can identify a *responsive* human component in such faith. This component includes an agreeable human response to something presented to a human. In the case of faith in God, the response is to *God*; otherwise, it would not be faith in *God*. This fits with an influential Christian view that *God* is the primary gift of grace in faith in God. The response would include an agreeable response to an intervention of God in one's awareness or experience. Otherwise, one would lack a more or less determinate divine object (as subject) to which to respond. One could respond to a merely apparent divine object in experience, but that would not be a response to God and hence would not qualify as faith in God. (Chapters 3 and 5 return to the epistemological matter of how one is to distinguish between the two kinds of objects of response in human experience.)

The role of human response in faith in God includes a role for human *decision* in faith in God. Three options for decision are: (a) a *positive* response whereby one commits to cooperate with God's self-manifestation in one's experience, in keeping with God's will; (b) a *negative* response whereby one commits to rejecting cooperation with God's self-manifestation; and (c) an *indifferent* response whereby one withholds commitment to cooperate with God's self-manifestation, neither committing to cooperate nor committing to reject cooperation. These options are *roughly* analogous to the options of theism, atheism, and agnosticism, but there is a key difference. Options (a)–(c) can be *de re* in the following sense: A person can satisfy one of those options without having *de dicto* content regarding God, that is, without having conceptual or propositional information regarding God. A person would not have to believe that God exists, to satisfy one of those options.

One's response could be *de re* in that one responds to the goodness of God's character self-manifested in one's experience without conceptualizing either God or the goodness as being from God. From a conceptual standpoint, one's commitment could be non-theological, but from a *de re* standpoint, it still could be a commitment *to God*. Here we find a major difference between faith *in* God and faith *that* God exists, at least in the taxonomy I recommend. The suggested *de re* approach has important benefits for religious diversity, because people across varying religious belief-systems, and even people without a religious belief-system, can have faith in God. So, one could have faith in God but not know that one does. This would be in keeping with a morally perfect God, who would not block people from relating to God solely on the basis of their lack of *de dicto* commitments regarding God. Otherwise, God would be morally superficial and morally defective. (For the bearing on religious diversity, see Moser 2010, chap. 5.)

The human response included in faith in God, being *de re*, is not a response merely to conceptual or propositional content; otherwise, it would be *de dicto*. Instead, it is a response to a distinctive *intentional power* or *energy* characteristic of a morally perfect God: namely, divine *agapē*. As suggested, *agapē* is unselfish, compassionate love that seeks what is best, all things considered, for others, even for one's enemies. God's *agapē* would be an agent-based intentional power or energy, because it would include the empowered *willing* from God, and not just divine reflection or ideas. It thus would have motivational influence, but it would not coerce humans against their own wills regarding God. As indicated, God would not want to exclude humans as voluntary participants in relationships of *agapē*.

Faith in God goes beyond trust in God to the human appropriation of the intentional power of divine *agapē*. This is human appropriation *from* a direct acquaintance, an I–Thou encounter, with God, and it is appropriation *to* the human who has faith in God. If an instance of faith is not a response to, and ultimately empowered by, divine *agapē*, it is not faith *in God*, because it is not suitably related to

God's distinctive moral character of perfect love. By title, God would be morally perfect and hence not be God in the absence of such a moral character. This moral character would be inherent to being God, and one's encountering God would include one's encountering this moral character. A suitable approach to faith in God must accommodate this widely neglected lesson.

The divine *agapē* central to faith in God would not be reducible to a discrete event or episode in human experience. Instead, it would be a key component of a *relationship* of divine–human fellowship or *koinonia* sought by God. Such a relationship would be redemptive and corrective, or curative (at least ultimately), for humans in thought, feeling, and action, and hence would be promoted by a morally perfect God. Faith in God thus would include one's entering in to a *koinonia* relationship with God empowered by divine *agapē*. Such entering can arise from one's deciding to cooperate with the goodness, including the *agapē*, presented to one by God. As suggested, this deciding can be *de re* in a way that allows one to be innocent of a concept of God. It is a positive decision toward a morally relevant *reality* presented to one by God, even if one lacks corresponding conceptual resources about God. (Chapter 5 returns to the relevant notion of *koinonia*.)

Faith, Knowledge, and Hope

We now can approach the question of why a perfectly good God would promote human faith in God rather than mere knowledge that God exists. Paul suggests a noteworthy answer: "For this reason [God's promise of redemption] depends on faith, in order that the promise may rest on grace and be guaranteed to all [of Abraham's] descendants, not only to the adherents of the law but also to those who share the faith of Abraham (for he is the father of all of us)" (Rom. 4:16). The key idea is that God would aim to relate to humans ultimately by a divine *gift* of "grace" (*charis*) rather than by human earning or meriting relative to God.

A divine motive for grace would fit with what would be the redemptive reality given a morally perfect God: The ultimate power of redemption, including lasting good life, would come from *God* rather than humans. Paul assumes this lesson in the following remark: "We have this treasure [of redemption] in clay jars, so that it may be made clear that this extraordinary power belongs to God and does not come from us" (2 Cor. 4:7). Paul is referring to the divine power to which faith in God is related, in a way that mere factual knowledge (that something is true) is not. Faith in God serves as the way to receive, cooperatively and without merit, God's intentional power on offer, particularly the power of righteous love in interpersonal relationship (see Phil. 3:8–9).

Faith in God is closely related to hope in God, at least in its orientation toward divine goodness being realized in the future, and Paul affirms this. In Romans 5, Paul begins with talk of faith in God and moves straightaway to talk of hope in God. His key remark is: "Hope [in God] does not disappoint us, because God's love [*agapē*] has been poured into our hearts through the Holy Spirit that has been given to us" (Rom. 5:5). Paul would say the same of faith in God, and he has in mind something offered to humans as a gift of grace, and not as a human earning from God. The thing being offered is a powerful relationship of divine *agapē*, to be received by faith and hope in God, and it reflects the center of God's character as morally perfect and worthy of worship. Faith in God is a cooperative response by a human to this offer from God, and it includes human self-entrustment *de re* to God.

De dicto hope in God can include hope that God somehow brings good out of the hardship of one's being morally overwhelmed and out of the evils in human life. Like hope in God, faith in God is irreducible to knowledge or belief that God is such-and-such. Ideally it would be accompanied by evidence, knowledge, and belief that something is the case regarding God, anchored in divine self-manifesting. It is not reducible, however, to any or all of those three, given its role for volitional resolve toward God's will into the future. Faith in God ideally includes a resolved human venture of endurance toward a future with God, even if in a *de re* case one has not acknowledged or conceptualized God at all. It thus differs from mere knowledge or belief that God is such-and-such, and it figures in a relationally curative process when it becomes a direct avenue to the reception of divine love in interpersonal relationships for a human.

De dicto faith in God is exclusive in its resolve to let God *alone* be supremely authoritative in *all* things, even in matters of moral overwhelming and hardship for humans (not to be confused with evil). Despite human failures in practice, no exceptions to the goal of this resolve would be allowed, lest God be denied as supremely authoritative. Idolatry, with its lesser gods, is the constant threat in this regard, as it offers sources of authority and power in conflict with God. The resolve in question requires human willingness to die to the authority of all powers in conflict with God and God's power, for the sake of living for just one ultimate personal Power. This is the heart of monotheistic *de dicto* faith, in *one* God, and it is more robust, demanding, and adventurous than mere belief or knowledge that God exists. Such faith in God, then, concerns the authoritative power for which one lives and dies.

The model test of the resolve of faith in God for humans (and not just for Jesus) is a Gethsemane context. This is the context of ultimate decision regarding the supreme authority of God's will for Jesus and for all other humans. Gethsemane is the standard for faith's trial, inviting a struggle to conform with the resolve of faith to God's perfect will, even in moral overwhelming by God. If a human is free of any such struggle, that human is at odds with the God relationship, because God's perfect character would call for this kind of struggle among humans. The aim of the struggle would be redemptive, or curative, and the struggle would be ongoing for humans, and not just momentary, given that human lives extend over time. In addition, an actively redemptive God would bring about a duty for a human, at some time or other, to face a struggle with God's will. Paul states the point bluntly: "You were bought with a price [by God]; therefore glorify God in your body" (1 Cor. 6:20). A big question concerns how humans can perceive their indebtedness to God via responsible inquiry.

Jesus set the standard for faith in God with his ultimate resolve in Gethsemane to let God alone be supremely authoritative in his life, particularly regarding his anticipated crucifixion by the Romans. Having linked human life with God with human dying (Mark 8:34–35), Jesus prayed in Gethsemane: "Abba, Father, for you all things are possible; remove this cup from me; yet, not what I want, but what you want" (Mark 14:36). The clause following "yet" identifies the hallmark of Jesus's relating to God in *koinonia*, and it arguably emerges as a standard for all people, upon willingly being convicted by God, in their relating to God in *koinonia* as supremely authoritative. In this perspective, Gethsemane is not just for Jesus.

Gérard Rossé has observed that the obedient response from Jesus in Gethsemane "release[s] the unfolding of the passion [of Jesus in the Synoptic Gospels]," and is "for the [New Testament] evangelist the key to all that is about to happen, a warning to read all that follows in this light" (1987, p. 63). This seems plausible. The key is Jesus's resolve, upon willingly being convicted by God, to put God's will and power above his own to the bitter end, even to the extent of undergoing feeling forsaken by God and dying on the cross.

Rossé adds: "At the moment in which he appears forsaken, he is identified more than ever with the divine will. . . . In this weakness without end, Jesus finds himself 'delivered' without reserve to the Power of the Father, totally open to the creative act of the resurrection" (1987, p. 68). We may think of this as Jesus's commitment to die to his own will in order to live to God's perfect will. This kind of cooperative commitment to God's will is at the heart of faith in God, and it is expected to endure through moral overwhelming by God.

The challenge of Gethsemane launches and guides the obedient, kenotic attitude toward God that led to Jesus's cry of forsakenness, his death, and his being "delivered without reserve" to God (see Rossé 1987, pp. 45, 102; cf. Rahner 1964, pp. 217, 219–20). In subjecting his own will to God's perfect will, Jesus resolved to live by the supreme authority of God's will for his life. This kind of subjecting is crucial to the relationally curative process that would be offered by a God worthy of worship. It would enable God to be supremely authoritative in the relationally curative process for humans by enabling God's will to integrate a human life with God's life, thereby removing its relational alienation from God. This factor is at the core of the God relationship under scrutiny, because it is at the center of the needed *koinonia* relationship. Even though a person does not incorporate God's goodness in an instant, and hence can be unrighteous and ungodly (as in Rom. 4:5), one's imitating Jesus in Gethsemane could begin a relationship with God that leads over time to character-transformation toward God's goodness in *koinonia*.

A key lesson from a relationally curative God would be captured by the previous phrase "in this weakness [of Jesus] without end." Such weakness includes the Gethsemane weakness of yielding one's own will fully to God's perfect will, even in the face of death. This would include a human moral struggle in many cases. Paul highlights this lesson in his Corinthian correspondence, where the significance of the crucified Jesus is at stake. For instance, Paul writes of Jesus that "he was crucified in weakness, but lives by the power of God" (2 Cor. 13:4). The contrast is between the accepted weakness of Jesus, relative to his submission to

God's will and power, and the resurrection power of God extended to the obedient Jesus (cf. Phil. 2:5–9). The relevant weakness, then, is accompanied by distinctive power from God that brings lasting life with God out of the accepted human weakness. So, the volitional weakness underlying human faith in God does not obstruct life with God, but instead launches a person in such life, in letting God be God with the supreme authority of God's will.

Paul's statement of the divine purpose for human weakness identifies the previously noted aim that "it may be made clear that this extraordinary power belongs to God and does not come from us" (2 Cor. 4:7). Paul's notion of the power that "does not come from us" bears on his understanding of God's challenge to human self-trust without reliance on God. He remarks: "We felt that we had received the sentence of death so that we would rely not on ourselves but on God who raises the dead" (2 Cor. 1:9). In Paul's perspective, this remark about what humans "rely on" concerns what humans have trust or faith in, and Paul regards God as seeking to undermine human self-trust that does not yield to trust in God. In opting for self-trust, humans opt out of suitable trust in God, which includes trust in God alone as supremely authoritative. Instead, they put themselves in a role properly reserved for God alone, as only God has the needed life-giving power to be received in faith. This move blocks the God relationship for humans, because it blocks a *koinonia* relationship with God.

God's distinctive intentional power, including resurrection power, would be *sui generis* and hence is not to be confused with what mere humans have to offer on their own. The contrast with human weakness puts this lesson in sharp relief, thereby highlighting the uniqueness of the divine power needed by humans. John Hick identifies the contrast: "To become conscious of God is automatically to be judged by the almost blinding contrast between our own self-centredness and God's perfect, because universal, love; but it is also to have opened before us the possibility

of a new and better life and to hear ourselves called for-
ward into that life" (1978, p. 41). Perhaps humans prefer a
mere divine supplement to enhance or approve their own
power and will, but neither Gethsemane nor Calvary enables any such easy compromise. God would not be a subor-
dinate for the provision of human power; otherwise, God
would cease to be God, because human power then would
set a standard for divine power. (For the distinctiveness of
Paul's lesson of the cross of Christ in his historical context,
see Hengel 1977 and Savage 1996.)

Paul ties together the previous observations about faith,
divine power (including grace as a relational gift of interpersonal reconciliation), suffering, and hope:

Since we are justified by faith, we have peace with God
through our Lord Jesus Christ, through whom we have
obtained access to this grace in which we stand; and we boast
in our hope of sharing the glory of God. And not only that,
but we also boast in our sufferings, knowing that suffering
produces endurance, and endurance produces character, and
character produces hope, and hope does not disappoint us,
because God's love (*agapē*) has been poured into our hearts
through the Holy Spirit that has been given to us. (Rom. 5:1–5)

Faith in God, according to Paul, gives humans access to
God's power, particularly the power of grace, because
the resolve of faith in God puts that power in the place of
supreme authority for humans, as Jesus did in Gethsemane
and on the cross. (For Paul's emphasis on the unmerited character of divine grace, see Barclay 2015; see also
Schillebeeckx 1980.)

Our having divine power in "clay jars," according to
Paul, shows that it does not come from us or our self-
sufficient efforts. Instead, this power must come from God,
and human faith in God is the human means to receive it
directly from God. Such faith, however, brings human suffering, given the world's opposition to it, but the suffering

can serve God's redemptive purpose for a human. It can contribute to an enduring moral character that abides in a relationship of hope in God, particularly, hope in God's sustenance in the suffering, as an alternative to the world's despair. In this respect, at least, God's power can be relationally curative even in a context of human suffering, including the suffering of being morally overwhelmed by God.

Paul is not engaged here in speculative or wishful thinking. Instead, he observes God's self-manifested reality in the unique power of unselfish love (*agapē*) that God has given people of faith through God's Spirit. God's distinctive power is, in Paul's account, a present reality of the relationally curative renewal of humans with divine love. It cognitively anchors and ratifies human faith and hope in God, thereby removing the disappointment of despair. So, owing to the received power in question, such faith and hope in God are an alternative to speculative or wishful thinking for receiving evidence from God. They are an affirmative human response to the divine power on offer in human experience, and, as such, they appropriate unique evidence from God. If one holds that faith and hope in God are a gift from God, one still should acknowledge a cooperative human role in the reception of that gift.

Paul speaks of a present human renewal that anticipates a resurrection of humans by God: "Even though our outer nature is wasting away, our inner nature is being renewed day by day" (2 Cor. 4:16). Timothy Savage refers to this as "the *present* experience of future resurrection" (1996, p. 182, citing Hooker 1979). A related idea emerges in Romans 6:13, where Paul encourages the Roman Christians to "present yourselves to God as those who have been brought from death to life," courtesy of the power of God. An adequate characterization of faith and hope in God must acknowledge their cognitive anchor in the present reality of divine self-manifesting to humans, particularly, the self-manifesting of God's power of love. In the absence of that reality, we will have counterfeits unable to weather the overwhelming hardships of human life and death. The counterfeits are unable to contribute to a relationally curative renewal from a perfectly good God. *Agapē* from God would have a unique curative role toward cooperative humans.

God's relationally curative renewal in love, according to various New Testament writers, is at the heart of Gethsemane and the cross. Rossé explains: "If the Father had intervened before the death, if he had interrupted the experience of abandonment with an act of power before it was fully finished, an abandonment which for Jesus meant complete, unlimited gift of himself, he would have limited the love of Jesus for him, he would not have allowed him to express his filial *relationship*, his being Son, to the full. But by this very fact, he would not have been fully Father" (1987, pp. 136–37, italics added). This filial relationship with God does not depend on a current experience of God.

Jesus acknowledged "My God" in his experience of God's forsaking him, thus suggesting that a present *experience* of God is secondary to something else: namely, a loving *relationship* with God, which may or may not include a present experience of God. This lesson is lost in much philosophical and theological discussion of God's reality, but it merits attention if a perfectly loving God would seek a *koinonia* relationship irreducible to present experiences, thoughts, feelings, or actions regarding God. Such a relationship can endure in the absence of present experiences, thoughts, feelings, or actions regarding God. An effective way to understand this relationship is to examine the relationship between Jesus and God.

Rossé concludes: "The abandonment [of Jesus], then, reveals to a maximum degree the being of God: Love. One understands what an upset such a fact must have been for the common mentality, for philosophy, and even for the behavior of those who were already 'following Christ'" (1987, p. 139; cf. Savage 1996, pp. 187–88). If this love is central to what Abraham Heschel (1962) calls the motivating "*pathos*" of God (as a lived, engaged concern for the world), and humans are to share in this *pathos*, then humans should have cruciform love as an abiding motive in all human action (see Phil. 2:5–9).

Gethsemane and the cross of Christ define the life of faith in God, particularly its distinctive motivating power of love that seeks to be relationally curative for humans. Paul remarks: "In Christ Jesus neither circumcision nor uncircumcision counts for anything; the only thing that counts is faith working through love" (Gal. 5:6). His talk of "faith working through love" is talk of faith being *energized* or *empowered* (*energoumenē*) through *agapē*. Separating faith in God from this empowerment will remove its stable epistemic and psychological base for humans.

We must face the reality of human failure to have faith and hope in God. This widespread failure can emerge in various ways, as suggested by Jesus's parable of the sower (Mark 4:3–20). A common shortcoming is human failure to enter the "weakness without end" where God's power alone guides ultimately in a person's life. Jesus entered this weakness with genuine struggle via Gethsemane, but many humans refuse to follow suit, thereby resisting the relationally curative renewal on offer. This renewal depends on humans being willing to struggle to submit their wills to God's perfect will; it thus depends on human cooperation in *koinonia* with God's will. In the absence of such cooperation, a human relationship with God would lack a volitional basis for renewal in the moral image of God. God's image, being irreducibly moral, includes God's perfect will at its center, and this will is the ultimate moral guide for the God relationship of *koinonia* with humans.

It would not add explanatory value now to invoke a lack of human *trust* in God, because we are trying to illuminate a failure of *faith* in God. Trust and faith are too closely related here. Perhaps we have in part a failure of human courage, as Rahner suggests in noting the courage of Jesus in committing himself to God (1964, p. 219; cf. Rahner 1960,

p. 56). Correspondingly, we may suspect human fear to be at work, including fear of missing out on something one seeks, even something one deems good, such as autonomy in ethics. In this perspective, the main challenge to faith in God is not intellectual doubt but rather fear of Gethsemane that includes fear of not satisfying one's own settled preferences. Such fear can include the concern that God is not genuinely good and hence will fail to supply what one finds good. In this perspective, God seems to be harmful rather than relationally curative toward humans, at least in some cases.

Fear aside, one might simply fail to see or find a relationally curative God at work in human weakness or in the kind of moral overwhelming that creates human hardship. One thus might doubt the reality of God, on the ground that needed evidence is lacking. Some people fail to see a curative God's involvement; other people see it. The difference between the two groups may seem clear in general, but it eludes quick explanation. Perhaps some *want* to see, whereas others do not, given that ultimate human authority is at stake (see Baillie 1956, pp. 140–42).

Augustine offers a pointed response: "Why does [one] not see God? Because he has not love itself. That he does not see God is because he does not have love; that he does not have love is because he does not love his brother. The reason then why he does not see God is that he has not love. For if he had love, he would see God, for 'love is God'" (402/2011, Homily 9, on 1 John 4:17–21). Even if this diagnosis applies to some people, it does not easily generalize to all people who fail to see a relationally curative God at work among humans. We need a more complex explanation, given the evident differences among relevant humans.

Timothy Savage has suggested that some fail to see God "because the new life comes to expression in the humility of faith, a trait viewed with scorn by those absorbed in the self-exalting outlook of their day" (1996, p. 186). We might say that my self-indulgence obstructs my seeing God at work in characteristic unselfish love. This answer may not apply universally, but volitional resistance to the weakness of faith in God can cloud human apprehension of its value in relation to God's power of love. Even if God is often morally overwhelming in the unique power of divine love, this love may need to be suitably apprehended and received only in the weakness of human faith in God. In that case, human neglect or disregard of the weakness of such faith will include failure to apprehend and receive God's definitive power and thereby *God* in a suitable manner.

The absence of faith could block a willing apprehension and reception of divine love, and thereby cloud the unique reality and value of this love, particularly if God intends this love to be received in faith. It does not follow, however, that faith in God must *precede* having evidence for God's reality, love, or goodness. Instead, faith in God may arise along with, as a concurrent positive response to, an episodic human experience of God's relationally curative love on offer. So, fideism does not threaten here, and that is a benefit for an account of faith in God. (Chapter 3 explains that a distinctive kind of evidence has a vital role in faith in God.)

Opponents of faith in God may or may not have compelling reasons for their opposition. In either case, we should acknowledge the real downside for humans of not having an opportunity for a faith relationship with a perfectly good God. It seems doubtful that we have a better alternative or even an equally good alternative to a God who is perfectly good toward humans and therefore seeks enduring *koinonia* relationships with them. This consideration does not bear on the available evidence for God's reality, but it does bear on the *value* of such evidence *if* it is available to humans. In addition, we should acknowledge that the evidence for God's reality may vary among humans. We have no reason to suppose that if one person lacks evidence for God's reality, then no person has such evidence. God could have good reasons to allow for variability of evidence here, if only because some people are not ready to receive the evidence in a redemptive manner, in keeping with its divine intent. (Chapters 3 and 5 return to the latter topic.)

4. GETHSEMANE, DERELICTION, AND INQUIRY

In the Gethsemane story of the Synoptic Gospels, Jesus prayed as if God could have changed the redemptive plan. Perhaps he thought that God could provide a way to avoid what would be his felt abandonment by God on the cross. At least Mark's Jesus, at one place, seems to be open to a change in redemptive plan (see Mark 14:36). The use of "must" in "the Son of Man must suffer" (Mark 8:31) is not that of absolute necessity; instead, it is the "must" of a requirement in God's initial plan. The plan evidently haunted Jesus in Gethsemane, at least for a time, and hence led to his initial prayer for an alternative. We might say that, by way of anticipation, he felt the scandal and the desolation of the cross, and he initially preferred an alternative. Even in John's Gospel, the thought of an alternative occupies Jesus's mind, if only briefly (John 12:27).

Perhaps the most troubling question is: Why would God say "No" to Jesus regarding his request for a change of plan? Part of the problem with this question is that it fails to capture the complexity of the situation. Arguably, God did not really say "No," because Jesus quickly changed his request. Jesus seems to drop his initial request without delay and to yield, in agreement, to what God asks of him. We plausibly can acknowledge here the difference between an *initial* request (perhaps under duress) and a *settled* request (perhaps upon reflection).

The request from Jesus to "take this cup from me" (Mark 14:36) was evidently an initial, unsettled request under duress, and God would have known this. His settled response was "Father, let Your will be done," and God

would have known this, too. (In John's Gospel, the settled
response is "Father, glorify Your name" [John 12:28].) So,
God would not really be saying "No" to Jesus, because the
initial request had vanished altogether with the emergence
of the settled response. Jesus and God would have been on
the same page, after all. As for the unsettled request, Jesus
was human, and his decision to self-identify with humans in
suffering, death, and felt abandonment by God (to demon-
strate God's love for humans) would have been traumatic
and unsettling. One might suggest that God should have
proceeded with Jesus's initial request for an easier path, but
it is unclear what kind of obligation, or sense of "should,"
would motivate such a suggestion, given a divine plan of
redemption through death and resurrection. In any case, we
gain little, if anything, by ungrounded speculation here.

We now can speak of the faith of Jesus in God, if we
understand such faith in terms of his positively responding
to God by resolving to yield his will to God's perfect will.
(This point holds quite apart from the extensive debate
over the meaning of *"pistis christou"* [faith of/in Christ]
in the New Testament; we need not digress to that topic.)
Jesus willingly received God's call to obey, even in the face
of death, and he followed through obediently, instead of
pursuing an escape or a delay. In this regard, his response
in Gethsemane becomes a model for human faith in God,
including in situations where one is morally overwhelmed
by God. The faith response of Jesus in Gethsemane enables
his being overwhelmed by God to become redemptive for
others, at least by offering a model to be imitated by them.
It thus can advance God's intention for volitional cooperation in *koinonia* for the benefit of humans through Jesus.
The faith of other humans also could become redemptive
in following suit. In this perspective, Jesus serves as God's
gift to humans by modeling, and inviting humans into, a
God relationship of *koinonia*.

The challenge of Gethsemane bears not just on cooperation with God but also on inquiry about God. Owing to

what would be God's unique moral character, it introduces a key normative component in such inquiry and hence recommends the ethics for inquiry about God. The ethics correspond to the offer and demand of what would be God's perfect relational goodness, in order to maintain responsibility to the subject-matter of the inquiry. It requires that inquirers be available to assessment by that goodness, including in their mode of inquiry about God. The relevant mode is interpersonal rather than scientific, in the manner illustrated by Chapter 1, and it bears directly on the morally relevant intentions of inquirers.

If God intends salient evidence of divine reality to be redemptive and hence morally transformative of humans, then God would expect that evidence to be received for what it is and hence to be received in accordance with the moral character on offer. In effect, the relevant evidence would offer God's moral character to humans for their full cooperative participation in it. Such participation would be an ideal of the *koinonia* central to the God relationship. As Chapter 1 suggested, inquiry about God should allow for God's being redemptive in a manner that bears on suitable human appropriation of faith, evidence, knowledge, wisdom, and meaning regarding God. It should allow that God would seek, particularly via humans willingly being convicted by God, an interpersonal relationship of sympathetic cooperation with God's will. Otherwise, a misleading bias in inquiry will threaten.

Ethics enters inquiry about God as the ethics for inquiry *responsible* to the subject-matter regarding a morally perfect God who is worthy of worship. A key component of that subject-matter is the standard of perfect divine *agapē* in interpersonal relationships. So, inquiry about God cannot properly be divorced from a standard of goodness in relationships with others, aside from how the question of God's existence is ultimately settled. Inquirers who neglect or shun this standard will hinder themselves from being in a responsible position to receive what would be salient interpersonal evidence of a perfectly good God. They will be out of a responsible position to be conformed to the moral character of that evidence and thereby to receive it aright, as it would be intended to be received. In contrast, inquirers who intend to cooperate sympathetically with the moral standard will be in a responsible position to receive the interpersonal evidence for what it is: an invitation to moral transformation toward God's moral character in *koinonia*.

We can formulate various normative principles based on the standard of God's morally perfect character. The ethics for responsible inquiry about God can start with a twofold base principle: Given an opportunity, a person should inquire about God's reality, owing at least to the potential for supreme moral benefit in apprehending perfect divine goodness; and an inquirer about God should put himself or herself in a good position to receive available salient evidence of God's reality and perfect goodness.

Three core sub-principles are noteworthy. They stem from an assumption that responsible inquiry about God requires one to be fully agreeable toward apprehending the kind of perfect goodness characteristic of a God worthy of worship.

1. Inquiry about God should include an inquirer's *self-reflective candor* about his or her moral standing relative to what would be God's morally perfect character.

2. Inquiry about God should include an inquirer's *intending to conform* sympathetically to God's morally perfect will upon receiving salient evidence of God's will (including evidence from uncoercive pressure in conscience on one's will, and perhaps from one's willingly being convicted, toward perfect goodness).

3. Inquiry about God should include an inquirer's *seeking evidence* for God and perfect divine goodness, and not just one's waiting for it to come to one.

The twofold base principle and principles 1–3 are normative standards for inquiry about God's reality. They concern what is, all things considered, *responsible* in human inquiry about God. Inquiry that is "all things considered" responsible will give special attention and respect to relevant conceptual, evidential, and moral factors in inquiry, in order to avoid debilitating bias against the subject-matter in question. It will seek to honor and preserve those factors in inquiry, even when apparent conflicts arise. The aforementioned principles direct one toward the kind of perfect moral goodness under inquiry, in keeping with the distinctive subject-matter regarding a God worthy of worship.

Responsible inquiry about a perfectly good God would concern acquiring truth about God's reality, but it would not be limited to this concern. It would be concerned to uphold inquiry respectful of the distinctive subject-matter of the inquiry: particularly, the kind of perfect moral goodness in question. Respectful inquiry would not obscure the reality of such goodness from the start with the use of questionable assumptions about evidence (as in strict empiricism, for instance), semantic meaning (as in verificationism, for instance), or goodness (as in sensory hedonism, for instance). In addition, it would not wield a mode of inquiry incompatible with an interpersonal mode, such as an exclusively mathematical or scientific mode. Instead, it would be attentive to, and respectful of, the considerations in inquiry that bear on the question of the reality of perfect moral goodness in an agent. In doing so, responsible inquiry would attend to whether human inquirers are in a responsible position to apprehend such goodness. It thus would explore the conditions for one's putting oneself in such a position. In that respect, responsible human inquiry about God would become self-reflective in part.

A perfectly good God would promote the normative requirements of the base principle and principles 1–3. The goal would be to encourage humans to undertake responsible inquiry about God and, as a result, to undergo transformation toward God's moral character. Just as inquiry is active, the ethics for inquiry about God is active in its requirements for *putting oneself* in a responsible position to receive salient evidence of God's reality. It is, in short, the ethics for *pursuing* God's reality and goodness responsibly, all things considered. It values evidence in a way that honors the importance of obtaining *truth*, or the fact of the matter, about God's reality and goodness. Our inquiry allows that one may fail to find salient evidence of divine reality and goodness; so, agnosticism is not excluded at the start for a person. This result is fitting, given the variability in salient human evidence regarding God's reality and goodness.

Principle 1 is a normative requirement of self-disclosure. It requires one to be honest, at least to oneself, about one's moral status relative to perfect goodness, including what would be God's perfect moral goodness and love toward others, even enemies. Such honesty can temper self-righteousness and moral self-pride in a manner that highlights one's need for moral change toward relational goodness. It can identify one's need for a perfectly good God who can initiate and sustain the needed moral change toward *koinonia* in interpersonal relationships. Upon identifying this need, perhaps by being morally overwhelmed by God, one can be motivated to pursue salient evidence for God's reality in a manner free of bias against God. In addition, one then can appreciate the importance of such evidence and have a sympathetic attitude toward it, when it becomes available to one. So, the requirement of self-reflective candor can contribute to the suitable, responsible appropriation of salient evidence for God's reality and goodness.

Principle 2 is a normative requirement demanding an inquirer to intend to conform sympathetically to God's perfect will upon receiving salient evidence of it. In lacking this intention, I can hinder myself from receiving direct familiarity with the kind of intentional power, and hence the kind of direct evidence, characteristic of a morally perfect God. God would intend such power and evidence to be appropriated by humans with an intention to conform sympathetically, and the conformity would be to God's morally perfect will represented in the power and the evidence. The absence of this intention would disable one from appropriating the power and evidence for what God would intended them to be: a means to intentional sympathetic conformity with God's moral character by humans.

God plausibly could withhold the relevant evidence in the absence of a human intention to conform to it. So, we need not assume that the evidence is always present to one. The required intention to conform, in any case, could figure in the suitable, responsible appropriation of salient evidence for God's reality and goodness by humans. There is a fact of the matter about the evidence for God's reality, but human appropriation of this evidence, even under conditions of being morally overwhelmed, may depend on the relevant intentions of humans (or the lack thereof) toward it. One's intentions should allow for a reordering of one's moral priorities in the presence of divine priorities.

Principle 3 is a normative requirement of seeking evidence for God's reality and perfect goodness. It figures in inquiry about God that is responsible, all things considered, in virtue of the following fact: The required seeking would be a component of one's being fully agreeable toward apprehending the kind of perfect goodness in question. It is noteworthy that the principle fits with the recurring biblical injunction to seek God (see, for instance, Isa. 45:22, 55:6, Amos 5:6, Deut. 4:29, Matt. 7:7–8). The required seeking could be prompted by being morally overwhelmed by God, but, in any case, God would intend it to put an inquirer into a responsible and responsive position to receive salient evidence of God's reality and goodness. God would intend it to engage an inquirer to act in a way that approaches such evidence in an interested manner. God, however, would not require one to *act as if* one has received such evidence when one has not.

The required seeking would include an active interest on the part of the inquirer, at least in virtue of the goal-directedness of the seeking. This interest would prepare one to apprehend the evidence without a history of full resistance or indifference to it. The seeking could prompt one to appreciate the value of the evidence and thereby to become receptive and cooperative toward it. So, the requirement of seeking evidence for God's reality can contribute to the suitable, responsible appropriation of that evidence. It could enable one to become ready, to some extent, for the kind of reordering of one's moral priorities demanded by God's moral character.

5. SYMPATHETIC FAITH

We can clarify the God relationship by attending further to the issue of why a redemptive God would invite faith in God from humans. The God of Jesus Christ reportedly sent Jesus to call for faith in God as including trust in God and in the good news from God. According to Mark 1:14–15: "Now after John was arrested, Jesus came to Galilee, proclaiming the good news of God, and saying, 'The time is fulfilled, and the kingdom of God has come near; repent, and believe in the good news.' " On another occasion, Jesus commands: "Have faith in God" (Mark 11:22). This call for faith in God and in the good news involved Jesus himself in such a significant manner that Jesus as the messenger from God became part of the message from God.

One of the best summaries of the message, from Paul, is: "In Christ God was reconciling the world to himself, not counting their trespasses against them" (2 Cor. 5:19). Many Christians thus came to understand faith in God as faith in God *as represented* in Christ, or for short, faith in God in Christ. Sometimes this was understood, in shortest form, as "faith in Christ" (see Gal. 2:16). In the Synoptic Gospels, Jesus commends people who show their trust toward him, as if it represents trust toward his divine Father (see Mark 2:5, 5:34, 9:23–25, 10:51–52; cf. Mark 11:22–23). Faith in Jesus, then, evidently emerged before his resurrection, and it was closely related, at least by Jesus, to faith in his divine Father. (The New Testament Gospels, however, do not give Jesus a status equal to his Father; see, for instance, Mark 10:18, John 17:3.)

Faith in God or Christ, as suggested, has features that distinguish it from factual knowledge that some claim is true. Such faith is relational toward a person; it includes an affirmative, agreeable response of trust toward God or Christ. In this response, one commits to yielding one's will to the will of God or Christ. So, the faith in question is not a leap in the dark, merely wishful thinking, or just assent to a claim. It is a positive response of trust toward the intervention of God or Christ in one's experience. Faith without a basis in such an experiential intervention by God or Christ is not faith *in* God or Christ. We shall see how the present lesson allows us to regard faith in God or Christ as grounded in evidence.

In his Epistle to the Romans, Paul offers an illuminating approach to faith in God. He uses the faith of Abraham to illustrate the nature of faith in God:

What does the scripture say? "Abraham believed God, and it was reckoned to him as righteousness." Now to one who works, wages are not reckoned as a gift but as something due. But to one who without works trusts him who justifies the ungodly, such faith is reckoned as righteousness. . . . For this reason it depends on faith, in order that the promise may rest on grace and be guaranteed to all [Abraham's] descendants, not only to the adherents of the law but also to those who share the faith of Abraham. . . . No distrust made him waver concerning the promise of God, but he grew strong in his faith as he gave glory [*doxa*] to God, being fully convinced that God was able to do what he had promised. Therefore his faith "was reckoned to him as righteousness." (Rom. 4:3–5, 16, 20–22)

By implication, Paul presents Abraham's faith in God as involving a need for a *decision* to trust in God's redemptive promise: "No distrust made him waver concerning the promise of God" (Rom. 4:20). More literally, Abraham refused to decide, in distrust, against the promise of God. Instead, he decidedly allowed himself to be persuaded, to have the conviction of trust, that God would deliver what he promised (Rom. 4:21). By Paul's lights, then, Abraham's faith in God has a decisional element relative to trusting God and God's promise or will. When this faith is *de dicto*, one will have, and endorse, the propositional content that God will deliver on the divine promises.

Human trust in God requires a struggle for resolve, for a resolute decision, to trust God (at least *de re*), even when hope seems hopeless. In making the right decision, Abraham became not only the recipient of God's reckoned righteousness (Rom. 4:3, 9, 22), but also the father of all those who walk in his steps of faith, whether Jew or Gentile (Rom. 4:11–12, 16). We should not take Abraham's response to be mere wishful thinking, a blind leap in the dark, or otherwise irrational. Instead, he was deciding to allow his evidence regarding God is to prevail over his fears and doubts regarding God.

In Paul's understanding, God self-manifested God's faithful character to Abraham, and then asked Abraham to decide in favor of trusting God as supremely authoritative in his life. In order to justify the ungodly (such as Abraham), whose own righteousness fails by a divine standard, God credits human faith in God as the kind of needed righteousness for humans. This credit includes approval before God that humans fail to earn or merit on their own (Rom. 4:5). Righteousness for humans before God becomes entering into a right relationship of faith in God, where God's righteousness is cooperatively received by humans as a gift. The God relationship thus figures in divine approval or justification of cooperative humans.

Faith in God is not mere intellectual assent to a claim. It includes resolute obedience in trust, or cooperative self-entrustment, toward God's will, call, promise, or good news (see Rom. 10:3, 16), whereby one submits one's own will, cooperatively and sympathetically, to God's will. So, Paul speaks of the "obedience of faith" (Rom. 1:5, 16:26) and even of "obedience, which leads to righteousness" (Rom. 6:16). (The latter talk is incompatible with any view that excludes obedience as a component of faith.) Such faith in God, as a kind of obedience in trust as cooperative self-entrustment toward God, is not a "work" that, in Paul's occasional technical sense, seeks to merit or earn God's approval and thereby obligate God to approve of a person (Rom. 4:4).

Abrahamic faith in God, according to Paul, includes a decision of trust to "give glory [or, honor] to God" (Rom. 4:20; cf. 1:21, 3:26–27) by submitting to God's will. In giving honor to God, one *decides* to act in a certain way. For instance, one intentionally gives credit to God for human redemption, among other things, and does not take self-credit for God's gracious approval of humans who have the faith of Abraham. Paul links "being empowered in faith" with "giving honor to God" and thereby undermines any role for human self-righteousness in faith in God.

Human faith in God, if God exists, involves a presentation–response dynamic that includes interpersonal mutuality, that is, an I–Thou interaction between a human and God, even if the person with faith has no concept of God. At the opportune time, God would initiate this interaction by challenging and perhaps even convicting a person, in God's preferred manner, to obey in trust toward God. In a faith response to God, this person would decide to yield to God in trust, even if the person has not categorized God as God but still relates favorably to God *de re*. This faith decision would be a kind of yielding in obedient trust toward God, as God challenges one to make such a decision. So, faith in God, if God exists, is inherently *personalist* in that it includes personal interaction whereby a person responds affirmatively in obedient trust as self-entrustment toward a personal God.

The personalist component in question underwrites *personalism* about human faith in God: the view that such faith should be understood in terms of an I–Thou person-to-person interaction between a human and God. Paul illustrates his personalism: "You have died to the law through the body of Christ, so that you may belong to another, to him who has been raised from the dead in order that we may bear fruit for God" (Rom. 7:4). This is personal belonging (and knowing) in that one belongs to (and knows) the personal God in Christ. Many accounts of Christian faith neglect this personalism, but it is at the heart of an adequate understanding of Christian faith in God and of what Paul calls "newness of the Spirit" (Rom. 7:6, my trans.; cf. Rom. 8:9). (Chapter 5 returns to the role of God's Spirit in knowledge of God.)

Faith in God, we now see, is not identical with belief or even knowledge that a claim is true. For instance, my believing or knowing that God exists does not require that I trust in God at all. As the writer of the Epistle of James says: "You believe that God is one; you do well. Even the demons believe – and shudder" (Jas. 2:19). Mere factual belief or knowledge that God exists omits something crucial to what God would seek in a curative relationship with humans: namely, human faith or trust in God that figures in a *koinonia* relationship. Such faith includes a personalist *endeavor* of trust in God in a way that mere factual belief or knowledge does not. In this endeavor, one decides (often repeatedly) to let God be supremely authoritative in one's life, as one submits in trust as self-entrustment toward God and God's perfect will.

An endeavor of faith can include a struggle to overcome distrust toward God, just as Abraham refused to decide, in distrust, against the promise of God. Mere factual belief or knowledge that God exists lacks this kind of trust-endeavor characteristic of faith in God. We should not, however, identify faith in God with the endeavoring in question, because, like the God relationship, faith is a dispositional state (which can be had while one is asleep) whereas endeavoring is an episodic intentional action. A dispositional state of faith can be episodically dormant at a time, whereas endeavoring is action-based in a way that brings faith to a life of action.

We now can elaborate further on the question of why God would seek human faith in God, beyond mere belief or knowledge that God exists. The answer has two parts. The first part of the answer is contained in the personalism mentioned previously. A God worthy of worship would seek the uncoerced redemption of humans, and therefore would aim for personal interaction and engagement with them for the sake of a *koinonia* relationship.

The desired engagement would invite and empower humans to respond to God with candor and commitment, beyond any fear or shame toward God. It also would seek, at least eventually, human endeavoring *with* God, where one struggles to obey in trusting, and thereby honoring, God as supremely authoritative in one's life. Such endeavoring would be a cooperative struggle that includes humans in the redemptive work of God. They thus would become co-workers and even co-creators with God toward the renewal of the world, including the reconciliation of humans to God (see 1 Cor. 3:9). Human life would take on new meaning or purpose in this way and thereby avoid the despair that can destroy a human life (as Chapter 4 contends).

We need to introduce an important but widely neglected qualification that corresponds to the character of a perfectly redemptive God: *sympathetic* endeavoring, trust, and faith. Just as a perfectly good God would be sympathetic toward humans in a compassionate effort to redeem them in a reconciled relationship, so also God would expect humans to be sympathetic toward God in their cooperative response by sharing in divine *pathos* as lived, engaged cares and concerns for other agents. God would intend to have self-manifested features of the divine character sympathetically (rather than, say, grudgingly) received and reflected (to others) by humans.

The endeavoring, trust, and faith sought by God among humans would be sympathetic and hence inclusive of a feeling component in humans who have faith in God. H.S. Holland has spoken of the need of believers to have "sympathetic appreciation" or "likeness of temper" toward God's motive in coming to humans, in order for them to be able to enter into the divine motive of redemptive mission (1923, p. 154). I am suggesting, however, that sympathetic *cooperation* with God is closer to the needed obedience of faith, because it would move beyond appreciation to an affirmative volitional position regarding God and God's perfect will. (On the role of sympathy and *pathos* in the Hebrew prophets, see Heschel 1962, pp. 221–31, 247–67, 307–23; Heschel does not attribute sympathy to God in the way I do, nor does he portray faith or trust in God as sympathetic.)

Sympathetic endeavoring with God, in trusting and honoring God, would be profoundly formative for a person in making that person increasingly renewed in the moral image or character of God. The renewal would stem from one's being sympathetically receptive toward God's self-manifested character traits. Sympathetic endeavoring, in response to God, would enable one to share in God's character traits and thereby come to image God in some distinctive ways, such as in imaging divine righteous love for others. It also would form and deepen one's faith in God as it forms and deepens one's disposition to trust God in various new situations, including situations that are difficult and even morally overwhelming for one.

As perfectly compassionate, God's character traits self-manifested to humans would be sympathetic toward humans for the sake of their benefit. In addition, God would intend these self-manifested character traits to be sympathetically shared by willing humans in trust toward God, for the sake of their redemptive transformation toward the divine character. God would seek to have divine sympathy met with freely given human sympathy, because the latter sympathy would enable a heartfelt understanding, reception, and motivation among humans toward God's self-manifesting to them.

God could arrange for the lack of sympathy toward God in humans to result in their failing to understand adequately God's redemptive purpose and work (cf. 1 Cor. 2:14). Such an arrangement could be a divine effort to save people from premature final rejection of God and God's redemptive work. In contrast, part of the transformation arising from a sympathetic reception would be a reconciled relationship with God as one yields cooperatively, in the spirit of Gethsemane, to God as supremely authoritative in one's life. This kind of yielding can supply the kind of ongoing resolve against distrust toward God that Paul identifies in Abraham's faith in God.

Paul refers to the Christians at Colossae as having "clothed yourselves with the new self, which is being renewed in knowledge [*epignōsis*] according to the image [*eikōn*] of its creator" (Col. 3:10). They were "being renewed" in "the image" of God in Christ, who himself is "the image [*eikōn*] of the invisible God" (Col. 1:15; cf. Phil. 2:6; 2 Cor. 4:4). The formative renewal of humans in the image of God in Christ is no purely external or behavioral matter. Instead, it is personally inward owing to an inward intentional *agent-power* (and not a mere event-power). Paul remarks: "I have been crucified with Christ; and it is no longer I who live, but it is Christ who lives in [*en*] me. And the life I now live in the flesh I live by faith in the Son of God, who loved me and gave himself for me" (Gal. 2:19–20; cf. Gal. 1:16). This faith includes one's sympathetically endeavoring to conform to the moral character of the God in Christ who calls from within one.

The second part of our answer acknowledges that God would use the receptive nature of faith in God to maintain the key role of divine grace as a humanly unearned gift in the redemption of humans. This strategy of grace would undermine any practice of humans to boast of their (having earned their) own righteousness before God. Paul thus remarks: "For this reason it depends on faith, in order that the promise may rest on grace and be guaranteed to all [of Abraham's] descendants, not only to the adherents of the law but also to those who share the faith of Abraham" (Rom. 4:16). The grace on offer, then, is universal, transcending all ethnic and national boundaries, in keeping with perfect divine love. So, God's promise of redemption would rest on a divine gift of grace, and not on human merit or earning, or any other kind of human righteousness.

Sympathetically receptive faith in God, including receptive endeavoring with God, would be the divinely chosen means to appropriate redemption from God, because such faith, in trust, receives from God rather than self-credits before God. Paul thus asks: "Then what becomes of boasting? It is excluded. By what law? By that of works? No, but by the law of faith. For we hold that a person is justified by faith apart from works prescribed by the law" (Rom. 3:27–28). Here we have an effective way to recruit faith to deflate human pride and supposed self-righteousness before God. Properly understood, the sympathetic receptivity of a divine gift in faith would remove any place for human pride or self-righteousness before God. In doing so, it would enhance the opportunity for sympathetic cooperation in *koinonia* with God.

Human endeavoring with God, like faith in God, largely would be a gift of divine grace and not a human earning at all. Humans would not merit their endeavoring with God or their faith in God, as if they had done something or become righteous in a way that obligates God to approve of them. Instead, God's grace would enable the redemptive import of human endeavoring with God and human faith in God. I have said that human endeavoring with God *largely* would be a gift of divine grace, because humans would have a causal role to play, beyond God's causal role.

Humans would not simply receive a gift of endeavoring without their cooperation. So, the story is not altogether passive for humans, contrary to some misunderstandings of divine grace (for details, see Moser 2013, chap. 4).

The causal role for humans would include their endeavoring to cooperate sympathetically with, and thereby to obey in trusting, the God who seeks their new life of *imitatio Dei* and *koinonia*. Even so, divine grace would require that human endeavoring with God be sympathetically *receptive* toward what God offers in redemption, including love, forgiveness, reconciliation, and hope from God. Such receptive endeavoring would be at the heart of faith in God, and it would fit with honoring God by giving God credit for redemption and its benefits. It invites Paul's challenging questions: "What do you have that you did not receive? And if you received it, why do you boast as if it were not a gift?" (1 Cor. 4:7; cf. John 3:27). In emphasizing divine grace, Paul also emphasizes the role of intentional human receptivity toward God and God's offerings. Human endeavoring with God in trust would be intentionally receptive toward divine grace and therefore would not be *just* a gift of divine grace.

One might propose that God gives one faith in God and endeavoring with God, in keeping with a suggestion of Ephesians 2:8–9 that faith is a gift of divine grace. One could talk this way, as long as one is careful not to make faith or endeavoring *wholly* a causal product of God. God could give the opportunity and the needed divine power for faith or endeavoring, but there still must be an enduring human decision to trust God. In this regard, faith in God, including endeavoring with God, would be personally *interactive* between God and a human, over time.

Both sides of the I–Thou interaction have a causal role to play, because both sides are intentionally active. As Pascal suggested in his *Pensées* (1662, sec. 234), God seeks to move the human will, and not just to prompt human reflection, but we should not take God to coerce the human will in deciding for or against God (contrary to the Jansenism evidently accepted by Pascal in the wake of the later Augustine; on which, see Moser 2018a). For the sake of an *interpersonal* relationship, sympathetic human agency would figure centrally in human faith in God, as Paul suggests with regard to Abraham's faith.

God's purpose would be clear: Divine love would be volitional, not merely reflective, and God would aim to encourage people to receive and to practice divine love toward all agents, even enemies. The desired receiving and practicing likewise would be inherently volitional and sympathetic, and not just reflective. If a person just reflected about God, even in ways that include having correct beliefs about God and Christ, something important would be missing. The person still would need to undertake the volitional struggle to receive God's unselfish love and thereby to be sympathetically conformed to its compassionate ways toward others. Dietrich Bonhoeffer characterized the struggle in a Christian life of faith: "We throw ourselves utterly in the arms of God and participate in his sufferings in the world and watch with Christ in Gethsemane" (1953, p. 169).

As the means of appropriating divine grace, faith in God would receive affirmatively and sympathetically what such grace offers, including God's powerful love and hope. Paul identifies the role of hope in connection with Abraham's faith (Rom. 4:18), and he links faith in God with the "hope of sharing the glory of God" (Rom. 5:2). A key part of his remark cited previously is: ". . . suffering produces endurance, and endurance produces character, and character produces hope, and hope does not disappoint us, because God's love has been poured into our hearts through the Holy Spirit that has been given to us" (Rom. 5:3–5). Paul links faith in God, then, with a kind of hope that does not disappoint persons of such faith because God has already done something definitive for them: "God's love has been poured into our hearts through the Holy Spirit that has been given to us." Paul elsewhere refers to this as the present "guarantee" from God regarding the coming fulfillment of God's redemptive promise (2 Cor. 1:22, 5:5; cf. Eph. 1:13–14).

Paul's idea of hope from God "not disappointing us" has, as suggested, an epistemic component. That is, the pouring out of God's love (*agapē*) into a willing person is experiential *evidence* from God, and it can be salient for a person. This evidence, when sympathetically received, can make a person morally new by giving that person God's unselfish love as a default motivation for action. So, Paul can say that "the love from Christ compels us" (2 Cor. 5:14, my trans.), thus suggesting that unselfish divine love becomes an important motivation for the followers of Christ.

Only God ultimately would provide the kind of love in question for humans, because only God self-sufficiently would have the kind of self-security (and thus resistance to fear of loss prompting selfishness) required by consistent unselfish love that extends even to one's enemies. (On the role of security, see Niebuhr 1937, chap. 5, 1941, chap. 7.) This divine love, and hence faith in God as a response to it, would be decentering and recentering for a human. They would displace a human from himself or herself as the priority center of perceived value by placing God (and God's unique love) there. If one lacks such decentering and recentering, then one also lacks sympathetic reception of God's distinctive love and hence faith in God. We have here a significant test for the redemptive work of God (or the lack thereof) in one's life (see John 13:35, Matt. 7:15–21). It fits well with Paul's injunction: "Examine yourselves to see whether you are living in the faith. Test yourselves. Do you not realize that Jesus Christ is in you? – unless, indeed, you fail to meet the test!" (2 Cor. 13:5).

Paul brings the distinctive role of divine love out of the realm of generality into actual practice, in clarifying the idea of "having the same love" (Phil. 2:2): "Do nothing from selfish ambition, . . . but let each of you look not [only] to your own interests, but [also] to the interests of others"

(Phil. 2:3–4). Paul has Jesus in mind, as the perfect representative of God's love (see also 2 Cor. 8:8–9). So, he says in
the same context:

> Let the same mind be in you that was in Christ Jesus,
> who, though he was in the form of God,
> did not regard equality with God
> as something to be exploited,
> but emptied himself,
> taking the form of a slave,
> being born in human likeness.
> And being found in human form,
> he humbled himself
> and became obedient to the point of death –
> even death on a cross.
>
> (Phil. 2:5–8)

Paul thinks of the self-giving of Jesus in obedience to God
as central to the love from God. He remarks: "God proves
his love for us in that while we still were sinners Christ
died for us" (Rom. 5:8). In Paul's thinking, the self-giving
love from Jesus for even his enemies is God's distinctive
love for humans, without exclusion.

How might others receive and give divine love as Jesus
did, and thereby realize both sympathetic faith in God
and its ground? Paul's illustration of divine love in terms
of Jesus's obeying God "to the point of death" recalls,
and presupposes, the Gethsemane crisis faced by Jesus.
In that crisis, we saw, Jesus prays to God: "Abba, Father,
for you all things are possible; remove this cup from me;
yet, not what I want, but what you want" (Mark 14:36).
This Gethsemane prayer brings us to the heart of *de dicto*
endeavoring with God and thus of *de dicto* faith in God.
Jesus prays to his Father to have his own will conform to
his Father's will. This is the core of "the obedience of [*de
dicto*] faith," the kind of endeavoring with God that figures
in *de dicto* faith in God. Such endeavoring has an I–Thou

component in prayer to God, and it includes a sympathetic decision to place God's will first, above one's own, with the aid of God's power.

Jesus does say, "Remove this cup from me," but, as noted, this is only an initial, revisable request that is followed by his settled request to put God's will first. If we omit the role of Gethsemane prayer to put God's will first, we omit the kind of endeavoring with God that is crucial to sympathetic *de dicto* faith in God. An adequate treatment of Christian faith in God, then, must come with a central role for Gethsemane prayer. Such prayer is crucial to receiving and giving divine love as Jesus did. It thus is crucial to realizing sympathetic *de dicto* faith in God. Philosophers and theologians often overlook this important lesson, but, in doing so, they obscure a central feature of the *koinonia* that a perfectly good God would seek.

6. FRAGILITY FOR FAITH

A Gethsemane trial for compassion with God, for the sake of prompting faith in God, fits with the reality of *human fragility*, that is, the tendency of human life to destruction. Such fragility prompts the following question: If God is worthy of worship and hence perfectly good, why is human life so dangerously fragile in ways that seemingly preclude a redemptive, or relationally curative, process for many people in this world? Innocent babies often die in birth and even in the womb; little children often succumb to deadly infections; young adults often undergo heart failure; and so on. The tragedies for many humans seem endless at times, and we see no good resolution at hand. If this world is God's "curing room" or "testing ground" for humans, why do so many people not have a chance to complete, or even to begin, the curing or testing? Is there a deep lesson here about God or humans? If so, what exactly is it? These questions are important even if we end up with incomplete answers.

The problem of human fragility is *not* the problem of suffering for theism. We can imagine that some people, without suffering, fail to begin the curing or testing process. If this failure is an evil, then the problem of human fragility is a variation on the problem of evil regarding theism. We need at least a partial answer to the problem, if we are to think of God as perfectly good and compassionate toward all humans. The problem raises the difficult question of how a perfectly good God would act in self-manifesting toward fragile humans. This question can help us to sort out relevant evidence for or against God's reality and to clarify how God would be present in a human trial with God.

The relevant "testing" of humans by God, as indicated, would include something like that suggested by Paul (2 Cor. 13:5–7): testing, including self-testing, to reveal whether people are living by faith in God. Paul links such testing to the question of whether God is at work in a cooperative person's life. Regardless of the answer, the testing in question would seek to promote human reconciliation and *koinonia* with God and others, and thus it would purport to be beneficial to human relationships. It also could be ignored or rejected by humans as divine testing. Paul thinks of the testing as occurring in a context of divine activity of the following kind: "The creation was subjected to futility, not of its own will but by the will of the one who subjected it, in hope that the creation itself will be set free from its bondage to decay and will obtain the freedom of the glory of the children of God" (Rom. 8:20–21). In this perspective, God subjects creation to futility in order to reveal who will emerge as the children of God, that is, those cooperative with God's redemptive will.

Paul imagines that one could fail to meet God's test and hence need to start over in relation to God. God's trial for humans thus could reveal where people stand in relation to God, and this would be important because people are easily deceived about where they stand relative to God. Many people, including many religious leaders, think that they are highly approved by God, despite the conflict of their actions with the moral goodness that would characterize God. This may be self-deception, or it could arise from confusion of a different sort. In any case, suitable testing could bring needed correction about a person's relation to God.

A perfectly good God could have various purposes for allowing the fragility of human life. Two points seem clear. First, the person who dies before entering this world's testing ground would not be lost automatically relative to God, because God still could offer that person an opportunity to know God in obedience and *koinonia*. Human death would not be an insurmountable obstacle for God, if God is the creator of human life. In fact, a harder time of testing may apply to the humans who remain in this world's strife and temptation.

Second, God could seek to test and build human faith and hope in God out of human fragility. Such faith and hope would be direct avenues for people to receive God's distinctive power of love. The fragility of human life could offer crucial opportunities for this testing and building, because it could invite humans to seek, and to trust and hope in, a divine power stronger than themselves. That intentional power would be God, who in valuing divine love for and among humans would value and promote the human seeking, trusting, and hoping in God invited by the fragility of humans.

Humans do not have now a full explanation of the purpose of human fragility, if there is such an explanation. God, however, would value the faith and the hope in God that emerge sometimes from human fragility, even if we cannot remove the accompanying anguish. God could encourage among humans at least freely given faith and hope in God, and such faith and hope could build unselfish love and compassion in humans of the kind inherent to a God worthy of worship. In God's suffering love, otherwise known as "compassion," humans could learn to love too, even in the grips of frustrations and sorrows the purpose of which we cannot fully explain. Perhaps humans can learn to live in faith and hope, without full explanations of the traumas in their fragile lives, particularly if God is present. We shall see, in any case, that the redemptive work and the salient evidence for humans of a redemptive God would not depend on our having a theodicy that includes a full explanation of God's purposes in allowing evil.

Human inquirers about God often have much to say about their expectations for God, especially regarding suffering and evil. They often neglect, however, what would be *God's* expectations for human inquirers. This neglect hinders responsible inquiry about God, because it omits what would be God's distinctive contribution to the inquiry, if God exists. It leaves humans with an inadequate conception of what would be the relevant evidence from God in a human inquiry. So, one easily can overlook salient evidence from God that is available to humans but not (yet) acknowledged or appropriated by them. We do well to consider that God, rather than humans, would set the conditions for how, and when, God is self-revealed to humans and thereby experienced by them. I have suggested that the idea of a human trial with God for compassion in *koinonia* contributes to this matter.

Perhaps a perfectly good God would seek, above all, to be with humans in *koinonia* as communion of a relationally redemptive sort. In that case, much would need to change in familiar human inquiry about God, because inquiry itself will need to become attentive to what would be God's redemptive expectations for humans. This book explains how, particularly in connection with the aforementioned roles of trial, reciprocity, and *koinonia* in the redemptive process. Its talk of a "relationally curative" process invites us to think of divine redemption as aimed at repairing or healing a wayward, alienated relationship humans have with God. Divine forgiveness, guidance, and power for humans would figure directly in this process, because humans need more than advice or information for their redemption. They need at least release from condemnation in addition to volitional conviction and correction relative to God's will. The latter conviction and correction can emerge from a human trial for compassion with God. Responsible inquiry about God needs to attend to such considerations.

While humans inquire about God, they may need to open themselves to inquiry *from* God, including God's expectations, trial, and offer of *koinonia* for them. In that case, they themselves would become an object of divine inquiry and trial regarding their being (or not being) suitably motivated, responsible inquirers about God. As suggested, a redemptive God in search of divine–human reconciliation would care not just about the questions raised by humans, but also about the motives for the questions and the intentions for having answers. In this regard, inquiry about God would become normatively robust in virtue of its subject-matter regarding perfect divine goodness. Divine testing in a receptive human conscience can figure in the redemption on offer, for the sake of bringing humans into *koinonia* with God. Responsible inquiry about God will attend to a role for such redemptive factors in the appropriation of salient evidence for God's reality and goodness.

The English term "communion" can translate the Greek term *"koinonia"* (fellowship) and is associated with the classical Latin term *"communio,"* which is related to the Latin terms *"cum"* (with) and *"munus"* (gift). Some theologians find here an etymological suggestion of one's self-giving to another person as a gift of being with that person. The *Oxford English Dictionary*, second edition, includes the following terms in its definition: mutual participation, possession of common qualities, union, community, fellowship, mutual association, intimate engagement of a spiritual nature. Perhaps the phrase "sympathetic cooperative engagement of a moral and spiritual nature" best captures a prominent biblical notion of communion with God, if we understand this engagement to include a sharing of volitions and affections between God and a human.

A perfectly good God could choose not to remove human fragility, but to use it to prompt humans, in their felt need, to explore the option of needed *koinonia* with God. In exploring this option, humans would be considering something more interpersonal than merely obeying a moral rule. They would be exploring the option of a personal encounter and relationship with God for the sake of cooperating sympathetically with God, even in the grips of human fragility. God could seek to commune with humans in their ongoing fragility for the sake of their reconciliation to God and redemption by God. This would be an important part of a human trial with God.

In *koinonia* as communion with God, a sharing of mere ideas or thoughts will fall short, because it will omit the sharing of such motivational factors as volitions (from the will) and affections (from feelings). The latter factors would be crucial in communion with God, because they would have a central role in divine righteous love (*agapē*), which includes compassion for others, as the basis for the communion that a perfectly loving God would seek. Such a God would aim to motivate people to act out of unselfish love and compassion for others, and this would take people beyond reflection to suitable motivational attitudes. One cannot have *agapē* and compassion for others without suitable volitions and affections toward others.

If God is worthy of worship and hence morally perfect, as some variations on Abrahamic monotheism suggest, then God is inherently loving toward all people, even toward God's enemies. Moral perfection requires being morally good, or positively morally valuable, without defect or deficiency; it thus precludes moral failure or inadequacy. If God is inherently loving toward all people, we should expect communion or *koinonia* with God to promote divine love for others in a redemptive manner that seeks divine–human reconciliation and human–human reconciliation. (Chapter 5 considers how *koinonia* does this.)

If God is morally perfect and has ultimate authority over all other persons, we should acknowledge God's volitions and affections to be authoritative over human volitions and affections. We then should regard God's volitions and affections to be the normative standard for humans, who should try to have their volitions and affections brought into conformity with God's. So, if God unselfishly loves God's enemies, as required for moral perfection in an agent, then humans should follow suit, in volitions and affections. Perhaps, however, humans lack the resources to follow suit on their own; maybe they need divine help, including divine power, to approach conformity with God's moral character. In that case, humans may need to seek to receive divine help. Actively seeking God, then, may be crucial to the redemptive process that brings humans into conformity with God's volitions and affections. A trial with God under human fragility could bring humans to cooperate in that process, with more or less sympathy.

The redemptive process would call for human seeking, unselfish love, and *koinonia* toward God, because a certain kind of misplaced, defective love would need to be cured in humans. Love and *koinonia* toward God would contribute to the cure in an irreplaceable way. John's Gospel mentions a certain "crisis" (*krisis*) faced by God and humans, namely: "people loved darkness rather than light because their deeds were evil" (John 3:19). This may seem to be an unduly harsh assessment, at least in the eyes of many observers. It becomes plausible, however, if it intends to capture the reality of human self-centeredness of various sorts that interfere with unselfish love and compassion toward others. If the redemptive process aims to heal such self-centeredness, it must work at the level of what people seek and love. It then must relate people, via *koinonia*, to one who can empower them to overcome their self-centeredness cooperatively. Perhaps, in that case, humans tend to trust too much in themselves and need to trust sincerely in one who can empower unselfish love and compassion in them toward others.

In the scenario under consideration, God and humans share a significant problem in a shared trial for them, namely: How can unselfish love and compassion toward others become freely located in, and commonly practiced by, humans who tend to be self-centered? Responsible inquiry about a perfectly loving God will attend to this problem. Perhaps humans will freely bear and commonly practice love and compassion toward others only as they directly experience and receive such love and compassion without defect. In that case, humans in this world will freely bear and commonly practice unselfish love and compassion only via faith and hope in God, because such faith and hope are the only means to receive God's unselfish love and compassion directly. We shall identify, in Chapter 3, the relevance of this perspective to responsible appropriation of divine evidence in a human trial with God. We shall allow, however, for people being good, in any familiar sense, without their believing that God exists.

Perhaps the love generated just by humans falls short of the unselfish love that would be expected and offered by a perfectly loving God. The latter, divine love would involve self-giving and even dying for others, and it would be, in many ways, more self-secure and demanding than what we ordinarily call "human love." For instance, a morally perfect God would call for loving one's enemies in an unselfish manner, without an overriding fear of loss prompting selfishness, and this would be in one's best interest. This kind of loving, however, is at best rare among human love and even among conceptions of love without a perfectly loving God. Merely human love, then, seems inferior to the morally perfect love that would be characteristic of a God worthy of worship. In addition, divine love would not be coercive or mechanical toward humans, but would be freely relational and in intention curative, and it could be appropriated by humans in imperfect ways. Even if humans receive divine love via faith and hope in God, they can taint the process to some extent with their own selfishness. The history of religion confirms this abundantly and painfully.

A redemptive God may want humans to receive and to practice unselfish love via direct reliance on its perfect source, God. Otherwise, a counterfeit, misplaced love would be a serious, ever-present threat to humans. God would want the reliance in question to include trust and hope in God, because these are effective direct avenues to receive divine love without inflating human self-trust or pride in human accomplishments. In addition, God would want people, in sympathetic cooperation, to practice, and not just to reflect on, the love received from God for the sake of others, including their enemies. So, the divine love under consideration would not be held selfishly if one cooperates fully with God's perfect will. (Chapter 3 will clarify the nature of such love in connection with the problem of divine hiding from humans as part of the divine trial for humans.)

Responsible human seeking of God, as suggested, would be active, and not merely reflective, intellectual, or emotional. It would require the exercise of one's will in actions of various sorts, including the action of gathering available evidence regarding God. It also would require one's yielding oneself sympathetically to God's will as one receives salient evidence of God's will. Such yielding is an intentional action, and cannot be reduced to mere reflection or emotion. This kind of action figures in what we may call "active foundations for faith in God." It suggests a new emphasis on faith in God and its foundations: an emphasis on responsive intentional action rather than on something merely reflective or emotional.

7. CONCLUSION

God's moral overwhelming of humans would aim to contrast human power in its inadequacy for lasting good life with the alternative, relationally curative power of God.

Given that this divine power would be *sui generis* in its moral overwhelming of humans and would be crucial to who God is, we may say that God would sometimes be *overwhelmingly other* relative to humans. It does not follow that God would be *wholly* other, because humans may share in the image of God, at least in virtue of being morally responsible agents. Gethsemane and the cross can illustrate God's being morally overwhelming in the divine power at work.

The divine love received by humans in volitional weakness relative to God's will would not be a divine–human hybrid, even if humans are called to cooperate sympathetically with it via faith in God. Instead, it would be uniquely divine, and it would underwrite human faith and hope in God. Such faith would be energized, or empowered, by God's unique love, and it thereby would be ratified on the basis of unique evidence from a self-manifesting God (cf. Gal. 5:6).

The weakness of faith, as suggested, is not the weakness of its object, namely God. Instead, the weakness is in the relevant human will in relation to God and God's relationally curative power. Gethsemane and the cross can highlight this human weakness without diminishing the strength of God's power. Even so, the strength of God's power would be distinctive and even enigmatic relative to coercive powers, because it would be the relationally curative strength of self-giving love. It would offer what is relationally good, and would not take or coerce for selfish purposes. So, Paul remarks: "God's weakness is stronger than human strength" (1 Cor. 1:25). This "weakness" is seen in the *power* of the message of the cross; so Paul is being ironic. Divine love may look like weakness to humans, but this is mere appearance. God's cruciform power of righteous love, represented in Christ crucified, ultimately would overcome any conflicting human power, even though it must be received by humans in Gethsemane weakness.

Faith in God as outlined here is inherently personalist, owing to its focal role for an irreducible I–Thou relation, and this relation is modeled by Jesus in Gethsemane as he endeavors sympathetically with God. Faith in God thus would become Gethsemane faith, because it would rest on the decentering and recentering power of God in a Gethsemane situation. This would be the power of God's righteous love, and it would need to be intentionally and sympathetically received by humans as they endeavor with God.

Cooperative humans would live with an ongoing challenge to receive, to be convicted by, and to manifest God's recentering love. When faith in God conforms to this challenge, Paul suggests, all things become new in significance, starting with inquirers themselves. The remaining question is whether inquirers of God are *willingly* up to the challenge to be remade in *imitatio Dei*, through sympathetic faith that sometimes faces the moral overwhelming of humans by God. We turn now to what salient evidence of God's reality and goodness would be and how it would function relative to humans open to the God relationship. Such evidence takes on a new look under the relationship theism on offer.

[handwritten annotations:]

sui generis: unique

imitatio dei: imitation of God is the religious percept of man finding salvation by attempting to realize his concept of supreme being

→ even if I don't know who the president is,
→ I believe the president is commander in cheif.

de dicto: individual has a certain property or plays a certain role

de re: pick out an individual via some property/role they play.
 └ I believe of the president that he is commander in chief.

3

⚝

The God Relationship and Evidence

Chapter 2 indicated that the God relationship would include, if God exists, a faith relationship that puts a human in a trial for compassion with God. A test for the reality of the God relationship would call for the ethics for inquiry about God, owing to the importance of responsible inquiry about God, all things considered. We have seen that the relevant ethics for inquiry calls for an inquirer's being in a responsible position to receive salient evidence of God's reality and goodness. Given perfect divine goodness, we may expect such evidence to be available to humans under certain morally relevant conditions, if God exists.

The question of God's existence seems not to be conclusively settled, either pro or con, by sound deductive or inductive (including abductive) arguments for any sizable group of people free of prior commitments on the question. Could this indicate something important about the God in question? We shall pursue this question to illuminate the kind of responsible inquiry suited to a God worthy of worship. We do well to follow Aristotle's suggestion, in the *Nicomachean Ethics* (1094b13), to seek the amount of precision available in our actual subject-matter, without assuming that all topics allow for the same exacting precision. Precision in inquiry about God may differ from precision in, say, inquiry about the Pythagorean Theorem.

Perhaps typical philosophical inquirers about God's existence have a misplaced emphasis on an argument-based mode of inquiry. Perhaps they confuse evidence and argument, as many people do. This chapter contends that important corrections are needed here, particularly if a God worthy of worship would self-manifest the divine character toward humans. In that case, we shall see, the place of arguments for God's existence must yield to a more important kind of evidence for the existence and character of God.

This chapter identifies the shortcoming of a kind of "intellectualism" that limits the relevant evidence to evidence already possessed by a person. If God is truly redemptive and hence relationally curative in seeking divine–human reconciliation, we should expect the evidence for God to be correspondingly redemptive and curative. The implications of this lesson for religious epistemology are significant but widely neglected. This chapter draws out some of these implications and explains why the evidence for a relationally curative God resists any quick and easy dismissal on epistemological grounds and instead offers a profound existential challenge for inquirers about God. A redemptive God would come with a distinctive kind of evidence that is often neglected by inquirers about God. In keeping with the ethics for inquiry outlined in Chapter 2, the chapter explores such evidence in connection with the topic of divine hiding.

1. WHOSE EXISTENCE?

Chapter 1 suggested that as responsible inquirers we should settle what we mean, at least roughly, by the slippery term "God." Otherwise, the nagging question "*Which God?*" will not go away, and our progress in inquiry will suffer accordingly. Alleged gods come in many different forms and characters, and therefore uncritical talk of "God" yields semantic and epistemological obscurity in inquiry. In that case, we end up with something akin to Lewis Carroll's problem of the hunting of the Snark. We then risk having not only false expectations for God but also misleading standards for what qualifies as suitable evidence for God. So, self-conscious clarity in our use of the key term "God" can save us from unnecessary problems in inquiry.

Perhaps God could inform us about how to use the term "God," but we would need to identify somehow that the information offered comes from *God* rather than an imposter. In any case, the world beyond us humans will not impose a semantic decision on us regarding the use of the term; we have a voluntary role here. Chapter 1 suggested that we set the bar as high as possible at the start and use the term as a perfectionist title. Specifically, the term "God" is a title requiring worthiness of worship and hence self-sufficient moral perfection in a titleholder. We can lower the bar later if we wish, but we would be ill-advised not to consider this perfectionist title as fitting for one who is divine. One important advantage of this use of a title is, as suggested, that we can ask about God's existence even if God does not exist. A title can have clear semantic sense even if it lacks an actual titleholder, that is, a referent. So, in using "God" as a title, inquirers about God need not beg key questions against atheists or agnostics.

We can get some help by understanding the term "God" via the familiar properties of omnipotence, omniscience, and omnibenevolence. The abstractness and generality of these properties, however, can hinder illumination and decision-making regarding questions about God's existence. We can avoid undue abstractness if we understand the title "God" to connote the kind of worthiness of worship that includes *perfect redemptive love* (*agapē*) in virtue of perfect goodness. Such a title, however, could lack an actual titleholder who is worthy of worship.

A divine agent with perfect redemptive love would actively seek what is morally best for all agents, even for those opposing God. What is best in this regard would include an intended reconciliation of humans to God through divine forgiveness, in order to empower humans to share, sympathetically if imperfectly, in God's perfect moral character and purposes. So, God would undertake intended redemptive interventions in human lives, including in the lives of people opposed to God who have not finally rejected God. Any alleged god who fails to undertake such interventions would fail by the standard of worthiness of worship and hence would fail to be God. So, in the absence of enemy-love and corresponding action, a candidate for being God will fall short of actually being God.

God's intended redemptive interventions would not need to be the same for all people. God could intervene in ways sensitive to the varying receptivity or the lack thereof in humans. For instance, God could use the most advantageous timing for the various interventions aimed at human redemption. It could be pointless and even counterproductive, for instance, to intervene in a case where a human is not ready at all to receive that intervention in a redemptive manner. So, God could hide from some people at times, at least until they are ready to respond in a suitable manner.

God would be elusive toward humans in ways required by perfect redemptive love, including self-sacrificial love. So, God would not be transparently ever-present in the way a conclusion of an argument can be. This lesson fits with the nature of the God represented in important strands of Judaism, Christianity, and Islam – the three main heirs to Abrahamic monotheistic faith in God. It fits with the nature of the elusive God of Isaiah, Jesus, and Paul, who sometimes hides from people for their own redemptive good. As truth-seekers and responsible inquirers regarding the existence and character of God, we should be conceptually open to this kind of God from the start, even if we find the supporting evidence inadequate in the end.

2. ARGUMENTISM ABOUT GOD

Let's call "argumentism about God" the view that one's knowledge of God's existence would depend on one's having some argument or other for God's existence. Many theist, atheist, and agnostic philosophers assume argumentism about God, if uncritically, and they are not alone in assuming it. Perhaps such a view is an occupational hazard for philosophers in particular, given their preoccupation with arguments on various topics of philosophy. We need to be suspicious of argumentism about God, however, because it does not fit well with a God of perfect redemptive love. Perhaps it fits better with lesser gods, but we need not digress.

An argument is simply a finite series of claims, some of which – the premise(s) – are intended to support, via an inference, some other claim(s) in the series – the conclusion(s). The intended inferential support can be either deductive or inductive (including abductive), and inductive inference can confer probability on a conclusion in various ways, one of which is an abductive, or explanatory, inference. Philosophers disagree on the exact conditions for when an explanatory inference confers reasonableness on a conclusion, but we need not pursue that complex topic. (For my own view, see Moser 1989.) Our present concern is much bigger than that of when abduction yields reasonable belief. Our main concern is whether human knowledge of God's existence would depend on an argument.

The God of Abrahamic monotheism contrasts with many other (alleged) gods, including many gods of philosophical theism. One difference is that Abraham's God offers a promise of a redemptive, or curative, relationship with God and others for all cooperative people, even God's enemies. It is difficult to identify any other initially plausible candidate for such a God of redemptive promise concerning interpersonal relationships. The gods familiar in ancient Babylon, Egypt, Greece, and Rome do not offer the universal redemptive promise of Abraham's God or anything like it (see Wright 1950). People have characterized the moral character of the God of Abraham in various ways, but I shall attend only to a use of "God" that requires moral perfection.

We should not expect to find the God of Abraham, Isaac, and Jesus as a reality in the conclusion of a philosophical argument or any argument. This God, if real, is no conclusion, statement, or proposition of any sort. This should be an obvious conceptual point, beyond plausible denial. A God worthy of worship would be a living person and thus intentional agent with a morally perfect will and corresponding purposes. As perfectly good, God would come to cooperative humans directly under certain conditions for redemptive purposes. A divine aim would be to invite cooperative humans to know and obey God without any needed argument for God's existence, because the aim would be for humans to know and trust *God*, beyond knowing arguments and their conclusions.

An argument, however compelling, could interfere with knowing and trusting God by directing human attention away from God and toward an argument. So, God may need to be intentionally active and challenging toward distracted humans in ways that arguments and their conclusions are not. Arguments and their conclusions do not have intentions, even if their human proponents do. Specifically, arguments cannot redeem humans at odds with God by morally overwhelming them, intentionally convicting and forgiving them, and offering them reconciliation with God. So, we do well not to conflate the distinct categories of God and argument.

As perfectly redemptive, God would be intentionally and compassionately forgiving and corrective in ways that arguments and their conclusions are not and cannot be. Arguments and their conclusions are not compassionate at all, even if their human proponents are. The God of Abraham, Isaac, and Jesus would offer receptive humans both a *personal* offer of forgiveness and reconciliation and a *personal* conviction of their need of forgiveness and reconciliation. Not being personal agents, arguments and their conclusions cannot deliver on this front. Specifically, arguments cannot *personally* offer forgiveness and reconciliation in a way that prompts personal indebtedness in recipients. Perhaps God could send his beloved son to show humans who God is and to manifest God's redemptive love for them; at least, this is supported by Christian monotheism. An argument, however, is no candidate for such a personal redemptive initiative, even if it can play an incidental role for some people.

As a perfectly redemptive agent, God would personally offer humans forgiveness, reconciliation, and life in communion as *koinonia* with God. Arguments and their conclusions, however, lack the power of redemptive agency to make any such personal offer, even if they can describe such power. It would be a category mistake to suggest otherwise. Arguments and their conclusions lack the intrinsic personal and intentional agency needed to offer an I–Thou interaction or an interpersonal relationship between themselves and humans. Not being a personal agent, an argument does not stand in an I–Thou personal relationship with anything. God, however, would be significantly different, owing to divine intentional agency and its corresponding redemptive purposes. So, belief *that* a conclusion is true cannot supply faith *in God*. As Chapter 1 indicated, such faith, as a cooperative self-response to divine self-manifesting to a human, would have a *de re* agent-to-agent, I–Thou feature that goes beyond merely discursive arguments and their conclusions.

Some gods of philosophical theism are explanatory postulates based on considerations of a best (available) explanation. The God of Abraham, Isaac, and Jesus, however, does not fit well with the familiar model of an explanatory postulate. Such a postulate is familiar in some of the natural sciences where a directly unobserved entity is postulated to make sense of some observed empirical data. In physics, for instance, one might postulate the existence of a subatomic particle to account for perceived data generated by an oscillating particle accelerator. Since the mid-1960s, our best physics has acknowledged the existence of quarks of various types even though quarks are not observed directly, because they are not individually isolated. Similarly, one might recommend God as an indispensable, or at least a valuable, explanatory postulate, on the basis of an abductive inference akin to familiar inferences in subatomic physics.

Let's acknowledge a distinction between an explanatory postulate and a *mere* explanatory postulate. The former may be directly observed by humans, whereas the latter is not subject to direct human observation. We do not ordinarily think, however, of something directly observed by us as a "postulate," given that we directly observe it. It strains ordinary use, for instance, to say that one's parents are explanatory postulates, because they are directly observed by some people. Some philosophers may talk that way on occasion, but such talk runs afoul of the mundane idea that one's parents do not need to be postulated because they typically present themselves to one in one's direct experience. So, we may ask why one would categorize one's parents as "postulates" when they can be directly encountered in one's experience.

Some philosophers will recommend God as an explanatory postulate on the ground that not all people have, or seem readily able to have, a direct experience of God. In this regard, God's reality is not a matter of direct experience for all concerned in the way the perception of, say, apples and oranges is. So, these philosophers might propose, we need to approach God as an explanatory postulate, at least relative to the experience of some people. Even so, we need another distinction: If some people have not directly experienced God, a perfectly redemptive God would have to be *available* (if at the redemptively opportune time) for direct experience by all cooperative people. Otherwise, God would be withholding something morally good from humans, and that would undermine divine moral perfection.

Given free human agency regarding a salient, or definite, experience of God, humans could exclude themselves from such an experience of God, say by resolving against God to make such an experience redemptively pointless for them. They thus could frustrate God's redemptive will, to their own detriment. Alternatively, humans could strive to become cooperative toward a salient encounter with God, in yielding to God's expressed will. An analogy comes from the perception of the stained-glass windows in a cathedral. If I insist on remaining outside, I may have no visual perception of the beauty of the windows, owing to the protective covering that hides the beauty from outside. In that case, I may decide not to appreciate the beauty available in the windows. Upon choosing to go inside the cathedral, however, my experience of the windows could change significantly, as I then could have a direct encounter of their beauty, and may even come to appreciate this beauty in a sympathetic manner. Likewise, in the case of encountering God, my will can be an impediment or an aid. So, I may have a role to play as a voluntary agent relative to available evidence for God's reality and character.

If a perfectly redemptive God is available for direct human experience, as many seemingly responsible inquirers testify, we should expect significant implications for knowing God's reality. In that case, we need not be limited to arguments as our evidence for God's reality, because we could rely on our direct experience of God as basic, foundational evidence for God's reality and goodness. Such foundational evidence can be defeasible (that is, subject to override by other foundational evidence), and it need not logically entail what it justifies (for details see Moser 1989). Even so, it is a viable candidate for the kind of evidence required by knowledge. A *belief* in God, in contrast, does not qualify as basic evidence, because such a belief needs support from evidence. A salient experience, however, can serve as such evidence, because it can be a (non-propositional) truth-indicator for a proposition for a person.

Evidence is not exhausted by arguments, given that the evidence provided by salient experience is not always an argument. My salient experience of my computer screen, for instance, is not an argument or even a claim of any kind, although it has qualitative content that can be a truth-indicator for a claim for me. I can make a claim *about* my experience, but that is another matter altogether. Likewise, a direct experience of God would not be an argument or a claim, even if one can make a claim about that experience. It would have, however, qualitative content that can serve as a truth-indicator for a person for a claim regarding God's existence and goodness. It might include a *de re* manifesting of righteous love to a person, and it might be welcomed by that person via willingly being convicted in conscience toward such love. Arguments and claims, then, do not have a monopoly on evidence, contrary to the suggestion of some philosophers.

If one can have a direct experience of God, and thereby have foundational evidence for God's reality, we need to ask what value, if any, there is in an argument for God's existence. The value would not be in the need of an argument to have human knowledge of God's reality, because the evidence component of such knowledge could be satisfied without an argument. Perhaps, then, an argument gets at least some of its value in the *presentation* or *communication* of one's having knowledge of God's reality. Such presentation, however, differs from one's *having* knowledge of God's reality, because one could have this knowledge without presenting or communicating it. The same point holds for one's knowing *that* God exists (if one wants to talk of purely *de dicto* rather than *de re* knowledge regarding

God's existence); it does not depend on its being presented or communicated. One's presentation of knowledge to others, then, is not to be confused with one's having that knowledge. A directly analogous point holds for evidence, whether *de re* or *de dicto*.

What is fitting for one's presentation of knowledge to others needs to be guided by what one's knowledge actually consists in. Otherwise, one's presentation will not represent one's actual knowledge. In some cases, one's supporting evidence in one's knowledge will not be publicly shareable in the way that, for instance, news about the weather is. This can result from the nature of the object known and the corresponding evidential experience. If, for instance, I have direct knowledge of my sporadic toothache, my knowledge that I have a toothache now will not depend on my presentation of this knowledge to others. Perhaps, then, nobody else knows about it. In any case, evidence and knowledge need not be publicly shared, contrary to some philosophers. Specifically, one could not bind God to give only public evidence.

When I present my knowledge of my sporadic toothache to others, I need to clarify that my knowledge of my sporadic toothache's reality does not depend on my having an argument that I have a sporadic toothache. I could have the former knowledge without having the latter argument. In addition, the failure in soundness of the latter argument, in terms of the validity of its inference or the truth of its premises, would not necessarily undermine my foundational evidence or knowledge of my sporadic toothache. So, the failure of my having an argument to convince others would not necessarily undermine my foundational evidence or knowledge. In general, then, one's failing to convince others of a conclusion does not entail that one lacks adequate evidence for that conclusion.

We can apply the previous lesson to knowledge of God's reality and any argument for God's reality. George Mavrodes has remarked:

Is there something that can be proved to everyone by some argument or other? Perhaps there is, though this also seems unlikely. If 'God exists' were to be a proposition of this sort then everyone would have to know something or other (not necessarily the same thing) that entails that God exists. . . . Perhaps everyone does know something of this sort, but there is no reason to think so. (1970, p. 47; cf. Hick 1971, p. 109)

It would be a big task to show that everyone knows something or other that entails that God exists. In any case, one's lacking a cogent argument that God exists would not exclude one's having foundational evidence or knowledge that God exists. Likewise, one's not being able to present or communicate such an argument could leave one's foundational evidence for God's reality unscathed.

Argumentism neglects that God could provide salient evidence of God's reality to humans, say by self-manifesting the divine righteous character to humans in a direct encounter, without any human reliance on an argument. If this evidence of God's reality does not face any undefeated defeaters, it could satisfy the evidence condition for knowledge of God's reality. In that case, a person's salient evidence and knowledge of God's reality would not need to rely on an argument possessed by that person. That person would not need to accept or to draw an inference from a premise to a conclusion regarding God's reality. So, such evidence and knowledge would not require one to have or to present an argument for either God's reality or one's knowledge of God's reality.

Argumentism suggests that we must rely on arguments to reason our way to genuine knowledge of God's reality. This suggestion, however, runs afoul of what would be the moral character of a perfectly redemptive God, the kind of God worthy of worship. Such a God would take the redemptive initiative toward humans, both in favoring humans and in seeking a redemptive and cognitive relationship with them. God would come to receptive, cooperative, humans with direct self-manifesting evidence of divine reality. Otherwise, humans would be at a loss to acquire salient evidence of God's reality, because we would lack an adequate proxy for (evidence of) God's unique character. The God of Abrahamic monotheism would be unable to find a twin to do God's redemptive and cognitive bidding among mere humans (see Heb. 6:13).

A perfectly redemptive God would have no good reason to produce or to underwrite arguments that bind agents generally, on pain of irrationality, to acknowledge God's existence. A divine redemptive plan would not suffer if, apart from direct experiential evidence from God, humans rationally could withhold judgment regarding God's existence. In that case, humans in general would not be rationally bound by any argument to acknowledge God's existence. As redemptive, God would seek a kind of volitional cooperation from humans, and arguments for God's existence would not have an essential role in that goal, even if they had an optional role at times. Philosophical inquiries about God's existence typically ignore this consideration, in their exaggeration of the importance of philosophical arguments as the evidence for God's reality. We should not expect, however, to gain salient evidence of God's reality just by an argument. A better alternative recommends, in keeping with Chapter 2, that an inquirer intend to cooperate with what would be God's perfect will.

We can formulate various arguments for God's reality, and many such arguments attract the careful attention of philosophers. Without a basis in evident divine interventions in human experience, however, the arguments will be dubious at best in failing to present a resilient evidential basis to responsible inquirers. These arguments then will lead to the kind of disappointing impasse we typically see in argument-based exchanges between philosophical theists and atheists or agnostics. We need to clarify the aforementioned concerns about argumentism in connection with a better understanding of the evidence for a perfectly redemptive God. This effort will contribute to an improved understanding of the ethics for inquiry about God.

3. A SELF-AUTHENTICATING GOD

Given God's perfect moral character, God would be not only redemptive but also self-manifesting toward (at least) humans willing to cooperate with God (cf. Rahner 1978, pp. 117–26). God would not offer revelation *only* as testimony to humans (of the discursive kind defended in Wahlberg 2014), because testimony from God would require for its evidential support a foundation in God's unique self-manifested character. In addition, given God's perfect moral character, we should expect God to be self-sacrificial for the moral good of humans. So, we should expect God to be actively self-giving in redemption, and not just discursive in instructing about redemption. Various parts of the Jewish Bible and the New Testament portray God as actively gracious and self-sacrificial in attempting to redeem humans from their alienation from God through forgiveness and reconciliation (for details, see Wright 1952, pp. 59–86, Baillie 1956, pp. 50–56, Knight 1959, pp. 218–29, 282–86, and Baillie 1962, pp. 189–212). This portrayal fits with what would be a morally perfect God, given a familiar understanding of moral perfection as including unselfish care for others.

If God is inherently self-sacrificial for others, opportunities presented to humans for self-sacrifice for the good of others can be significant for knowing God. They can include God's self-manifesting presence in offering to humans the opportunity to conform to God's perfect moral character. They can be opportunities for humans to participate sympathetically in God's moral character of self-sacrifice and even in God's powerful activity of self-sacrifice. Specifically, they can be opportunities for humans to *cooperate* volitionally with God's presence and activity of self-sacrifice. In cooperating thus, humans could come to know God in a redemptive or relationally curative manner and hence be renewed personally and morally according to the image of God (see Col. 3:10).

God's power and presence could become salient for humans as they cooperate in ongoing divine self-sacrifice when the opportunity arises. Perhaps God's presence is typically intended to be, and typically is, cooperative in this manner relative to humans. If God's distinctive causal power centrally and intentionally includes the power of self-sacrifice for the good of others, we should expect God's presence to include such power of self-sacrifice. We also should expect the evidence for God to become tenuous and elusive as we ignore or resist such power of self-sacrifice in our lives. (We shall return to this matter later in the chapter, in connection with the problem of divine hiding.) The power in question is *agapē*, as designated in the New Testament, and it can be present to humans even if they fail to classify it as *God's* power or presence. As Chapter 2 indicated, God can be present *de re* to humans even when they do not know or believe this *de dicto*.

God's moral perfection would require that God perfectly love all other persons, even resolute enemies of God. The New Testament endorses this requirement in various ways, for God and even for humans who cooperate with God (see, for instance, Matt. 5:43–48, Luke 6:32–36, Rom. 12:9–10, 20–21, Col. 3:13). So, God's self-manifesting toward humans would include the presence of redemptive love for them. Even so, humans could perceive their own inadequacy and unworthiness relative to this powerful *agapē*, and could even turn away from it rather than willingly being convicted toward it. God, then, would have no guarantee that humans will cooperate with the intended divine redemption offered to them. In this respect, humans could frustrate God's will. They could fail to empower God to bring about redemption as reconciliation with God, given divine respect for human agency.

Alan Richardson has commented on the divine evidence found in the self-manifesting of God's unique character:

I would . . . deny that my faith was self-induced and unsupported by any evidence; I would insist that it was the *intrinsic quality* of [for example] my doctor or my friend which had created my faith in him, not some subjective impressions of my own. So it is with faith in Christ: it is he who has awakened faith in us by being what he was and doing what he did. And when I find that my initial decision to trust him is confirmed by my actual experience of doing so, then I may say that I have 'proved' him . . . . (1966, p. 109, italics added)

The self-manifesting of God's distinctive moral character (or "intrinsic quality") of *agapē* could awaken faith in God for a suitably cooperative human. In the absence of defeaters, this self-manifesting could supply for a recipient undefeated evidence in support of faith in God. Such faith then would have a salient evidential ground in human experience of God, courtesy of God's self-manifesting to a human. So, it would not be self-induced, groundless, or suspiciously abstract regarding its evidential basis. Faith in God then could be above evidential reproach without relying on any philosophical argument, including any argument of natural theology.

As an intentional causal agent, God could authenticate God's own reality and character for humans. This self-authentication would include God's self-manifesting God's distinctive moral character to humans (perhaps in conscience) and producing traits of this character in the experiences and lives of cooperative recipients. So, as a self-manifesting agent with a unique, morally perfect character, God could be self-evidencing and self-authenticating toward humans. (For variations on this theme, see Forrest 1906, pp. 102–107, Mackintosh 1913, p. 312, 1921, chap. 2, Stewart 1940, pp. 87–88, Rahner 1978, pp. 203–206; cf. Moser 2013, chap. 3.) This widely neglected view does not reduce to the dubious view that a subjective human experience or a part of the Bible is self-authenticating regarding God's reality. God would be an independent moral agent and the ultimate base of *agapē* for humans, and therefore God would not be a subjective human experience or a part of the Bible. Divine agency, then, would be irreducible to subjective human experience and to the Bible. Such agency, in addition, would not need to be self-manifested in all of the events of human history, because God could choose to self-manifest in some events but not in others (see Farmer 1936, pp. 85–89).

As the supreme, uniquely perfect authority, God ultimately would testify to God for humans via self-manifestation. Neither mere claims nor mere subjective experiences are self-attesting in a convincing manner about objective reality. As an intentional causal agent, however, God would be self-authenticating in being self-manifesting and self-witnessing regarding God's reality and moral character (see Rom. 10:20, 2 Cor. 4:6, John 6:27, 14:21–23). This kind of self-authenticating fits with the biblical theme of God's confirming God's own reality for humans, given that God inherently has a morally perfect character and cannot find anyone or anything else with the needed quality of character to serve this purpose. We have noted the following New Testament remark on this theme: "When God made a promise to Abraham, because he had no one greater by whom to swear, he swore by himself" (Heb. 6:13; cf. Gen. 22:16–17, Isa. 45:22–23). God thus could invoke and present God's own unique moral character to underwrite the integrity, authenticity, and trustworthiness of God's reality, actions, and purposes.

My suggested position has major implications for a religious epistemology regarding human knowledge of God. One component of it may be called, following James S. Stewart, *the divine self-verification of Christ in conscience*: "This is a very wonderful thing which happens: you begin exploring the fact of Christ, perhaps merely intellectually and theologically – and before you know where you are, the fact is exploring *you*, spiritually and morally. . . . You set out to see what you can find in Christ, and sooner or later God in Christ finds you. That is the [divine] self-verification of Jesus" (1940, pp. 87–88; cf. Moser 2013, chap. 3). Responsible inquirers about God should investigate the prospect of this kind of experience (particularly in connection with the theme of 2 Corinthians 4:6), and not just philosophical arguments about the existence of God. Philosophical arguments can divert attention from, and obscure the importance of, this kind of experience of God's self-authenticating via self-manifesting for receptive humans. The "intrinsic quality" of God's self-manifested moral character, including its perfect love, in connection with Christ could authenticate the reality and character of Christ as God's representative.

We should expect God to be self-attesting and self-witnessing, if God is *sui generis* regarding worthiness of worship. A perfectly redemptive God would self-manifest, at God's preferred times, the divine character of *agapē* in the experience of cooperative humans, placing divine enemy-love in their motivational centers (see Rom. 5:5). This would be an ideal witness to God's reality and moral character, and it would be something only God could do. Mere humans and counterfeit gods, including imaginary gods, lack the needed power and moral character to witness in this way. No mere human, faced with fears of personal loss, would have the self-sufficient *agapē* character of enemy-love needed for the task; so, no mere human would be worthy of worship or be divinely self-manifesting. The same holds for false gods.

God's self-attesting would challenge, and perhaps even convict, potential recipients to move toward a life of enemy-love and forgiveness, away from destructive selfishness and pride. Ultimately, then, humans would not convince people regarding God's reality. God would do this, and humans could contribute by being in cooperative union with God, thereby manifesting the power, beyond the mere talk, of God's own *agapē*. Paul refers to the latter power in a number of his letters (1 Thess. 1:5, 1 Cor. 4:20, and Rom. 1:16, 5:5), in order to remind his readers of a unique formative reality in their lives. (Chapter 5 returns to the topic of convincing people regarding God's reality.)

A perfectly redemptive God, I have suggested, would want people to know God directly, in an I–Thou acquaintance relationship, without any dilution or distraction from philosophical arguments. Such a relationship would include a direct encounter with God, but, as a state, it would be irreducible to events of experience and would not require constant experience of God. God would want the central self-commitment of a human agent to be directed to *God*, not (in this context) to an inference or a conclusion of an argument. This fits with the biblical theme that God alone is the foundation, rock, and anchor for humans, including the cognitive foundation regarding God's reality, courtesy of divine self-manifesting to humans (see Ps. 18:2, 31, 28:1, 31:3, Isa. 44:8, Rom. 10:20, 1 Cor. 2:9–13, 2 Cor. 4:6).

A redemptive God would want to be one's ultimate evidential foundation for believing in God and for believing that God exists, and hence would not want an argument to assume this role. God would be the most reliable and secure cognitive basis for human knowledge of God, and the most redemptive too. The evidential foundation would be *God in God's self-manifesting interventions* in one's life, including in one's conscience, as God directly gives knowledge of God to receptive cooperative humans (see 2 Cor. 4:6). This would uphold God's vital and unique existential and cognitive significance for human inquirers.

Responsible inquirers would put themselves in a position to apprehend divine self-manifesting by being sympathetically open to receive and to participate in redemptive self-sacrifice, the hallmark of God's perfect moral character. The actual timing of the self-manifesting, however, would be at God's discretion. Humans should not expect to have control over divine self-manifesting or even its timing in their lives. Otherwise, they would wrongly tread on God's unique authority in self-revelation to humans.

An argument can obscure the importance of directly knowing God, and many uses of arguments by theistic philosophers actually do this. When familiar theistic arguments come under heavy fire from critics, many of these critics take the heavy fire to underwrite their agnosticism or atheism. This is misleading, because the key evidence for God's reality and character is not an argument. We could describe foundational evidence for God in a sound *first-person* argument, but such an argument cannot exhaust or replace the underlying experiential evidence from divine self-manifesting to a human. In addition, such an argument does not presume that everyone has the relevant foundational evidence. That evidence can vary among persons, with the result that some people lack it altogether. (On this matter, see Moser 2008, chap. 2; see also Richardson 1957.)

Philosophers often overlook the importance of a *nondiscursive* manifestational witness, in human experience, to God's powerful redemptive reality. In doing so, they overemphasize the role of discursive, intellectual reasons for beliefs regarding God. This deficiency may be the residue of a dubious kind of epistemic coherentism that lacks the needed resources of an experiential (non-Cartesian) foundationalism. Alternatively, it may stem from a confusion of the conditions for one's either having or manifesting evidence and the conditions for one's giving an argument. We do well, however, not to confuse evidence and an argument. If all evidence is an argument, we face a devastating epistemic regress problem of the sort suggested by Aristotle in his *Posterior Analytics* (see Moser 1989 for details, including criticism of epistemic coherentism).

An evidential component is *discursive* if and only if it uses assertive language to express a state of affairs. The New Testament category of "witness" (*marturia*) is broader than that of discursive evidence. A witness to God's reality and redemption may include discursive evidence, but it need not. A *nondiscursive* mode of human existing or relating can be a witness to God's redemptive character in virtue of manifesting certain properties of God's character, such as divine *agapē*, without making an assertion. (We should not confuse the manifestation of a property with an assertion.) This neglected point bears on an aim to manifest one's evidence for acknowledging God, including an aim to manifest a basis for the hope in God within one (see 1 Pet. 3:15). Even when a witness to God's reality includes a discursive component, that component need not be an argument. It could be a descriptive testimony to what God has done in one's life, free of reliance on the inference of an argument.

Foundational evidence or reasons need not be discursive, but could be non-propositional character traits supplied by God's self-manifesting intervention: love, joy, peace, patience, kindness, gentleness, and so on (see Gal. 5:22–23; cf. Col. 3:12–15). John's Gospel thus portrays Jesus as announcing that his disciples will be *known* by their *agapē* for others (John 13:35). Jesus himself did not mention or use any philosophical arguments with regard to the reality of God's interventions in human lives. The same is true of his followers represented in the New Testament. This noteworthy fact, moreover, does not qualify as a deficiency in their actual evidence or reasons.

Talk is cheap, and therefore many inquirers will wonder whether an argument has support from a corresponding nondiscursive witness, which can have power and cogency irreducible to statements, beliefs, and arguments. (On a nondiscursive witness in human *personifying evidence* of God, see Moser 2010, chap. 4.) We should expect a self-authenticating redemptive God to intervene with such a witness, at least for cooperative recipients. In addition, as Chapter 1 suggested, divine self-manifestation to humans could set an epistemic standard for knowledge of *God* over time, owing to the definite contours of God's moral character presented to humans. So, humans would not have to be creative in this area, owing to the contribution of divine self-manifestation.

4. WHITHER ARGUMENTS?

Perhaps we should anticipate that a philosophical exchange between theists and their critics would include an exchange of arguments, but to what end? *Philosophical* theism typically relies on arguments of natural theology, and, in this respect, is not to be confused with the theism of the Jewish Bible or the New Testament. The biblical writers do not offer their theism with philosophical arguments from natural theology. In this respect, biblical theism, including its epistemology of divine self-manifesting to humans, differs from philosophical theism.

It is doubtful, at least to many philosophers, that the familiar empirical arguments of natural theology, such as first-cause, design, and fine-tuning arguments, cogently yield a god who is a *personal agent*, even if they yield various impersonal explanatory postulates (see Moser 2010, chap. 3). We can coherently, and perhaps even plausibly, imagine an *impersonal* basis for such a contingent universe as ours, in keeping with certain metaphysical variations on Platonism and neo-Platonism (see Rescher 2010). This is true despite the report of one philosophical theist that he cannot imagine this and finds the suggestion astonishing (see Craig 2014). A familiar metaphysics from Platonism and neo-Platonism, however, is neither unimaginable nor astonishing; it is a historical reality with considerable influence among philosophers. An expression of astonishment does nothing to challenge this historical reality.

What does seem astonishing is that advocates of the philosophical arguments of natural theology typically neglect that the God of biblical theism is elusive and hides from humans on occasion. The purported evidence from the philosophical arguments of natural theology does not bob and weave in that manner for the redemptive good of human agents. So, that purported evidence easily can distract one from an intervening God who offers humans redemptive self-manifesting in an elusive manner. The evidence proposed by familiar natural theology does not fit in this regard with the God it aims to represent, but instead leave us with a serious disconnect.

Inquirers aiming to prevail in exchanges about theism and atheism with philosophical arguments would do well to consider the following observations from George Mavrodes:

Every valid argument is reversible. Someone who is determined to remain an atheist at all costs can always buy consistency by denying the apologist's premise, even if this means giving up some previously acknowledged conviction. (1983, p. 201)

We are . . . interested in whether there is any argument that will prove God's existence to everyone. Such an argument has apparently not yet been invented. If it is to be invented, there must be some set of propositions that everyone knows and that entail, by logical relations that are also known to everyone, that God exists. . . . [T]here is not much reason to believe that [this] is possible. (1970, p. 46; cf. Hick 1971, p. 109)

If these observations point in the right direction, we need to acknowledge that intellectual clashes between theists and atheists need to go deeper than arguments.

The following observation from H.H. Farmer suggests how the clashes go deeper than arguments: "The degree in which a reasoned cased for theism carries conviction (coercive logical demonstration not being possible) depends on the degree in which there is already present in the mind a disposition toward theistic belief; or in other words, natural theology can only make progress towards its desired haven when it allows its sails to be filled in part by the wind of natural religion" (1954, p. 13). A "reasoned case" still could figure in one's belief in God; it would not, however, be the full story of such belief. Something else would be a key part of the matter, and it would be motivational in a way that disposes an agent to be sympathetic to belief in God. This "something else" may be under an agent's control, at least indirectly, in the way an intention to cooperate sympathetically would be. We can clarify this lesson in connection with a recent philosophical exchange about theism and atheism.

William Lane Craig (2014) has offered seven quick arguments for the existence of God, without clarifying the defining parameters for being "God" in his perspective. A key question is whether his postulated God is worthy of worship and hence morally perfect. We are not told, but if we omit enemy-love, we omit the God of Jesus Christ. Alex Rosenberg (2014) finds Craig's arguments to be too quick and remains altogether unconvinced. So, we have an impasse between these philosophers, and they offer nothing to move beyond the impasse.

Craig's arguments have fallen short of one of their *apparent* goals: rationally to convince dissenting readers like Rosenberg, or at least to move them closer to theism. Why are we left with this impasse? Are the arguments inadequate for their own apparent purpose? Presumably, they are not designed just to satisfy readers already committed to theism. Craig, however, does not acknowledge that his arguments have failed to meet an apparent goal; nor does he specify what his goals are for his arguments. So, the exchange languishes. This is common, unfortunately, for philosophical exchanges between theists and atheists. It suggests that something is amiss in philosophical inquiry about God, and it recommends attention to the ethics for inquiry about God.

When philosophical theists present arguments for God's existence to an audience, they should accept a rational burden: rationally to convince (some) previously uncommitted people who read or hear the arguments. They should not want to give just arguments *they* deem sound, such as the following toothless argument noted by Mavrodes: "Either nothing exists or God exists; something exists; therefore, God exists" (1970, p. 22). Philosophical theists should want to give arguments where acceptance of the premises does not depend on acceptance of the conclusion. They should want to give *rationally cogent* arguments *for their audience*. Otherwise, they should scale back to a smaller group of recipients already agreeable to their conclusion. We do well to acknowledge the rational burden in question as it bears on philosophical theists presenting arguments to an audience. This matter bears on the presenting of arguments, and not on the mere having of evidence.

Craig's seven arguments face a serious problem arising from his unclarified talk of God as "the best explanation." Philosophical use of "an inference to a best explanation," or abduction, is typically inference to "a best *available* explanation," and not "the best explanation." The qualification is crucial, because we cognitively limited inquirers are not in a position to examine *all possible* explanations that bear on our relevant data. Craig's language of "the best explanation" assumes that he has surveyed all possible explanations and found one explanation to be "the best." He has not done so, because he, like other humans, does not enjoy access to all possible explanations in the domains in question. So, his language is overdrawn and misleading.

We have at best only the explanations now available to us, and not all possible explanations. So, we should settle for a best *available* explanation, and not use exaggerated talk of "the best explanation." The history of science recommends such cognitive modesty in our use of abduction.

The future can bring new explanations that we have not yet anticipated, as the history of science shows. Craig's seven arguments run afoul of this commonplace lesson. In addition, we may have to settle for "a" best available explanation, because we do not always enjoy a *singular* best explanation.

Given that our cognitive limits call for a restriction to our "best available explanation," we must ask: Best available *for whom*? For everyone? Evidently not, given that nontheists like Rosenberg (2014) and theists like me do not find Craig's arguments cogent (to us), on the basis of our overall available evidence. So, a neglected abductive question arises: What is the best available explanation of the impasse between philosophical theists of Craig's sort and dissenting inquirers like Rosenberg and me? Does this explanation involve an alleged deficit of rationality or intellect in those of us unconvinced by the arguments? If so, what exactly is this deficit, and how can it be removed, if it can? Here is where the exchange should begin, at a level where we are probing foundational issues, and not just throwing quick arguments at each other to score points in an ultimately inconclusive exchange. The ethics for inquiry about God would advise accordingly.

The data calling for explanation in the exchange are: the reality of contingent events, the origin of the physical universe, the applicability of mathematics to the physical universe, the apparent fine-tuning of the universe for intelligent life, the reality of consciousness, the reality of moral values, and various historical facts about Jesus Christ. At least for the first five or six categories of data, many theorists will find a theist's explanatory appeal to God to be theoretically too remote (perhaps even causally too remote) from the data, given their conception of a best (available) explanation. In addition, I remain unconvinced that those data yield, even abductively, an explainer who is a *personal* agent, let alone a personal agent worthy of worship.

If I had *only* the arguments in question, I would not be a theist, because the arguments fail to give us a God worthy of worship. Craig reveals his own tentativeness when he weakens some of his inferences to "plausibly" (2014, p. 15) – something much weaker than "the best explanation." A merely plausible inference will not settle the matter for most people free of an antecedent commitment to theism. They will hold out, understandably, for a more secure basis, given the high stakes involved. A plausible hypothesis need not be a rationally compelling hypothesis or a best (available) explanation of the relevant data.

The impasse stems from divergence among inquirers over *what it is to be* (that is, the constitutive conditions for) a "best (available) explanation." A key matter of divergence concerns the extent to which, or the way in which, a good or best (available) explanation can *exceed* relevant data and background commitments. The hypothesis of God as explainer *excessively* outstrips, and thus is theoretically *too remote* from, the data in question to qualify as a good or best (available) explanation, according to the constitutive conditions for such an explanation adopted by many inquirers, including many theists and nontheists. In addition, rationality seems not to require that the latter inquirers adopt either different conditions for a good or best (available) explanation or a notion of explanation friendly to natural theology.

The theorists unconvinced by philosophical theism are not necessarily rationally or intellectually inferior to a proponent of the abductive arguments in question. Instead, the former theorists may work with a more rigorously local understanding of what it is to be a good or best (available) explanation, and this need not be irrational. So, regarding the first five or six categories of data, they rationally can withhold judgment rather than postulate God as the best (available) explanation, as long as no rational error occurs in doing so. Perhaps, given their explanatory conceptual perspective, the hypothesis of God's existence is theoretically and conceptually too remote from the relevant data to serve the needed explanatory purpose. As a result, they would seek a more local explanation, and rationality seems not to bar that live option.

We need not insult the intelligence or the rationality of the unconvinced inquirers in the exchange. Instead, we should focus on why the abductive arguments in question fail to convince them, along the line suggested. An inquiry with this focus would prove fruitful in a way that typical exchanges between theists and atheists do not. A kind of question-begging about what it is to be a best (available) explanation often stunts those exchanges, and it gains us nothing to use a notion of "best explanation" as a blunt instrument to end careful discussion.

Craig mentions personal experience of God in passing, and contrasts it with an argument. Such experience, however, does not play a central role in his philosophical approach, at least by the standard of attention received. This is a mistake, because it shortchanges what would be key, salient evidence for God's reality. Due attention here would lead to pressing questions about why some people have the relevant experiences and others do not, and about the implications for the role of arguments in exchanges about theism. When such questions get no serious attention, we have a missed opportunity to explore the roles of volitional factors, personal discernment, and divine elusiveness in theistic evidence. We then fail to explore the deeper matters of religious epistemology, while staying at the surface and begging key questions in inquiry about God. This would not be responsible inquiry from the standpoint of the ethics for inquiry about God.

Some theists might balk at my agnosticism about Craig's abductive inference to God's resurrection of Jesus from the empty tomb of Jesus and the postmortem appearances of Jesus. He cites the view of N.T. Wright that the occurrence of these events is "virtually certain, akin to . . . the fall of Jerusalem in AD70" (2014, p. 18). Given the very limited and largely non-independent historical sources we have, we should regard this as misleading hyperbole at best. People without a prior commitment to the empty tomb of Jesus and his postmortem appearances to the disciples will properly expect a non-question-begging case for the bold claim to "virtual certainty," but we do not have one. The exaggerated rhetoric, at any rate, will not fill in for the needed case, and it only hinders responsible inquiry. (On Wright's mistaken abductive inference about the resurrection, and my positive alternative, see Moser 2008, pp. 189–99.)

Nontheists might oppose my foundationalist theistic evidence by offering a familiar defeater: horrifying evil in the world. Rosenberg (2014, p. 31) thus invokes a "logical" problem of evil, but he fails to convince here. Philosophers now widely recognize that, as the free will defense illustrates, there is no *logical* incompatibility between God's existence and the evil of the world. (See any recent careful treatment of the topic, such as Speak 2014.) Even though Rosenberg raises some serious questions facing the proposed arguments from natural theology, he offers no defeater for the kind of experiential evidence for God outlined in this book. In addition, a demand for a theodicy now will be misplaced, because we limited humans should not expect now to know God's full purposes in allowing evil.

Because this book's position does not depend on any argument from philosophical theism, it is unscathed by objections to the arguments of natural theology in question. I have suggested that philosophical theists should investigate why their widely used theistic arguments fail to convince many intelligent, rational inquirers of theistic and nontheistic persuasions. I also have proposed that we should not identify evidence for God's reality with an argument. We need to clarify further what the human reception of evidence for God's reality and character would include. To this we now turn.

5. INTELLECTUALIST UNDERPINNINGS AND SHORTCOMINGS

If we simply "think hard enough" about our current evidence, do we get an adequate answer to the question of whether God exists? If we answer *yes*, then we favor an *intellectualist* approach to the question of whether God exists. Such an intellectualist approach includes among its supporters atheists as well as theists. If one holds that the adequate answer received by thinking hard enough is *no*, then one is an atheist (for purposes of our discussion). In contrast, if one holds that the adequate answer is *yes*, then one is a theist.

We may call a proponent of an intellectualist approach, whether atheist or theist, an *intellectualist* about the question of God's existence. The discipline of academic philosophy houses a large representation of intellectualists offering views on God's existence, owing perhaps to its including some influential figures in the history of the intellectualist position. We may call their common position *intellectualism*. Bertrand Russell, for instance, was an influential proponent of intellectualism and an opponent of theism. He imagined himself protesting upon meeting God: "God, you gave us insufficient evidence" (1970; cf. Dawkins 2006, pp. 74–77). We shall see that intellectualism is suspect at best and arguably false. In doing so, we shall identify some widely neglected limits of human thinking relative to the evidence underlying human faith in God.

A person's "thinking hard enough," according to intellectualism, is not just a matter of having a lot of thoughts, as if the sheer quantity of one's thoughts was the key. The hard thinking in question includes one's using arguments, that is, one's using premises to infer conclusions, either deductively or inductively. This revives our previous question of the value of arguments regarding God's existence. Is our thinking hard about such arguments sufficient for our having an adequate answer to the question of whether

God exists? As suggested, the answer is no if humans can, and sometimes do, have relevant evidence independent of arguments regarding God's existence. If a human can have a direct experience of God, which is neither a thought nor an argument, there will be room for relevant evidence independent of arguments regarding God's existence. We should not exclude such experiential evidence at the start, in order to avoid begging some important questions about the evidence for God's existence. (See Moser 2008, chap. 2 for an attempt to make room for such evidence; cf. Farmer 1943, chaps. 3–4.)

When is an answer to the question of whether God exists "adequate"? An intellectualist will offer this reply: When an answer comes from our "thinking hard enough" about our evidence, it is adequate. Even so, a convincing reply needs to offer more, given that overall adequacy in an answer to our question comes from various domains. *Objective* adequacy requires the correctness or the truth of an answer, whereas *evidential* adequacy requires the suitable fit of an answer with one's overall evidence, but does not require the answer's truth. A person's overall evidence can be incomplete in a way that falls short of yielding truth in beliefs based on that evidence. For instance, widely shared astronomical evidence before Copernicus and Galileo was incomplete and misleading in this manner, at least in certain areas of inquiry.

Cognitive adequacy, let us assume, includes both objective adequacy and evidential adequacy. Genuine knowledge that a claim is true has this kind of adequacy, regardless of whether one knows that one has this knowledge. Many philosophers seek cognitive adequacy in their answers, because they want to know that their answers are true. For current purposes, we may sidestep the many complications arising from Gettier-style problems for the view that justified true belief is sufficient for knowledge that a proposition is true (for some relevant details, see Moser 1989, Shope 2002).

If intellectualists seek cognitive adequacy in their answer, they seek not only evidential adequacy but also objective adequacy. We have suggested, however, that the connection between evidential adequacy and objective adequacy is contingent, because the suitable fit of a contingent answer with one's overall evidence does not entail that the answer is true. This raises the issue of whether our thinking hard enough about our evidence will automatically yield an adequate answer to the question of whether God exists, if cognitive adequacy is the goal. The gap between evidential adequacy and objective adequacy in various actual cases recommends a negative reply.

It would be implausible to retreat to the view that we (should) care only about evidential adequacy, and not objective adequacy. Many people do care about objective adequacy, because they seek a *correct* answer to the question of whether God exists. In addition, evidential adequacy as characterized above is too limited for the purposes of many people. These people seek an answer that fits not only with the evidence we have now but also with the broader evidence *available* to us. The evidence we now have can be arbitrarily or prejudicially restricted by us, such as when we arbitrarily or prejudicially exclude the pursuit of relevant available evidence in a case. We may see broadly where our current evidence will lead us, perhaps even to new evidence, but prefer not to extend our evidence, given our perceived interests. Our available evidence, in contrast, transcends such arbitrary or prejudicial exclusion. So, seeking relevant new evidence can figure importantly in responsible inquiry, as Chapter 2 suggested in connection with the ethics for inquiry about God.

Consider a case involving my trusted employee who has always exhibited honesty and reliability at his job in the past. An equally trusted supervisor has just called my attention to what appear to be this employee's financial irregularities in some recent transactions at work. I now have a difficult choice to make, regarding whether to investigate my trusted employee by pursuing and gathering further available evidence regarding his reliability.

My current evidence does not indicate, in any preponderant way, that this employee is unreliable. On the contrary, my preponderant evidence, based on an extensive work history, indicates that he is reliable. As for available evidence I do not (yet) possess, it may undermine the previous evidence by indicating that the employee is actually unreliable. If I seek a responsible answer to the question of whether my employee is reliable, I will need to pursue further available evidence that I do not yet possess. Perhaps most employers would undertake this kind of pursuit, but I could refuse to do so, owing to fear of destroying my long-standing friendship with this employee. That kind of refusal could undermine responsible inquiry on my part.

We may have difficulty in specifying exactly when evidence is available in some cases. This general point, however, does not count against a distinction between the broader evidence *available* to us and the more limited evidence we now *have* or possess. For current purposes, we may suppose that we now "have" evidence only if we have had a salient awareness of it, but that we need not have had such an awareness of evidence merely available to us. This distinction will enable us to proceed with some clarity. (For an attempt to recruit this distinction to challenge evidence-based atheism, see Moser 2013, pp. 190–205, 2017.)

Evidence could be available to me but depend for its being *possessed* by me on a volitional stance or inclination of mine toward it, even if I do not actually possess the evidence. The volitional stance could include my being *willing* to love or to be faithful in a certain manner toward the source of the available evidence. If the source is a personal agent, that agent intentionally could supply the evidence of himself or herself accordingly. In this scenario, I could fail to possess the relevant available evidence as a result of my failing to be willing to love or to be faithful in a certain manner. I thus could be responsible, owing to my adopted volitional stance, for my not possessing evidence that is available to me. (Here, as previously, I use a conception of love or *agapē* requiring one's intentionally caring for what is good for people. For some helpful background for this conception, see Ramsey 1950, chaps. 1, 3, Furnish 1972; cf. Ferré 1961.)

Suppose that you refuse to confide in me regarding your deepest motives in life, because you know that I do not have the proper love or care for you and hence should not be trusted with evidence regarding your deepest motives. We might imagine that I am the town gossip who cares only about the favorable attention I bring to myself, even at the expense of others. So, you hide yourself from me in terms of who you really are, since I am a real threat to your good purposes, if not to your dignity as a person. It may be harmful to me as well as you to reveal your deepest motives to me, because I would handle this information in a bad way for all involved.

You would have no desire to enable, or otherwise to promote, my harmful tendencies in handling confidential information. So, you plausibly would withhold from me evidence regarding your deepest motives and hence regarding yourself, that is, evidence concerning who you really are. Even so, that evidence could be *available* to me, because (we may suppose) you would give it to me upon my coming to love you or to be faithful to you. We may call this *volitionally sensitive available* evidence, because my coming to possess this evidence would depend on my volitional stance toward the source of the evidence.

God could have good, redemptive purposes in making at least some available evidence of God's reality volitionally sensitive in its being possessed by humans. This evidence then would be sensitive to our volitional stance toward God and God's will. God could be evidentially elusive in this manner for purposes of redeeming humans via moral-character transformation toward God's character of perfect *agapē*. That is, God could hide or withhold evidence of God's reality for the good of potential recipients of this evidence. This divine hiding could save at least some people from rejecting God outright when they are not ready to receive God as the rightful authority of their lives. In that case, they would not be prepared to handle the evidence redemptively, in keeping with God's good purposes toward reconciliation and *koinonia*.

As perfectly redemptive (at least in purpose), God would care about *how* people respond, in terms of their motivating attitude, to evidence of God's reality, and would offer such evidence accordingly. So, God would not be a promiscuous exhibitionist or a superficial entertainer regarding the divine evidence offered to humans. The divine offer of such evidence would stem from God's profound moral character. God would preserve a redemptive role for available divine evidence by encouraging its pursuit with a cooperative, obedient, and even wholehearted human will. Such a human pursuit of divine evidence would contrast with any passive or casual reception of evidence by humans. (Chapter 2 noted the importance of seeking divine evidence, in connection with the ethics for inquiry about God.)

A number of biblical writers emphasize the importance of wholehearted human pursuit of God. For instance, the prophet Jeremiah assigns the following announcement to God: "When you search for me, you will find me; if you seek me with all your heart, I will let you find me, says the Lord" (Jer. 29:13–14; cf. Luke 11:9–13, Matt. 7:7–11). Wholehearted human pursuit of God and evidence for God could bring needed focus and integrity to human wills and lives, and it could prevent humans from becoming complacent, presumptuous, and conflicted relative to God. Such a pursuit, therefore, could contribute to the redemption of humans as reconciliation and *koinonia* with God.

God could bob and weave in divine self-manifesting to humans, for the sake of challenging people to approach God with due seriousness and reverence, and not to treat

God as a controllable or dispensable object. Some people may wake up to God as a valuable reality after feeling God's absence in their lives but then being confronted by God's self-manifesting to them, perhaps by the presentation of divine *agapē* in their conscience. We humans sometimes learn deeply from a sharp contrast between the absence and the presence of something in our experience, such as a human relationship.

A redemptive God would seek to elicit a human decision in favor of God's character and offered relationship of *agapē*, specifically a priority commitment that puts God and God's moral character first in human life, in terms of a relationship with God. In this respect, redemption would be cooperative, as humans resolve to share in God's moral character as a priority in their lives. This priority would call for a reordering of typical human priorities to conform to divine priorities, particularly regarding the priority of *agapē* toward others. (On the central role of human decision in redemption, see Minear 1966, chap. 3, Moser 2013, chap. 4.)

The idea of divine self-manifesting in *agapē* figures in Paul's understanding of the evidential basis for belief and hope in God (see, for instance, Rom. 5:5; cf. Rom. 10:20, 2 Cor. 4:6). Following Isaiah, Paul invokes God's self-manifesting to unexpecting humans (specifically Gentiles), and he understands it as seeking to "pour out" divine *agapē* within receptive humans. This self-manifesting of God's character, being redemptive, would seek to have humans put divine *agapē* for others first in their lives, above all the alternatives, in keeping with the greatest love command (see Ramsey 1943). Paul evidently holds that God's self-disclosure is sensitive, at least to some extent, to *human* disclosure to God, whereby one allows oneself to be known, and laid hold of, by God (see Gal. 4:9; cf. Phil. 3:12). In any case, we should allow that God can disclose God's will to a person, perhaps in conscience, without that person's knowing that it is *God's* will thereby disclosed. (On the role of conscience here, see Forsyth 1909, pp. 195–205, Forrest 1914, pp. 255–77, Häring 1978, pp. 224–82.)

We should not infer that a person must earn or merit (evidence of) God's self-manifesting or become morally perfect to be presented with it. Such an inference would seriously distort the moral character of a God who is worthy of worship and hence gracious and merciful toward morally imperfect people (in order to "justify the ungodly" by counting their faith in God as righteousness) (cf. Rom. 4:5). Instead, we should consider that a person may need to be willing to cooperate (if imperfectly) with God's perfect will if that person is to receive definite self-manifesting from God. The problem is not that God would be personally injured in a devastating way by uncooperative humans; it is rather that such humans could dishonor (the dignity of) God and themselves. In fostering such dishonor, one can bring about a kind of relational harm, that is, harm to a potential good relationship between humans and God. One thereby could harm the purpose of God's self-manifesting to humans, by frustrating a God relationship, thus harming oneself in turn. Such harm would obstruct what Chapters 1 and 2 outlined as God's "relationally curative" purpose for humans.

Suppose that God seeks to redeem all constitutive aspects of human persons, including not just human thinking but also the willing, or volitional, activity integral to intentional human agency. God then would offer a challenge to those aspects of human persons for the sake of their being transformed toward God's character and purposes, and thus their being included in a reconciliation to God in *koinonia*. This involves the question of what kind of person God would want one to be in relationship with God.

As a morally perfect agent, God would desire redeemed human *agents* who reflect God's moral character and agency in intention and action, and not just in thinking. The volitional activity central to human agency is not just thinking or even thinking hard about evidence. It involves intentions and decisions regarding the kind of person one aims to be, in terms of moral character and practice. So, moral responsibility looms large in the make-up of a mature human agent. In being perfectly redemptive, God would not neglect the volitional make-up of human agents, but rather would aim to lead it, uncoercively, into sympathetic cooperation with God's perfect will.

In the spirit of Job, humans often strive to understand God and God's providential ways to gain security and assurance for themselves. We should not expect God's security or assurance, however, to arise from mere human understanding, which is painfully limited in scope, especially regarding God's purposes in particular cases. Instead, we should expect divine security and assurance for humans to emerge from their volitional activity in response to God. This lesson fits with the following simple but profound remark from the prophet Micah: "What is good, and what does the Lord require of you but to do justice, and to love kindness, and to walk humbly with your God" (Micah 6:8).

In Micah's perspective, God aims for more than hard thinking by humans, even hard thinking with correct and well-grounded content. God aims, in addition, for volitional activity from humans that includes loving and obeying God. Such volitional activity is not captured by "thinking hard" about evidence. I can think hard about, and even accept, evidence for God but not welcome, love, or obey God at all. The volitional activity in question could be an avenue to more, and even better, evidence regarding God, as a human conforms to God's redemptive expectations. So, the evidence for God's reality from divine self-manifesting to humans could be sensitive to human wills, and it thus could allow for divine hiding in the face of volitional resistance.

In the portrait of God being developed, we cannot simply think ourselves into an objectively adequate answer regarding God's reality, because God would want, by way of redemption, more than our thinking. God would want to redeem our full agency, including our volitional features (such as our love), because God would want us to reflect divine moral agency in willing cooperation with God. If God would not want the latter, then God would not want what is morally best for us, and this would rob God of worthiness of worship.

One's being willing to obey God, in keeping with God's perfect will, mirrors the crisis of Jesus in Gethsemane, as Chapters 1 and 2 suggested. Seeking to obey God and thereby to inaugurate God's kingdom, Jesus found himself called by God to give up his own life in self-sacrifice to God for the sake of others. This was a temporary struggle between Jesus and God, where Jesus anticipated his arrest and crucifixion by Roman officials as part of God's plan of redemption. We have identified the heart of Jesus's obedience in the following response: "Abba, Father, for you all things are possible; remove this cup [of suffering and death] from me; yet, not what I want, but what you want" (Mark 14:36).

Gethsemane begins with a humanly experienced conflict between a human want and a divine want, but ends with a resolution in a human plea to God in favor of God's will and its priority. So, the Gethsemane approach to God puts God's perfect will first, even when a serious human want must yield to God's volitional challenge. The challenge from God could come in human conscience, where one is convicted by God of (potentially) wandering away from what is good or right in relation to God's will, and this challenge could be encouraged by other humans. The origin of the Gethsemane challenge, however, would be God's perfect moral character and will, and that challenge could convict one to move toward God's character and will.

Even if some people regard human conscience as just socially informed by humans, God still could work in conscience to challenge people to cooperate with God's will. In that case, receptive humans could find the God who hides, not in mere reflection, but instead in the experiential and volitional conflict of a Gethsemane-style crisis, where

God offers a new mode of life to humans on God's moral terms. In following the example of Jesus in Gethsemane, humans then would resolutely allow God to be authoritative at least in some area of their volitional and practical lives. This would be the beginning of human cooperation and *koinonia* with God.

We might think of a Gethsemane crisis as providing an opportunity for a kind of practical rationality toward God, via one's willingly moving toward cooperation with God. One's will could move toward God's will by one's responding in obedience to God's self-manifesting, and perhaps even convicting, in human conscience. If this is practical rationality toward God, its practicality consists in the uncoerced exercise of one's will to comply with God's will. It also would be substantive practical rationality, because it would encompass genuine goodness in cooperation with God's perfect will. It thus would not be purely instrumental practical rationality.

God's morally perfect will would represent a standard of goodness independent of the variability of human preferences or ends. As Chapter 2 suggested, God could nudge and encourage receptive people toward a Gethsemane crisis, and, therefore, they would not have to set up this crisis on their own. God would bring Gethsemane to humans as needed, at the opportune times, perhaps even with conviction allowed by free recipients. This process would be integral to God's being perfectly redemptive toward humans, at least in divine intent. God's morally perfect will would stand in sharp contrast to merely human wills, thus exposing their moral deficiency relative to God.

Intellectualism is an inadequate approach to the question of whether God exists. It neglects the plausible view that God would have definite redemptive purposes for humans and would reveal the evidence for God accordingly. God could provide available evidence for God's reality that is volitionally sensitive, in its being possessed by a human, to the direction of one's will relative to cooperation with

God's will. Many philosophers overlook this view, because they assume, in the tradition of Plato and Aristotle, that God is (or would be) immutable or static rather than purposively elusive. A God who is worthy of worship and hence morally perfect would have to be purposively elusive for the good of potential human recipients of salient divine evidence. Such a God would oppose half-heartedness in humans toward God, and seek instead their wholehearted commitment to God as supremely authoritative (see, e.g., Deut. 4:29, Jer. 29:13, Mark 12:29–30; on the idea of God as elusive, see Minear 1966, chap. 8, Terrien 1978, Moser 2008).

We can acknowledge some pre-cooperative evidence for God, where a person has initial evidence for God's self-manifesting (perhaps in conscience) but does not cooperate with God at all. Such evidence would be elusive, unstable, and thin, because God would not want people to rest content with it, apart from cooperating with God. Consider a resolute enemy of God such as the biblical character called "Satan," who believes that God exists but does not receive God cooperatively as authoritative for life. Satan could reasonably believe (on pre-cooperative evidence) that God exists, because God has self-manifested divine reality to Satan *to a very limited extent*. In rejecting God's will, Satan would freely prevent God from self-manifesting divine reality to a redemptive, cooperative extent, where God's powerful love would be poured out in his heart (cf. Rom. 5:5). In the biblical perspective, Satan is not volitionally receptive to God at all, and therefore his pre-cooperative evidence does not lead to the kind of salient transformative evidence arising from cooperation with God.

6. MOTIVES FOR INTELLECTUALISM

Proponents of intellectualism have various motives for their position, three of which merit attention here. First, they often seek aid from considerations about a needed method for inquiry. They adopt a method for belief formation and belief revision, and then wield it across the board in inquiry. This strategy is not mistaken in principle, but it needs to be handled responsibly, in a manner that does not preclude reasonable acknowledgment of genuine features of reality. The ethics for inquiry requires as much. For instance, we should be suspicious of any method that precludes reasonable acknowledgment of either human agents or such medium-sized physical objects as tables and chairs. We might say that a responsible method of belief formation will call for a responsible meta-method of belief formation: that is, a responsible method regarding (the identification of) a responsible method of belief formation. Inquirers must avoid, however, an endless regress of required methods, if only because we do not possess an infinite number of such methods in regress.

Two key questions arising from a meta-method about a proposed method of belief formation are: What does this method set as parameters for (evidential) acceptability in a set of beliefs? Does the method allow for (potential) reasonable acknowledgment of an elusive God who aims to redeem humans uncoercively? If it precludes such acknowledgment from the start, we may face a methodological bias that hinders the responsible and reasonable pursuit of truth. One might try to establish that our barring acknowledgment of an elusive God is well-grounded in our available evidence. That task, however, sets a tall order for advocates of the position in question, because our available evidence does not seem exclusive in the manner required. It seems more open-ended than suggested by the position at hand. At least, we now see where the burden would lie.

If God exists and is cognitively available to humans, a method for inquiring about God should fit with reasonable, evidence-based acknowledgment of the moral character and purposes of God, and not preclude such acknowledgment. Philosophers have sometimes adopted methods that settle the issue of God's existence in advance of due attention to the relevant evidence. For instance, a method that requires an evidential basis in mundane sensory evidence will represent a highly questionable bias, if only because much of ethics, aesthetics, mathematics, logic, and theology will be in evidential trouble. The same is true of a method that requires conformity either to a materialist ontology or to the kind of experimental procedures typical of a chemistry laboratory.

In general, we should not let a questionable method blind us from acknowledging genuine aspects of reality and the corresponding evidence. Instead, we should allow human experience of reality to play a key role in adjudicating among the many methods in circulation. Otherwise, we may have the proverbial oddity of putting the cart before the horse, or, at least, we may have an implausible bias in our method. More to the point, we should not allow a method to preclude volitionally sensitive evidence of God from the start. The ethics for responsible inquiry about God demands as much.

The second motive for some commitments to intellectualism comes from an unduly restrictive demand for evidence of God. As suggested, Bertrand Russell (1970) anticipated his response if God were to meet him, perhaps after death: "God, you gave us insufficient evidence." In the interest of gaining more truth, Russell might have considered a bit of modesty in the presence of God, perhaps by inquiring about available evidence of God that is volitionally sensitive in its being acquired by humans. In that case, Russell might have asked: "God, what purposes of yours led to your being subtle and elusive regarding the available evidence of your reality? Is such evidence volitionally sensitive in our acquiring it? If so, might this have a redemptive purpose?" Russell gave no indication of being aware of such plausible questions for a God who is redemptive toward humans. He should have asked about the moral character and purposes of a God worthy of worship, in order to avoid begging key questions about the evidence for God's reality. In that case, Russell would have had a potential challenge on his hands, or at least on his will, because *he*, rather than God, would be subject to potential challenge on volitional grounds.

The lesson is that intellectualism, advocating mere intellectual reflection on one's evidence to settle the question of God's existence, is existentially too thin (relative to the human will) for the kind of evidence suitable to a redemptive God. Humans in need of redemption should not expect to know a redemptive God on the cheap, as if no volitional challenge is needed. Just as there is no place for cheap grace in a robust theology of a morally perfect God, so also there is no place for redemptively cheap evidence of a gracious God who seeks the redemption of humans. Redemptive expectations would accompany the evidence as well as the grace.

Many proponents of the arguments of natural theology run afoul of the lesson at hand. They assume that if atheists and agnostics would just think hard enough on our common evidence, they would come to acknowledge the reality of God. These atheists and agnostics, they assume, then would see the crucial role in reality for a First Cause, a Designer, a Fine-Tuner, or a Perfect Being, which (at least according to Aquinas regarding the traditional empirical arguments) we all know to be God (see Moser 2010, chap. 3 for dissent from Aquinas's natural theology). The needed evidence for God, according to this position, is in our midst and even in our possession, but we need to think more rigorously to see its bearing on theism. That position, however, is too shallow, volitionally and existentially.

A serious problem is that the God of traditional natural theology (and its corresponding evidence) is not elusive in the manner to be expected of a redemptive God who bobs and weaves, and even hides, to challenge humans for their own redemptive good. This kind of redemptive God would not be the static solution to merely intellectual questions, but instead would seek to convict and to move humans, uncoercively, toward God at the level of their wills, to put God's will first in all things. This God would aim to redeem humans as intentional agents, and not just as thinkers. Like intellectualism, traditional natural theology neglects this key lesson, and therefore is defective. (For elaboration, see Moser 2010, chap. 3, 2012, 2013, chap. 3.)

We can put the problem at hand in terms of divine presence as divine self-manifesting to humans. If God self-authenticates divine reality for humans by self-manifesting God's unique moral character (including *agapē*), but seeks not to coerce humans to receive this manifesting, then God's self-manifesting is rejectable by humans. The self-manifesting of God's moral character to humans would not force the will of humans in a way that undermines their genuine agency in responding to God. So, God's self-manifesting would allow humans to say no to it by excluding it from their focus. As Chapter 1 suggested, God would be willing to withdraw or to postpone divine self-manifesting to leave room for genuine human agency regarding divine presence. Such basic evidence of God's reality, then, would not be static across human experience. It could vary relative to the volitional stance of its potential recipients, in order not to trivialize or to obscure the redemptive intent of divine intervention in human experience.

The third motive is not an avowed reason for intellectualism, but it still plays a psychological role in some commitments to intellectualism. The unexpressed motive, I propose, is desired avoidance of a volitional struggle with a redemptive God. Such avoidance has a range of detrimental results, including a coupling of intellectualism with a destructive kind of intellectual pride. This pride manifests itself in the common attitude that opponents of intellectualism, of a theistic or an atheistic variation, are intellectually dim in a peculiar manner. Such an attitude emerges even from many proponents of natural theology when their favored evidence fails to convince critics.

This book offers an alternative to misplaced human pride by shifting attention to volitional sensitivity in humans, beyond their intellectual skills. In doing so, it acknowledges the significance of the kind of volitional attitude candidly expressed by Thomas Nagel: "I want atheism to be true . . . I hope there is no God! I don't want there to be a God; I don't want the universe to be like that" (1997, p. 130). Nagel worries that the existence of God would pose a serious "cosmic authority problem" for us. The obstacle for Nagel, among many others, is volitional, and not (just or even primarily) intellectual. Even so, Nagel is right: The existence of a perfectly loving, redemptive God would raise a cosmic authority problem for us humans, because God's perfect will would challenge our imperfect wills. Contrary to Nagel's assumption, that would be a *good* situation for us, owing to what would be divine moral perfection.

7. DIVINE SELF-HIDING AND SACRIFICE

Divine Self-Hiding

A religious epistemology that neglects the prospect of occasional divine hiding from humans will fail to explain human evidence and knowledge of the God of Abraham, Isaac, and Jesus. It also will be inadequate in explaining human evidence and knowledge of a God worthy of worship who self-manifests at times but also hides from humans on occasion for redemptive purposes. Such an epistemology thus will fail to capture a key feature of the God relationship that does not require constant awareness or experience of God, even if experience of God is available on occasion.

The God of Abrahamic monotheism does not appear constantly in the awareness of all people, because this God hides from some people at times. Chapter 1 offered the following quotation: "Truly, you are a God who hides himself" (Isa. 45:15). A similar theme recurs in the Psalms; for instance, the psalmist asks God: "Why do you hide your face? Why do you forget our affliction and oppression?" (Ps. 44:24). Jesus himself reiterates the theme of divine hiding regarding the things of his own ministry and gives thanks to God for this hiding: "At that time Jesus said, 'I thank you, Father, Lord of heaven and earth, because you have hidden these things from the wise and the intelligent and have revealed them to infants'" (Matt. 11:25; cf. Luke 10:21). In a similar vein, Paul speaks of God's "hidden wisdom," specifically the treasures of God's wisdom "hidden" in Christ (see 1 Cor. 2:7, Col. 2:3). We should hesitate, then, to suggest that God is constantly obvious to all people or even ever-present to their awareness. Blaise Pascal points us in the right direction: "God being hidden, any religion which does not say that God is hidden is not true. And any religion which does not give the reason why does not enlighten" (1662, sec. 242).

Some philosophers of religion have identified a "problem" of divine hiddenness. They ask whether a perfectly loving God could fail to be self-revealed in a manner that removes all reasonable human doubt about God's reality. Some of these philosophers hold that perfect love would preclude God's hiding from humans in a way that leaves reasonable human doubt about God's existence. If they are right, one must face the consideration that God's existence is not beyond reasonable doubt by the evidence of many normal adult humans. The latter humans, one might propose, may reasonably deny that God exists or at least refrain from believing that God exists. A consideration about divine hiddenness, then, can figure in a case for atheism or at least agnosticism.

God's hiding from some people does not entail either God's hiding from *everyone* always or *everyone's* lacking salient evidence for God's existence. In addition, God's hiding from some people does not entail anyone's lacking *available* evidence for God's existence, beyond the evidence one actually has. Evidence regarding God's existence can be variable among persons in a way that the truth about God's existence is not. One reason for this variability is straightforward: People can have different experiences regarding God, including with different degrees of salience. In this regard, evidence for God's existence is akin to a lot of ordinary empirical evidence.

The Freedom Response to the problem of divine hiddenness, suggested by John Hick (2010), proposes that God would hide at least to some extent to enable people *freely* to love, trust, and obey God, that is, to avoid the divine coercion of humans toward God. If God self-revealed without any hiding, according to this response, humans would be overwhelmed in a way that precludes their free response to God. It seems, however, that God could supply a less elusive or less obscure self-revelation without precluding human freedom in responding to it. A self-revelation of God with a bit more salience would seem not to overwhelm people by precluding freedom in their response. So, it is doubtful that the Freedom Response will supply a full response to the problem of divine hiddenness.

The Proper-Motivation Response, suggested by Blaise Pascal (1662), claims that God would hide to avoid, or at least to reduce the likelihood of, a human reply to God from such improper motives as selfish fear or pride. God's self-revelation without hiding, according to this response, would prompt humans to have selfish fear or pride in their response, owing to the unique intensity of the revelation. God would hide to discourage such fear and pride, because such fear and pride do not fit with the kind of moral character sought by God. It seems, however, that God could give a less elusive or less obscure self-revelation without eliciting improper motives in a human response. A little more clarity in God's self-revelation would seem not to require human selfish fear and pride in response. So, it is doubtful that the Proper-Motivation Response would supply a full response to the problem of divine hiddenness.

The Divine-Purposes Response proposes that God would restrain divine self-revelation, at least for a time, to at least some humans in order to enhance the satisfaction of *various* perfectly loving purposes God has for humans. This response, I have contended (see Moser 2008, 2010), allows that the amount and the kind of God's self-revelation can vary among people, and the variation can come from God's perfectly loving purposes in self-revelation. If these purposes are perfectly loving, God can be perfectly loving in giving varied and elusive self-revelation to humans. God's exact purposes sometimes could be unclear to humans, as we should expect given God's cognitive superiority relative to humans. Even when unclear on the exact divine purposes, however, one could know and reasonably trust the God who hides for a time, if God has intervened in one's experience with adequate evidence. So, a general argument for atheism or agnosticism will have no footing here, contrary to Schellenberg (2006) and some others.

If God is perfectly redemptive toward humans, in seeking their well-being all things considered, then, as Chapter 1 noted, God's self-revelation would come with redemptive purposes for them. As suggested, we should not expect this self-revelation to be just an intellectual matter, as if God aimed merely to prompt humans to believe that God exists. Instead, we should expect God's self-revelation to encourage people to cooperate with God, in loving God wholeheartedly above all else, and in loving others as God loves them, even one's enemies. Such cooperation from humans would be a fitting response to a God who is worthy of worship and hence self-sufficiently morally perfect. It also would enable the reality of human *koinonia* with God, in reconciliation to God, and thereby restore humans from their alienation from God. In that regard, human cooperation with God would be relationally curative for humans, relative to human spiritual sickness from God's perspective (cf. Mark 2:17).

A problem for a perfectly redemptive God would be that many people are not ready or willing to enter into cooperation with God. Their own commitments and plans interfere with such cooperation, and they are aware of this, sometimes painfully (see Mark 10:17–27). So, God may decide to hide from them for a time, to avoid deepening their antipathy toward God or the purposes of God. The problem would stem from a failure to follow Jesus in Gethsemane, where he yielded his will to God, even when death was the result. This is more than an intellectual problem; it goes to one's moral character as a volitional agent in relation to God. As perfectly redemptive, God would choose to bob and weave toward humans, looking for a relationally curative opportunity, in order to begin or to deepen the God relationship with humans. So, God would have profound redemptive purposes, and they would account for occasional divine hiding, even when humans, like Job, are unable to comprehend those purposes. Cognitive modesty, then, is well-advised in the area of explaining divine hiddenness.

Paul Minear has linked divine hiddenness to the need for human seeking toward God:

The very hiddenness of God marks his superiority to idols. It is his hiddenness that requires that men seek him with their whole heart. They must seek him in a different way from that in which they seek an idol. As Subject, God calls for men to seek him; an idol is an object which men themselves decide to seek. (1966, p. 191)

If God were present to humans transparently and conveniently, idol-like, they may come to expect too much of God's agency and shirk their own responsibilities, in the pattern of a spoiled child. How then should humans seek God with wholeheartedness? We shall explore this in the light of a unique requirement on God's character: self-sacrifice.

Divine Self-Sacrifice

If God is inherently intentional *agapē*, as parts of the Christian tradition suggest, and such *agapē* is self-sacrificial in a redemptive manner, then God would be self-sacrificial in that redemptive manner. This widely neglected lesson is required by worthiness of worship and has significant implications for the topic of divine self-manifesting and self-hiding. It suggests how the question of God's existence could challenge humans not just to think but also to exist and to act in profoundly redemptive ways. In doing so, it offers a new practical alternative to familiar ways of inquiring about God's self-manifesting and self-hiding. It also prompts us to think of God as inherently relationally curative toward humans, owing to the divine effort to free people from their alienation from God, including their tendencies to self-destruction and moral failure by divine standards. In this perspective, our problems regarding divine hiddenness are not purely intellectual or cognitive, but are profoundly moral and existential in involving human wills in relation to God's perfect will. So, this perspective bears directly on the ethics for inquiry about God.

We can imagine an illuminating scenario regarding God. Being self-sufficiently morally perfect, God is worthy of (and hence merits) worship as adoration and full love, trust, and obedience. God thus seeks uncoercively what is morally best for all humans, even for the resolute enemies of God. In doing so, God does not opt for the immediate extermination or the coercion of humans. Instead, God makes a divine self-offering to humans that invites them freely to cooperate with God's purpose of redemption as reconciliation in *koinonia*. We might think of this as God's "peace offering" to humans that offers forgiveness as a release from divine condemnation and as an entryway to a reconciled relationship of *koinonia*. The desired reconciliation is no *mere* agreement among persons, of the kind had by partners in crime, for instance. Instead, it conforms to

God's perfectly good moral character and hence is robustly normative and righteous.

In an ancient Jewish tradition, the divine offering emerges in God's "bending low" in various ways to sustain and to rescue Israel, despite Israel's frequent resistance to God (see Hosea 11:1–4). In addition, God's sacrificial offering is anticipated in Abraham's remark to Isaac that "God himself will provide the lamb for a burnt offering" (Gen. 22:8). In the canonical Christian tradition, the divine offering culminates in God's sending Jesus as the Son of God to offer himself for humans on God's behalf (see Rom. 3:24–26; cf. 1 Cor. 5:7, Heb. 9:11–15, John 3:14–17). This self-sacrifice emerges in the enacted parables of the Last Supper in the Synoptic Gospels (see Mark 14:22–25) and the foot washing by Jesus in John's Gospel (see John 13:3–15).

In Paul's message, the death of Jesus Christ is where *God* proves his righteous love (*agapē*) for humans (Rom. 5:8, 10; cf. Rom. 8:39). This divine self-offering aims for what is best for humans, all things considered. It aims to prompt their reciprocating toward God, that is, their offering themselves wholeheartedly to God in obedient and sympathetic cooperation with God's perfect will. This reciprocating self-offering to God forms the center of human faith in God, because it is the means of intentionally receiving and manifesting God's redemptive self-offering to humans. This key component of faith in God is, however, widely neglected among theologians, philosophers of religion, and many others, perhaps owing to an excessively intellectual understanding of faith. God's self-offering would aim to be freely received and *re-manifested* by humans as personal agents who intentionally image God's moral character of *agapē* in *koinonia*. God thus would seek a world of mutual self-sacrifice for the moral good, including the reconciliation and *koinonia*, of all concerned.

In the imagined scenario, humans lack the power to live self-sufficiently, independently of a stronger intentional power. They lack the resources of their own to extend their lives for the indefinite future, and their impending deaths confirm this. They also lack the power of their own to flourish lastingly in a morally good community of humans. Left to themselves, humans face a bleak future, as Bertrand Russell acknowledges in "A Free Man's Worship" (1903). In our scenario, God has a vital educational and relationally curative project aimed at personal reconciliation: a project to lead people uncoercively to recognize, value, and participate in their needed cooperation with the divine power that aims to sustain them in a flourishing community. A perfectly redemptive God would confront the reality that humans need to be redeemed of their contrary tendencies on this front.

The needed divine power contrasts with the kind of power that dominates power-exchanges in cases of exclusive competition. It centers instead on the kind of redemptive self-sacrifice that seeks reconciliation among all agents and fits with a divine standard of worthiness of worship, moral perfection, and perfect love. The divine project therefore faces the difficulty of going against typical human selfishness in order to promote the moral good of all concerned. It would call for, and offer to empower, the replacement of human selfishness with redemptive self-sacrifice that promotes reconciliation and *koinonia* with God and humans. Sympathetic cooperation with this ongoing project of human renewal would be the way to enter and to abide in the kingdom of God. This challenging kingdom would stem from the power of redemptive self-sacrifice, beyond talk and even sophisticated philosophical talk. It thus would offer distinctive power that opposes one's living mainly for oneself or for one's clan. The God relationship would underwrite this kind of kingdom and power.

The redemptive self-sacrifice in question includes, as its motivation, what various New Testament writers call *agapē*, and it figures in the striking claim that "God is *agapē*" (1 John 4:8, 16). We may translate the latter claim as: "God is intentional self-sacrifice" (of the redemptive kind just sketched). This translation is preferable to the familiar translation, "God is love," given the merely sentimental uses of "love" common to contemporary English. A God worthy of worship, being morally perfect, would be anything but merely sentimental. The writer of 1 John thus characterizes *agapē* in terms of intentionally active self-sacrifice for the good of others. One pertinent statement from 1 John is: "We know love by this, that he [Jesus] laid down his life for us – and we ought to lay down our lives for one another" (1 John 3:16; see 1 John 2:1–5, 4:9, and, for the writer of John's Gospel, see John 15:12–14).

Paul relates *agapē* with intentional self-sacrifice in the following remark about Jesus: "The life I now live in the flesh I live by faith in the Son of God, who loved me and gave himself for me" (Gal. 2:20). He also relates grace (*charis*) with intentional self-sacrifice: "You know the generous act (*charis*) of our Lord Jesus Christ, that though he was rich, yet for your sakes he became poor, so that by his poverty you might become rich" (2 Cor. 8:9). This intentional self-giving of Jesus is inherently sacrificial for the good of others, and it occupies the center of Paul's thought and message (see Phil. 2:5–8, Rom. 3:24–26). The relevant love, then, does not reduce to anything merely sentimental, but includes intentional self-sacrifice for the good of others.

In our imagined scenario, God offers a self-sacrifice to humans for their good: particularly for their being invited to a reconciled life of sympathetic cooperation and *koinonia* with God. This offer prompts some simple but formative questions. What, if anything, would we humans do in response? Would we just think and talk about the offer, and avoid conforming to it? Would we demand some kind of "proof" of its veracity, and, if so, what kind of proof? Would we follow the rich young ruler of Mark 10:17–22 in turning away with some regret? (See Thielicke 1962, pp. 55–57.) Would we turn away, instead, without any regret? Alternatively, would we let the offer grip us in a manner that redefines us, in thought, attitude, and action?

Would we let the author of the offer make us new in God's image, come what may? One answer does not fit all humans, given the wide variation in human motives and goals. Even so, our scenario would leave us humans with a crucial decision bearing on the basis and direction of our lives. (On such a decision and its role in obedience to God, see Minear 1966, pp. 72–93.)

Seeking full human redemption for each human, God as relationally curative would want people to decide to enter in wholeheartedly to the life of divine self-sacrifice. God thus would want people to experience, welcome, and manifest this life rather than just to think, talk, or even know about it. This divine want would fit with God's desiring the willing redemption of the whole person, not just a single human aspect, such as the human intellect. So, God would want to engage and even uncoercively to convict the human will, to encourage free human compliance with God's perfect will. This compliance would include a primary self-commitment to, and a consistent practice of, redemptive self-sacrifice of the kind manifested by God, even if people making this commitment fall short at times. We should expect such falling short if God's aim is to "justify the ungodly" by counting their faith in God as righteousness (Rom. 4:5). The divine challenge for humans, then, would call for an internal and an external manner of existing and living, in terms of internal commitments and outward practices suited to God's character of unselfish love. Anything short of this goal would be redemptively inadequate by a divine standard of moral perfection.

We should clarify how self-sacrifice figures in worthiness of worship and bears on divine hiddenness. If we lack an adequate understanding of God's moral character, we will be unable to make needed sense of divine hiddenness. I do not expect, however, that humans will reach a full explanation of divine hiddenness on their own, because the redemptive purposes of God are not fully available to humans.

The English term "sacrifice" derives from the Latin term "*sacrificium*," which stems from the terms "*sacer*" ("sacred") and "*facio*" ("do, make"). The idea of "making something sacred," by an offering in relation to God, looms large in the etymology of the term "sacrifice." Perhaps the most common notion suggests something consecrated, or solemnly offered, by humans *to* a divinity. It would be a mistake, however, to regard this notion as having a monopoly or even the priority relative to its alternatives.

Our imagined scenario, in keeping with some prominent strands of the Jewish and Christian traditions, portrays *God* as taking the initiative in self-sacrifice in order to reconcile humans to God. Just as various biblical writers suggest that God first loved us humans, they also suggest that God first offered self-sacrifice on our behalf, and that our self-sacrifice (to God and others) is to be a fitting, imaging *response* to the divine initiative (see 1 John 4:10, 19; cf. Rom. 3:24–26). Our scenario likewise suggests that we put first things first, relative to *God's* initiative in sacrifice as a sacred, grace-based offering for the redemption of humans.

Human self-sacrifice, like human freedom and love, is not intrinsically good, because we can sacrifice to bad things, just as we can freely choose and love bad things. For instance, we can sacrifice to destructive idols of greed, hate, and death rather than to the God worthy of worship. Human history illustrates this problem with seemingly endless examples. Some of the history in the Jewish Bible, for instance, confirms this lesson, even in the presence of divine challenges to avoid idolatry and other destructive sacrifices.

Bad sacrifice need not be obviously destructive from the perspective of all observers. When sacrifice is altogether morally superficial, such as in the case of empty religious ritualism, it can be bad, even when some people fail to recognize this. Some of the Hebrew prophets had genuine concerns in this regard (see, for instance, Micah 6:6–8), and such concerns should persist in the face of empty ritualism in religion, which lacks redemptive self-sacrifice. Good sacrifice is intentionally redemptive in conforming to the divine project to reconcile humans to God and to each other. So, we have a definite contrast between good and bad sacrifice, including good and bad self-sacrifice.

If God is inherently self-sacrificial for the redemptive good of all concerned, some important consequences emerge for divine self-manifesting and self-hiding. If God is inherently self-sacrificial in moral character, then divine self-manifesting to humans would likewise be self-sacrificial, given that it would represent God's moral character. Divine self-manifesting would include the essential motive of being self-sacrificial for the redemptive good of all concerned. In that regard, divine self-manifesting would be morally robust in what it includes and may call for human sensitivity to its moral robustness.

If God's power alone, rather than human power, is the ultimate source of redemptive self-sacrifice, certain results are noteworthy. Wherever redemptive self-sacrifice occurs, the power of God would be present too, as would divine self-manifesting, even if humans overlook or ignore this power. Divine self-sacrifice would not owe its reality to our embracing or even acknowledging it. If God first self-sacrificed for us, divine self-sacrifice would not delay in waiting for our invitation, acknowledgment, or approval. Instead, it would come first, aiming to prompt our response in kind, by our chosen reliance on the divine power of self-sacrifice. Our opposing or even ignoring the reality or the importance of redemptive self-sacrifice can obscure divine reality for us, leaving it hidden from us. For instance, if I hold that God would never stoop to redemptive self-sacrifice, I will not (consistently) recognize or acknowledge God in such sacrifice.

The human sacrificial response to God would characteristically fall short of divine perfection, given human frailties. Vincent Taylor thus remarks: "No Hebrew could think of offering himself as he was, frail and sinful, to a holy and righteous God (cf. Isa. 6:5–8), while the idea of a purely spiritual offering would have seemed to him abstract and meaningless. The life offered must be that of another, innocent and pure, free from all impurity and sin, and yet withal the symbol of an ideal life to which he aspired and with which he could identify himself . . . ." (1937, p. 60). This perfectionist standard suits the moral character of a God worthy of worship, but it raises a problem for morally imperfect humans (cf. Heb. 7:11). The problem concerns how humans can supply the needed redemptive perfection in their sacrifices.

Left to our merely human resources, we lack a sacrifice that accurately images or reciprocates God's perfect self-sacrifice for us. Our own resources fall short of willingly offering a morally perfect self-sacrifice for the sake of redemption as reconciliation. Taylor identifies a key part of the problem: "The main obstacle to a healthy development [of the idea of self-sacrifice in the Jewish Bible] was the passive character of the Levitical offering; the worshipper faced the demand of identifying himself with that which could neither will nor experience the glory of vicarious sacrifice . . . ." (1937, p. 60). Despite human alienation from God, the ideal sacrifice is an intentional self-sacrifice that draws from and manifests the moral perfection of God in order to offer human redemption as reconciliation to God.

From the standpoint of available resources, only God would be able to deliver the ideal, perfect sacrifice. Mere humans, lacking the power of perfect love on their own, will fall short of any perfectionist standard for self-sacrifice. If the perfect sacrifice is to be a *human* sacrifice to God, only God would be able to supply the human who can serve this redemptive purpose with perfection. That is, the needed human mediator for redemptive self-sacrifice must come from God in order to supply redemptive perfection.

The good news of the Christian message is that God has supplied the needed self-sacrifice in Jesus Christ as God's morally perfect Son, Mediator, and Priest (see Mark

14:22–24, Heb. 7:14–28, 9:14, 1 Cor. 5:7). This divine offering through Jesus aims to meet the perfectionist standard that was only approximated in the Levitical system of sacrifices and could not be met by humans alienated from God. The divine offering in question includes redemptive suffering that can transform human sin as disobedience against God into divine grace aimed at human redemption, as seen in the crucifixion and death of Jesus (see Robinson 1942, chap. 13).

A twofold theme of the Christian message is that, courtesy of God, Jesus supplies the representative human self-sacrifice on behalf of humans, and other humans can, and should, share in this offering by "faith" in God and Jesus (which God credits to these humans as righteousness, according to Romans 4:5). Such faith, as Chapter 2 indicated, is no mere assent to information, even theological information about redemption. Instead, to be redemptive, it must provide human union with the self-sacrifice of God, whereby humans willingly share in the perfect self-sacrifice offered on their behalf. It is thus active, obedient trust in God that goes beyond belief that something is true (see Jas. 2:17–20; cf. Matt. 7:21). The key role of self-sacrifice in human faith in God is widely neglected in theology and the philosophy of religion, and therefore we need to introduce an important correction here.

The New Testament evidence for the needed sharing in redemptive self-sacrifice is clear. The Gospels portray Jesus as saying: "If any want to become my followers, let them deny themselves and take up their cross and follow me" (Mark 8:34; cf. Luke 9:23, Matt. 16:24). Even more strongly: "Whoever does not carry the cross and follow me cannot be my disciple" (Luke 14:27). His talk of the cross here suggests that his disciples must image him in self-sacrificial commitment and action, in redemptive obedience to God. Faith in God, then, would not replace the need for self-sacrifice. Instead, it would enable self-sacrifice to be empowered by God's unique character, purpose, and power of self-giving *agapē* directed at the redemption of humans.

Paul echoes the call of Jesus to self-sacrifice in his remarks that he is to "complete what is lacking in Christ's afflictions for the sake of his body, that is, the church" (Col. 1:24), and that the Roman Christians are "by the mercies of God, to present [their] bodies as a living sacrifice, holy and acceptable to God, which is [their] spiritual worship" (Rom. 12:1; cf. Rom. 8:36). Similar confirmation comes from the author of 1 Peter: "Let yourselves be built into a spiritual house, to be a holy priesthood, to offer spiritual sacrifices acceptable to God through Jesus Christ" (2:5; cf. 2:21). The latter sacrifices are "through Jesus Christ" at least in that they follow his self-giving redemptive path in obedience to God. (For related discussion, see Richardson 1958, chap. 13, John Taylor 1992, pp. 202–205, Bradley 1995, chap. 4, Daly 2009.)

What Paul calls "the obedience of faith" (Rom. 1:5, 16:26; cf. 10:15–17) is best understood as the self-sacrifice characteristic of faith in God, after the pattern of Jesus. In this obedience, people offer themselves, if imperfectly, to God for the sake of redemption as reconciliation and *koinonia*. Such self-sacrifice to God would include one's receiving God's power of self-sacrifice and thereby giving oneself to God in similar self-sacrifice. This kind of self-sacrifice does not include any human earning or meriting of redemption, and therefore it does not qualify as what Paul calls "works" in contrast with faith, in some contexts (see Rom. 4:4). So, this self-sacrificial component of faith is compatible with Paul's understanding of faith in God that excludes the human earning of redemption. (For a detailed treatment of Paul on faith and works, see Moser 2013, chap. 4.)

If redemptive self-sacrifice is the locus of divine self-manifesting, where humans can meet and commune with God, a question arises. Why does God offer redemptive self-sacrifice to humans and then demand similar sacrifice from them? An answer now emerges. As morally perfect,

God would seek what is best (all things considered) for all concerned, and hence would seek the reconciliation of humans to God's character of redemptive *agapē*, or righteous love. If genuinely good relationships and communities among intentional agents require self-sacrificial *agapē*, a morally perfect God would need to offer such relationships and communities on the basis of such *agapē*.

A genuinely redemptive God would put self-sacrifice front and center on the stage of personal life, both for God and for humans, in order to reconcile all agents under God's perfect moral character. This redemptive mission would encompass the ultimate meaning of life for God and for humans (on which, see Chapter 4), even if some humans ignore or resist it and thereby ignore or resist God. So, this mission also would include the path to human self-fulfillment: self-fulfillment as redemptive self-sacrifice in cooperation with God. Selfishness, by contrast, would fall short of lasting self-fulfillment, because it would run afoul of God's moral character and the corresponding redemptive mission.

8. SELF-SACRIFICE IN EVIDENCE FOR GOD

Is our scenario regarding God pure fiction, just a wishful fairy tale? It *could* be, but our answer should depend on the actual evidence available to us. The word "available" is crucial to the previous claim, because our coming to have the needed evidence of God's reality may require our seeking it in a particular way, in accordance with the ethics for inquiry about God. So, we should not settle for the evidence we happen to have, apart from our seeking (and perhaps acquiring) relevant evidence in a suitable way. We need to explore this matter to be in a position to comment on the reasonableness of our scenario.

Inquiry about the evidence for God's reality can benefit from reflection on the kind of moral character God would need to be worthy of worship. Such reflection can calibrate our expectations regarding the evidence for God's reality. To be morally perfect, and not just morally tolerable, God would have to be inherently self-sacrificial toward a redemptive end for everyone. Here we have an indicator of where we may expect to find God's salient presence: in redemptive self-sacrifice as we ourselves participate in it.

The writer of 1 John states: "Whoever does not love does not know God, for God is love" (1 John 4:8). A more suitable translation is: "Whoever does not self-sacrifice, redemptively, does not know God, for God is redemptive self-sacrifice." So, coming to know God via acquaintance with God's self-manifesting would not be a spectator sport or an armchair pastime. It would require one's joining, by one's own commitment, in what is inherent to God's moral character: redemptive self-sacrifice. Such knowing is foreign to certain modern conceptions of volitionally disengaged knowledge, but it fits with the expectations of a redemptive God, who would seek human cooperation in redemption for the good of all concerned. Knowing God, then, would be morally robust in a way that some mundane knowledge is not.

If we are not expecting God to aim to redeem humans via divine self-manifesting in self-sacrifice, we may overlook salient evidence for God, even when it is close at hand. In that case, the self-sacrificial death of Jesus on the cross may appear to be a place just of human suffering, and not God's aiming to reconcile the world via divine self-manifesting in self-sacrifice. In overlooking what would be God's redemptive purposes, we also may overlook divine redemptive actions, and hence God may seem hidden from us.

Alan Richardson explains:

God's acts are so intimately bound up with their meaning that apart from the apprehension of their meaning they are invisible, or . . . apart from faith there is no apprehension of the revelation. The *kerygma* [the good news of God in Christ] is

expressed and communicated in images, not in abstract conceptual terms, because its comprehension requires not an act
of intellect alone but also an act of will – the trust and obedience which . . . in the biblical view [is] the only means by
which men can attain the knowledge of God. Once we have
discarded the dogma that scientific knowledge is the only
kind of truth, we shall realise that the imagination, using the
word in such a way as to include the act of will, is the only
means by which ultimate or existential truth can be apprehended and communicated. (1956, p. 44; cf. Richardson 1957)

This perspective gains credibility if God would want
humans to be sympathetically interested in, and volitionally
engaged with, the divine redemptive purposes stemming
from God's character. God would want such sympathetic
interest if God wanted humans to love what God loves and
to love how God loves. God thus would want human wills
to be engaged cooperatively with what God wills, for the
sake of volitional agreement and *koinonia*. The redemptive
truths on offer would be existential, then, and not merely
intellectual. They would be profoundly person-involving
relative to God and God's will. They would advance the
God relationship, in accordance with the ethics for inquiry
about God.

Paul's theological epistemology suggests that a person
needs to rely on "spiritual discernment" to apprehend
things revealed by God (see 1 Cor. 2:14) and that this reliance includes one's having the "mind of Christ" (1 Cor.
2:16). Paul does not elucidate his notions of spiritual discernment and the mind of Christ in the ways a contemporary philosopher or theologian might, but he does leave
readers with some clues. He introduces these notions in a
context that is explicitly concerned with redemptive self-
sacrifice, both from God and (in response) to God.

Paul suggests that having spiritual discernment and the
mind of Christ includes being (in) "God's temple" (1 Cor.
3:16–17; cf. 2 Cor. 6:16), which is a place of redemptive

self-sacrifice from and to God. Paul likens Christian life to the Passover sacrifice (cf. Exod. 12:21, 27): "Clean out the old yeast so that you may be a new batch, as you really are unleavened. For our paschal lamb, Christ, has been sacrificed" (1 Cor. 5:7). The Passover shows both sides of redemptive self-sacrifice: God's self-sacrifice (now paradigmatically in Christ) for humans and the response of human self-sacrifice to God (in the obedience of faith in God). The omission of either side undermines human redemption by God, because it leaves out either the crucial divine role or the crucial human role in redemption.

"The mind of Christ," being that of a willing Passover lamb for God, is now seen to be inherently redemptive and self-sacrificial, in willing obedience to God. So, we now see that the mind of Christ is the mind of Gethsemane (Mark 14:36), where a human will offers itself in redemptive obedience to God. Perhaps Paul's clearest linking of knowing God's Son and one's sharing in his redemptive suffering is: "I want to know Christ and the power of his resurrection and the sharing of his sufferings by becoming like him in his death, if somehow I may attain the resurrection from the dead" (Phil. 3:10–11; cf. 1 Cor. 2:2). By implication, this links knowing God (in Christ) with the *imitatio Dei.*

We should expect God to reveal God's self-sacrificial character directly, by self-manifesting the divine moral character to cooperative humans. This fits with the suggestion of some New Testament writers that God self-authenticates divine reality by direct self-manifesting to some humans (see Rom. 10:20, 1 Cor. 2:4; cf. John 14:23). There would be no better way to reveal who God truly is, because other, indirect means fall short of the needed perfect moral character and are easily distorted by humans. If God works by such self-manifesting, there are definite consequences for knowing God, which cannot be reduced to knowing that God exists. Even if God's perfect self-manifesting is in Jesus Christ, we should not limit God's self-manifesting to the historical Jesus. Divine self-manifesting could continue in the risen Christ and his Spirit (see Forrest 1906, pp. 332–99, Mackintosh 1913, pp. 310–20). God would be a cognitive and redemptive failure if divine self-manifesting ceased some 2,000 years ago.

God would have the final decision on when to self-manifest to humans; it would be odd if the situation were otherwise. Even so, we can put ourselves in a responsible position to apprehend divine self-manifesting, particularly by willingly being open to receive and to participate in redemptive self-sacrifice, the hallmark of what would be a divine moral character. Human indifference or resistance to such self-sacrifice could interfere with the reception of foundational evidence for God's reality, because it would put one in a disadvantaged position to discern the evidence for what it is.

As suggested, God would be self-authenticating regarding divine reality in a way that arguments are not and cannot be, given that arguments are not a causally interactive personal agent. By self-manifesting God's moral character to a receptive human, God could self-authenticate divine reality. This would be roughly akin to one human's self-manifesting her reality as a person (and not just a body) to another human. In addition, a redemptive God would sustain a flourishing human life in a way that arguments cannot. Arguments are not a causal personal agent; they do not have the intentions needed to sustain human lives in their fragility.

A perfectly redemptive God would want divine self-manifesting to provide the ultimate reason for human hope in God. Directly knowing God in encounter and *koinonia* thus would be central to a flourishing, lasting life for humans (see John 17:3). Such knowing would include foundational evidence from experiencing divine self-manifesting, but, as noted, it would not need to wait for an argument that God exists. A commitment to this kind of position on direct knowledge of God accounts for the absence of the traditional arguments of natural theology in the Jewish Bible and the New Testament. As indicated, the relevant evidence can be non-propositional character traits presented by God in self-manifesting: love, joy, peace, patience, gentleness, and so on (see Gal. 5:22–23; cf. Rom. 5:5).

Having outlined the kind of evidence to be expected of a God worthy of worship, we need to clarify the human contribution in its appropriation. We have noted the relevance of "spiritual discernment," which calls for a personal undertaking. Paul offers direction: "Do not be conformed to this world, but be transformed by the renewing of your minds, so that you may discern what is the will of God – what is good and acceptable and perfect" (Rom. 12:2). I have referred to the needed transformation as an "undertaking," because it includes intentional action on the part of humans. The discernment in question is not passive, and it calls for an ongoing struggle, even against some of one's own tendencies.

As mentioned, Paul identifies the relevant intentional action in terms of a kind of redemptive self-sacrifice: "I appeal to you therefore, brothers and sisters, by the mercies of God, to present your bodies as a living sacrifice, holy and acceptable to God, which is your spiritual worship" (Rom. 12:1; cf. Col. 1:24). A role for such sacrifice rarely emerges in contemporary writing on knowing God, moral transformation, or discernment of God's will. An excessive focus on relevant intellectual content may account for this deficiency, but, in any case, a correction in emphasis is needed. Otherwise, a religious epistemology will fail to capture how profoundly redemptive a God worthy of worship would be, including in the area of human knowledge of God.

In order to discern God's will, according to Paul's epistemology, humans need a moral transformation that requires their self-sacrifice to God as a way of sharing, by the obedience of faith in God, in Christ's perfect sacrifice. This includes dying to one's selfishness and pride in order to flourish in life with God, who seeks to kill selfishness and pride (see Rom. 8:13). We may understand this transformation in terms of the need to undergo the crisis of Gethsemane, yielding one's will to God's perfect will, in order to be in a position to discern further aspects of God's will. This Gethsemane experience, involving obedience to God, is the core of the needed redemptive self-sacrifice to God, as one shares in the exemplary sacrifice by Christ to God for all humans (see Phil. 2:8). This obedience need not be blind for humans, if God has self-manifested to them the divine moral character as a trustworthy basis for human cooperation.

Paul's ideas of spiritual discernment and sacrifice may seem too messy for some theorists who seek cut-and-dried principles, arguments, and algorithms. Such a concern should subside, however, when we consider that our ultimate audience would not be a logical principle, an argument, or an algorithm, but would be an intervening divine Spirit who is inherently self-sacrificial and can self-manifest the divine moral character to humans. Relative to this God, the cardinal human failing would be alienation whereby we fail to cooperate with God in a manner that shows and empowers us how to love God and others as God does.

The cardinal human failure, relative to a perfectly good God, would not be a failure to have or accept a conclusive argument for God's existence. The challenge for humans would be much deeper relative to a purposive God who seeks to be relationally curative toward humans needing redemption. The challenge would include a needed realignment of human wills to conform to God's perfect will, in sympathetic cooperation with God. *Talk* of such realignment may be straightforward and even easy, but the *practice* of it is full of challenge and struggle, including struggle against one's own tendencies toward selfishness. The latter tendencies die hard, if they die at all. The demanded reorientation of one's lived values amounts to a daily struggle that defines who one is and how one lives, particularly in relation to others.

Human decision, but not blind decision, would play a key role in overcoming the alienation from God in question. Christian hyper-intellectualism implies that humans should be able to settle or resolve matters regarding Christian commitment with the giving of pro-Christian arguments. This view is naïve at best, in assuming that the conclusion of a sound argument would settle or resolve the matter of Christian commitment. The matter instead is irreducibly agent- and decision-oriented, because it involves a volitional, decisional response of one intentional agent to the expressed will and offer of another intentional agent. Such interactive, decisional agency requires the free self-commitment of a human will to another agent, and is not reducible to or settled by logical proof or any argument.

Logical proofs and arguments do not entail human decisions to self-commit to another agent. In addition, the latter decisions do not need to rely on such proofs or arguments for their reasonableness or evidential support. Even if an argument concludes with a recommendation for an agent to commit to another agent, the former agent still would need to *decide* on the recommendation: to endorse it, to reject it, or to withhold judgment regarding it. An argument cannot make this decision for an agent.

The needed foundational evidence from divine self-manifesting for an agent would be much more profound, existentially and experientially, than an argument. It would present one with the qualitative moral character of God, and thereby offer a sharp moral contrast with oneself. The contours of that character could serve as a personally manifested epistemic standard for deliberations about God and a standard for a need for human repentance, by way of contrast. A merely human will would pale in comparison with the morally perfect will of God, and a fitting result would be a perceived inadequacy in a human agent relative to

God. Many people would opt for a less challenging alternative, by turning away from the comparison.

The decisional interaction in question can develop with a cooperative human response of intentional self-commitment to divine self-manifesting, on the basis of one's experiencing its perfect goodness. Such interaction is central to a redemptive I–Thou relationship between God and humans. Even if a person can have pre-cooperative evidence from God's intervention, this evidence would deepen and expand upon being received cooperatively. It would become evidence central to the kind of moral agent one has become in relationship to God. In other words, it would become integral to who one actually is, as a moral agent before God.

The biblical injunction that humans "taste and see that the Lord is good" (Ps. 34:8) advises a firsthand acquaintance with God, particularly God's goodness, as a way of confirming God's reality and goodness. The recommended "tasting" is not casual, but fits with the demanding promise from the prophet Jeremiah noted previously: "When you search for me, you will find me; if you seek me with all your heart, I will let you find me, says the Lord" (Jer. 29:13–14; cf. Deut. 4:29). Seeking "with all your heart" seems appropriate relative to a God worthy of worship, but it does demand a kind of attentive and volitional rigor from humans. Many people will decide that the needed rigor is not worth their effort, given their other concerns.

It would be misleading to suggest that we should confirm God's reality first and then seek to confirm God's goodness. Being inherently good and redemptive, God would seek to keep the two together, and we should too. If a person needs firsthand acquaintance with God's perfect goodness, that person cannot experience God by proxy. You cannot experience God for me, even if you can witness to me regarding God (discursively or nondiscursively) on the basis of your experience of God. God would want each person to be redeemed *directly* into a life of *koinonia* with

God, in order to remove the wavering from lesser interme-diates in this role.

We sometimes talk loosely of human experience of God, but we can refine such talk to include human experience of *what God experiences* (see Moltmann 1981, pp. 3–5). We thus face the following existentially important questions. Are we willing to experience what God would experience? Are we willing to experience what would be God's self-sacrificial love for others and God's redemptive suffering for others? In addition, are we willing to go where God would go to experience such things? Are we willing to leave our sheltered experience to share in what would be God's self-giving experience in self-identifying with others in their troubles? The latter issue includes the question of whether we are willing to risk sharing in what would be God's redemptive experience. We can opt for avoidance and rejection instead of cooperation.

Our cooperating with God in the manner suggested would require our co-experiencing with God. It therefore would require our being willing to experience self-sacrifice with God for others. We may think of such willingness as central to sharing "the mind of Christ" (1 Cor. 2:16). This would include learning not just to think like Jesus Christ, but also to experience *with him*, to experience what he expe-riences in ongoing redemption for all humans. This would lead to a moral transformation for a human life, and the consequences for fitting in with one's peers would be sig-nificant. So, many people would pull back. The cost would be too high for many humans, and therefore God would face avoidance or rejection by them. We are not dealing, then, with a merely intellectual puzzle.

9. WHITHER HIDDENNESS?

We cannot solve "the" problem of divine hiddenness, if this requires our having the means to explain or to remove all such hiddenness for all people. Given our obvious human limitations in cognitive matters, that kind of solution would ask too much of us. If, however, God is at work, elusively and subtly, in the world's episodes of redemptive self-sacrifice, we have an option for drawing near to God: the option of voluntary participation in and cooperation with redemptive self-sacrifice. This option would include drawing near to God, because it would include drawing near to God's distinctive power and presence in the self-manifesting of the divine character to humans.

W.R. Matthews has identified a common human problem:

There are, I suppose, many in these days who long for the assurance that God is a reality and not a fiction, and the lover of men, but who are looking for that spiritual assurance in the wrong place. They turn over the arguments for and against the Christian belief in God, "and find no end in wandering mazes lost"; or they seek for some overwhelming religious experience which will sweep doubt away, only to be haunted by the suspicion that this experience when it comes is nothing but a drama played on the stage of their own minds. (1936, p. 182)

Humans need an alternative to being lost or haunted in those familiar ways of seeking God, and they may have such an alternative, at least if they are willing to cooperate with God's redemptive character and purposes.

Matthews explains, taking the lead from the author of 1 John:

The guidance which comes from the earliest days of our religion would not indeed lead us to despise intellectual enquiry and mystical vision, but it would not lead us to begin with them. It would tell us to start loving our fellows, to cultivate the settled and resolute will for their good. So by coming to know what "love" means we shall come to know what "God" means, and by realizing [love's] power, its reality as a human force, we shall be in contact with a power which is more than human, with the creative energy of the world. "Beloved, let us

love one another, for love is of God and everyone that loveth
is born of God and knoweth God. He that loveth not knoweth
not God, for God is love" [1 John 4:7–8]. (1936, p. 182)

This is no recipe to make God self-manifest to all people
whenever and however we wish. Formulating such a recipe would be simply presumptuous of humans relative to
God. Even so, if self-sacrificial love, when redemptive, is
"of God" and self-manifesting of God's powerful presence,
we can have some hope regarding divine revelation on
God's terms.

Matthews proposes that Christian belief in God as
inherently loving does not stem from speculative philosophical reflection or a theoretical assessment of prob-
abilities. Instead, this belief emerges (at least) from the
self-manifesting of God in Christ, although it is anticipated
in parts of the Jewish Bible (see Hos. 11:1–9; cf. Heschel
1962, pp. 39–60, 289–98, Levenson 2015). As Matthews
remarks: "Because we find God in Christ, we discover that
God is love" (1939, p. 223; cf. Hick 1978, pp. 39–41). So,
we are well-advised not to try to establish that God is love
on the basis of speculative philosophy. Instead, we would
do better to look to the prospect of ongoing experience of
God's love in redemptive, self-sacrificial action. The love
in question is no mere emotion, but originates in the will
of God for what is best, all things considered, for all concerned. Such love can manifest the stability of a divine
will that is morally perfect and hence redemptive toward
humans.

Our experiencing and cooperating with redemptive love
would entail our experiencing and cooperating with the
redemptive power and self-manifesting of God. The perfect human exemplar of this love, according to Christian
theology, is Jesus Christ, now risen to sustain and prolif-
erate God's redemptive love, even toward God's enemies.
One could cooperate with his power *de re*, without awareness *de dicto* of God's role in the power of redemptive

love from God. So, one's experiencing and cooperating with redemptive love does not require one's acceptance of a Christian account of such love. This lesson is important, because it enables people unfamiliar with a Christian account to experience and to cooperate with God (see Moser 2010, chap. 5).

People may desire fireworks and other diversions from heaven, but, being perfectly redemptive, God would be more profound and more subtle than any such desire. God's redemptive character inherently would be relationally curative in seeking to save people from everything alienating them from God, their sustainer of lastingly good life. Jesus put forth this neglected message: "Jesus ... said to them, 'Those who are well have no need of a physician, but those who are sick; I have come to call not the righteous but sinners'" (Mark 2:17). God could offer forgiveness as part of a relational cure for spiritually and morally sick people, but this offer by itself would not yield such a cure. Humans would need to receive or appropriate the offer in a manner suitable to what it seeks: the reconciliation of humans to God in a *koinonia* relationship. Chapters 1 and 2 proposed the same for the human appropriation of faith, evidence, and knowledge regarding God. (Chapter 4 offers a similar proposal for wisdom and the meaning of human life.) It would be irresponsible of inquirers to exclude this option at the start. The ethics for inquiry about God requires that this option be given due attention.

We can expand the point about forgiveness in terms of redemptive love, given that the relevant offer of forgiveness would include such love. Merely experiencing redemptive love will fall short of not only an I–Thou acquaintance with God but also a suitable appropriation of such love in a *koinonia* relationship. Something more is needed, and this "more" would stem from *God's challenge* to a human to cooperate with redemptive love, in *koinonia* with God. We may think of this as the *challenge of Gethsemane* where God seeks the yielding of a human will to God's perfect will, after the model of Jesus in Gethsemane. This challenge would be relationally curative in intent and the basis of all lasting spiritual and moral healing of humans.

God would challenge humans at the opportune time for redemption, by *God's* timing, and humans would do well to be ready for this challenge. Otherwise, they may miss God's vital challenge, owing to a less important focus that obstructs a suitable response. One's response of sympathetic cooperation would be crucial, because it would enable God's challenge to be redemptive for *oneself*, in virtue of being appropriated by being internalized and thus becoming motivational for oneself. This cooperative response would be the means of appropriating by "faith" God's offer of redemption. So, as Chapter 2 suggested, faith in God is not a leap in the dark; it is a positive response to something vital on offer from God. In a cooperative human response of faith and hope, as noted from Paul, "God's love has been poured into our hearts through the Holy Spirit" (Rom. 5:5). Redemption thereby begins to be realized in a human life, and it has a cognitive anchor in God's self-manifested power of redemptive love when cooperatively received.

The person who responsibly desires to overcome divine hiddenness should seek to experience and to cooperate with the self-sacrificial love on offer. In failing to do so, one may exhibit a misplaced desire *for* divine hiddenness, perhaps in the interest of full human autonomy, self-sufficiency, or some other kind of waywardness from God. For the sake of responsibility in inquiry, one should sincerely entertain the prospect of the priority of a question from God to oneself: In relation to God, "where are you?" (Gen. 3:9). Specifically, is one in a place of hiding that seeks to avoid the aforementioned divine challenge of Gethsemane? Perhaps hiddenness is ultimately more characteristic of humans than of God.

God's question "Where are you?" could reveal in a human an oppositional attitude toward God. It thus could reveal the following about a human, as indicated by Helmut Thielicke: "You do not really want the kingdom of God and in spite of your moral life and serious questions, you have no interest in fellowship with God. What you really seek is yourself" (1962, pp. 55–56). If this is true of a person, two considerations arise. First, this person is not in the best position to comment on the availability of evidence for God, because a motivational bias is present and easily can distort an examination of relevant evidence. Second, as relationally curative, God properly could withhold evidence, and thereby hide, from such a person, in order to avoid increasing that person's opposition to God. The person in question would not be ready to handle evidence from God aright, with suitable care, interest, and seriousness. So, divine hiding could serve a good purpose relative to such a person.

10. CONCLUSION

Finally, we face a question that is simple but vital. What do humans actually desire: divine hiding or divine self-manifesting? Only an individual person can answer for himself or herself. Our answers should be honest and responsible, as we patiently look for God's morally robust presence in the midst of a distracting world. This presence, coupled with a suitable human response, would begin to remove divine hiding faced by some people.

Responsible inquiry about God must entertain an option noted by Thielicke: "God never comes through the door that I hold open for him, but always knocks at the one place which I have walled up with concrete, because I want it for myself alone. But if I do not let [God] in there, he turns away altogether" (1961, p. 134). If we fail to see God's self-manifesting toward us, we should ask why some other responsible people testify to their having evidence from God's self-manifesting to them. We then should ask which places of our lives we have walled up. Our inquiry about divine hiding would then become honest and suitable to God, whatever the actual outcome.

The Divine-Purposes Reply to divine hiddenness, as suggested, neither offers nor promises a full explanation of God's purposes in hiding from some people at times, and this is appropriate given human cognitive limitations regarding God's purposes. Even so, one still could cooperate with the redemptive purposes suitable to a God worthy of worship, and this chapter recommends as much for responsible inquiry about God. One could acquire evidence of unique divine power in such cooperation, and this result could lead to further evidence of God's reality. In this respect, the relevant "proof," or at least the evidence, may be in the *practice* conformed to God's character. If a divine self-manifesting challenge in favor of renewal is also there, we will have the beginning of a new evidential situation, and perhaps a new life too. The matter is worthy of an individual's careful exploration, for the sake of truth that matters. A religious epistemology, therefore, should leave adequate room for such exploration of the available evidence.

God would seek to engage humans redemptively as agents, not just thinkers, and we should expect evidence of God to be elusive, variable, and challenging to that end. We should expect salient evidence of God to come through a Gethsemane crisis rather than mere casual reflection on our evidence. So, we should doubt any suggestion, such as that of Richard Dawkins (2006, pp. 52, 59), that evidence for God's existence is to be treated just like evidence for a scientific hypothesis. As an elusive personal agent, God would differ in significant ways from typical scientific objects, and this would yield a relevant difference in the two kinds of evidence. We beg a crucial question if, with Dawkins, we simply assume otherwise.

Responsible human inquiry about God is inextricably bound up with who a human intends to be, either in cooperation with God or in opposition to God, the latter including indifference toward God. The salient evidence for God would come not from speculative philosophical arguments, but instead from God's self-manifesting of the divine character to humans at God's opportune times. This self-manifesting could appear in human conscience, but it could not come just by human resources. Humans lack the power to manifest God's morally perfect character on their own, and therefore must be prepared to receive evidence of God as a redemptive gift rather than as a human earning or creation.

Conforming to the ethics for inquiry about God, responsible inquiry about God looks very different now, especially very different from the troubled positions of argumentism and intellectualism. It takes on an existential value involving the human will, and it calls for responsible allowance of the kind of evidence suited to a redemptive God: evidence intended to be received in a *koinonia* relationship with God. It suggests that inquirers of God may be under inquiry themselves by a redemptive God who seeks not just religious experiences or beliefs but the God relationship for humans.

Each inquirer must settle firsthand whether he or she is under divine inquiry, specifically regarding his or her own will relative to a morally perfect will. A theology accompanied by a volitional epistemology will be not only resilient in the face of familiar objections to theism but also existentially vital for cooperative humans. The outstanding question is whether we humans are sincerely willing to cooperate with God's perfect will if it engages us. We turn now to the bearing of the present account on the wisdom and meaning for life available to humans, on the assumption that the God relationship would include distinctive wisdom and meaning for human life.

4

~

The God Relationship, Wisdom, and Meaning

The God relationship, if genuine, would be a source of wisdom and meaning (or purpose) for human life. This wisdom and meaning would reflect God's morally perfect character and be appropriated by humans in a context of a *koinonia* relationship. We shall ask how faith in God is related to such wisdom and meaning. How, for instance, does faith in a God worthy of worship relate to wisdom found in philosophy as immortalized by Socrates and Plato? Jewish and Christian faith benefit from the Hebrew wisdom traditions, but this does not answer the previous question. The Hebrew wisdom traditions differ significantly from the wisdom of philosophy found in Socrates and Plato. This is no surprise once we see the sharp difference between the God of the Hebrews and the gods of Socrates and Plato. As one's God goes, we might say, so also goes one's wisdom and philosophy.

This chapter contends that the unique character of the Jewish–Christian God sets Jewish–Christian wisdom and philosophy apart from not only the gods of the ancient Greek philosophers (and of many subsequent philosophers), but also the wisdom and philosophy of those philosophers. Many writers have neglected this lesson, but this chapter will offer an approach that illuminates the God relationship and its parameters for wisdom, human life's meaning, and responsible inquiry about God.

193

We shall see that, in a Christian perspective, human wisdom and philosophy need to conform to God in Christ (in a sense to be clarified), "in whom are hidden all the treasures of wisdom and knowledge" (Col. 2:3). In that perspective, God in Christ would be authoritative not only over our behavior but also over our wisdom and philosophy, and therefore the latter would need to conform to, or align with, God's wisdom and will. A denial of this would entail a denial of the supreme authority of God in Christ. I contend, then, that wisdom and philosophy benefit Christian faith in a God worthy of worship only when they conform to the supreme authority of God in Christ. We shall see how this lesson bears on the God relationship in Christ and on human life's meaning.

Paul has a tenable account of divine wisdom in some of his New Testament letters, even though his account is widely ignored by philosophers of religion and theologians. We shall attend to some of his insights, because they contribute to an understanding of the God relationship. As before, we shall not simply assume that a God worthy of worship exists, or that a Christian perspective of God is true or even justified; nor shall we simply assume that biblical claims about God are true or even justified. We would gain nothing by begging controversial questions about God.

We shall consider what expectations about God and evidence for God's reality are satisfied in our experience as we seek to discern the available wisdom and meaning for human life. This task will call for more than intellectual reflection, because it is sensitive to the direction of our wills and feelings. This result should be no surprise if God has redemptive purposes that involve inquirers themselves not only in the God relationship but also in a broader redemptive process. A central aim will be to uphold responsible inquiry about God, in keeping with the ethics for such inquiry.

1. WISDOM: EVALUATIVE, PRACTICAL, AND PHILOSOPHICAL

We may think of wisdom as the special knowledge that enables us to prioritize our values and valued things and to guide our plans and actions in ways that are good. We can distinguish between evaluative wisdom (concerning values and valued things) and practical wisdom (concerning plans and actions). Both kinds of wisdom would be important to the God relationship, because God, as perfectly good, would want people to be responsible for good evaluation and good conduct. The neglect of either kind of wisdom would threaten to undermine a relationship faithful to God and a good human life as well.

Western philosophy began with the following concerns of Socrates about wisdom (*sophia*) and God.

I shall call as witness to my wisdom, such as it is, the god at Delphi . . . I am only too conscious that I have no claim to wisdom, great or small. So what can he mean by asserting that I am the wisest man in the world? . . . The truth of the matter . . . is pretty certainly this, that real wisdom is the property of God, and this oracle is his way of telling us that human wisdom has little or no value. It seems to me that he is not referring literally to Socrates, but has merely taken my name as an example, as if he would say to us, The wisest of you men is he who realized, like Socrates, that in respect of wisdom he is really worthless. (*Apology*, 20e, 21b, 23a–b, trans. H. Tredennick; cf. *Phaedrus* 278d)

Socrates seems underwhelmed by human wisdom apart from God's wisdom. He holds that "real wisdom is the property of God," and that wisdom apart from God is "really worthless." His perspective makes theology directly relevant, even indispensable, to an account of real wisdom in philosophy. Very few philosophers have followed suit. Many philosophers have tried to secure and explain wisdom without dependence on God as its source or sustainer and even without acknowledging the existence of God. The results could not be encouraging by Socrates's lights.

Wisdom, according to Plato, leads to happiness (*Meno*, 88c) but requires a kind of human "purification" (*Phaedo*, 69c), because it gives humans an escape from evil (*Phaedo*, 107c–d). I suspect that Plato and Socrates agreed on the latter point about wisdom. In the *Laws*, Plato has the Athenian say: "Righteousness, temperance, and wisdom [are] our salvation, and these have their home in the living might of the gods, though some faint trace of them is also plainly to be seen dwelling here within ourselves" (*Laws*, 10.906b, trans. A.E. Taylor). Socrates may have been more pessimistic here than Plato or at least than the Athenian, given his claim in the *Apology* that wisdom in humans apart from God is "really worthless."

Plato's "salvation," or redemption, through wisdom includes the deliverance of the human mind or soul from the world of change into an acquaintance with the immutable constituents of reality (see *Phaedo*, 79). Following Parmenides, Plato and Aristotle portray reality and God as immutable and impassible, and they evidently hold that perfection requires such features of God. So, God is unmoved and unmovable, without feelings or emotions. This view influenced Philo and Clement of Alexandria, among other thinkers in the Jewish and Christian traditions around the time of Jesus, and it still has many avid proponents today.

Contrary to Parmenides, Plato, and Aristotle, we should doubt that perfection in a personal agent requires immutability or impassibility. Change in an agent does not have to be change *toward imperfection*. It can be a change from one state of perfection to another state of perfection, particularly as circumstances change for the agent. Likewise, an agent with feelings or emotions could maintain perfection, because a change in feelings need not be a change into imperfection. These points are clear if we have the moral perfection of a personal agent in mind. The influence of Parmenides seems to have obscured these compelling points for Plato and Aristotle, among other philosophers.

The moral perfection of a personal agent seems to require change in response to varying circumstances, given that such perfection requires unselfish love or care toward others. In many cases, as the people loved by one change their attitudes or conduct, one must respond appropriately, and that often requires a change of some sort. It does not require, however, a change into imperfection, even if it includes a change from one state of perfect love to another state of perfect love. The Parmenidean theology of Plato and Aristotle cannot accommodate this lesson, and this fact counts against it. The biblical story of the active, self-manifesting God does not fit with their static portrait of God, and that is a virtue of the biblical story.

The lesson regarding perfection and change is important. If God, as perfectly compassionate, is affective with profound feelings, cares, and concerns for the world, then significant consequences follow for the God relationship. Those consequences bear on knowing God, faith in God, receiving wisdom from God, and the role of philosophy in knowing God, in faith in God, and in divine wisdom. (For discussion from a Jewish perspective, see Heschel 1962.) We shall see what these lessons are in connection with what would be a divine gift of grace, but we need to introduce some considerations about philosophy in connection with its wisdom.

I favor an approach to "philosophy" that has normative value (and so not just *anything* can qualify as philosophy) and fits with the broad etymology of the term. As a *practice*, it is the love and pursuit of *wisdom* of the broad sort immortalized by Socrates and Plato, where wisdom is an objective reality including the special kind of knowledge noted previously; it is not just what some person or group says it is. As *content*, philosophy is what qualifies as a suitable product of such a practice of the love and pursuit of wisdom. People can model the love and pursuit of such wisdom without paying dues to a professional society of philosophers or without teaching in an academic department of philosophers. In many Western societies, professional academic philosophy seems to have a monopoly on the discipline of philosophy, but that is more of an appearance than a reality. The discipline still allows for philosophers like Socrates, who had no professional or academic affiliation.

What of "Christian philosophy"? Perhaps there are as many views of what it is as there are Christian philosophers. We need at least a rough idea of Christian philosophy in order to understand how the philosophy espoused by some Christians bears on the God relationship and faith in God. Etienne Gilson has offered what seems to be a straightforward approach at first glance: "We call Christian philosophy the use made of philosophical notions by the Christian writers . . . ." (1955, p. v). The big question concerns when a notion is "philosophical" and when not. The issue is highly controversial among philosophers and resists any simple answer.

We get an idea of Gilson's position in his following remark: ". . . Christianity, itself centered upon the living person of Christ, is less a speculative view of reality than a way of life. It is not a philosophy; it is a religion" (1955, p. 5). In his position, a philosophy is a "speculative view of reality," and a philosophical notion is a notion that figures importantly (substantively, and not just formally) in a speculative view of reality. Gilson denies that Christianity, as a way of life focused upon "the living person of Christ," is a philosophy. He apparently finds its focus upon the person of Christ to be inadequately speculative as a view of reality to qualify as a philosophy. This seems plausible as a basis for a contrast with traditional philosophy. We shall return to a contrast between distinctively Christian wisdom and speculative philosophy.

Gilson finds the wisdom involved in Christianity to be different from the wisdom of the philosophers. He writes: "When Saint Paul wrote that Christ was 'wisdom' [1 Cor. 1:30], ... he was saying that what the philosophers had vainly expected from their so-called wisdom, the Christians had just received from Christ, and this was not a philosophical statement; it was a religious one" (1955, p. 6). In Gilson's perspective, philosophers have "so-called wisdom," and they "vainly expect" something important from it. In contrast, according to his view, people can receive wisdom from Christ that actually delivers what the philosophers had expected from their wisdom. Gilson evidently has the salvation or redemption of humans in mind, perhaps in light of the Platonic view, mentioned previously, that wisdom yields salvation for humans. This salvation would include human knowledge of God, but it is controversial whether the "so-called wisdom" of the philosophers includes knowledge of God. We shall return to the latter issue.

Abraham Heschel is not far from the general position of Gilson: "The disturbing fact is that philosophy remains the perpetual rival to religion. It is a power that would create religion if it could. Again and again, it has tried its talent at offering answers to ultimate questions and has failed" (1955, p. 11). Heschel includes questions about God's reality and presence among "ultimate questions," and he holds that philosophy does not offer adequate answers to such questions. He doubts that philosophy can show that God exists: "There are no proofs for the existence of the God of Abraham. There are only witnesses" (1962, p. 22). One problem, according to Heschel, is that the God of Abraham is a personal, passionate agent who hides from people at times in order to instruct them and to challenge them. So, this God is not constantly present to people for their convenient speculation or proof. This is therefore not the God of the traditional philosophers.

Heschel finds a special task for philosophy of religion in relation to religion and philosophy: "[Philosophy of religion's] task is not only to examine the claim of religion in the face of philosophy, but also to refute the claim of philosophy when it presumes to become a substitute for religion, to prove the inadequacy of philosophy as a religion" (1955, pp. 11–12). He would add that philosophy of religion also has the task to challenge the claim of philosophy when it presumes to offer a way to knowledge of God. He doubts that philosophy has that capacity. I share his doubt, and will explain the basis for my doubt, while contending that Christian philosophy must conform to God in Christ, in a manner to be specified.

2. GOD'S WISDOM AND REVELATION

However one understands the bearing of philosophy on faith in God, a distinctive kind of wisdom figures in the early Christian movement, starting with Jesus himself. According to Luke's Gospel, "Jesus increased in wisdom and in years, and in divine and human favor" (Luke 2:52). Luke portrays Jesus as linking wisdom to his ministry and remarking that "wisdom is vindicated by all her children" (Luke 7:35; cf. Matt. 11:19). Jesus suggests that he himself is superior to Solomon, the famous dispenser of wisdom in the Jewish Bible (see Luke 11:29–32; cf. Matt. 12:42). He offers the following promise to his disciples: "I will give you words and a wisdom that none of your opponents will be able to withstand or contradict" (Luke 21:15). In Mark's Gospel, some people in the synagogue ask the following about Jesus: "What is this wisdom that has been given to him?" (Mark 6:2; cf. Matt. 13:54). The Synoptic Gospels, then, portray Jesus as having a reputation for wisdom of a distinctive kind. We shall identify this kind of wisdom.

Paul on Wisdom

Paul offers a profound approach to wisdom in his letters, primarily in 1 Corinthians. He acknowledges God as the source of human wisdom via a divine gift in Christ, and he develops this approach in more detail than Socrates develops his God-oriented approach in Plato's writings. Paul agrees with the book of Isaiah that God aims to "destroy the wisdom of the wise" (Isa. 29:14, 1 Cor. 1:19; cf. 1 Cor. 3:18–20). The people called "the wise" here try to make do without God's gift of true wisdom, understood by Paul for his time as God's gift of wisdom in Christ. Paul contrasts "fleshly wisdom" with the "grace of God" (2 Cor. 1:12). God's wisdom, in his perspective, comes courtesy of a humanly unearned gift of divine grace and hence leaves no room for human self-credit or earning.

Joseph Fitzmyer remarks: " 'Human wisdom' . . . denotes the mindset of some Corinthian Christians who were denying the soteriological significance of Christ's cross or crucifixion" (2008, p. 157). The controversy, however, concerned more than the saving significance of Christ's cross; it included the matter of *knowing God* via human wisdom. In Corinth, some sought wisdom that had no need for God in Christ crucified, and therefore Paul countered with the central role of Christ crucified in God's wisdom and power. This led to Paul's striking remark: "I decided to know nothing among you except Jesus Christ, and him crucified" (1 Cor. 2:2). Paul had in mind the risen Christ, and not just the earthly Jesus.

Paul announces to the Corinthians: "My speech and my proclamation were not with plausible words of wisdom, but with a demonstration of the Spirit and of power, *so that* your faith might rest not on human wisdom but on the power of God" (1 Cor. 2:4–5, italics added). Paul desires that faith in God "rest not on human wisdom but on the power of God," because "in the wisdom of God, the world did not know God through [its] wisdom" (1 Cor. 1:21). This concern is important in understanding the evidential basis of faith in God and of the God relationship. Paul's approach to wisdom bears on knowing God, and not just on how God saves people. It has epistemological import (as emphasized by, for instance, Martyn 1967/1997 and Brown 1995, 1996).

Paul contrasts "God's wisdom, secret and hidden, which God decreed before the ages for our glory," with "human wisdom" (1 Cor. 2:7). He also contrasts "God's wisdom" with "the wisdom of the world" (1 Cor. 1: 20–23). The two contrasts seem to be substantially the same. One key difference between the categories contrasted is that only God's wisdom would have the divine power (*dunamis*), including the power of self-giving *agapē* (righteous love), to give cooperative humans a lasting good life in a *koinonia* relationship with God, as an alternative to despair. Humans and their wisdom lack such power, as human death and moral inadequacy illustrate. Only God's wisdom, then, can empower human redemption or salvation as a lasting good life anchored in unselfish interpersonal relationships under God's authority. Such life would be impervious to final death, just as its sustainer, God, would be.

God's wisdom, in Paul's account, includes the message of Christ crucified (1 Cor. 2:7–8), and he thus speaks of "Christ [crucified], the power of God and the wisdom of God" (1 Cor. 1:24). He reports that he did not proclaim the gospel "with eloquent wisdom, so that the cross of Christ might not be emptied [of its power]" (1 Cor. 1:17). Obscuring, diminishing, or ignoring the significance of the cross of Christ, in his perspective, would put one at odds with the wisdom God uses to undermine the wisdom of the world. Here we have a stark contrast between God's wisdom and power in the cross of Christ and the wisdom of the world, the kind of wisdom God seeks to destroy. We shall attend to this important contrast, in order to illuminate the God relationship.

God chose the wisdom in the cross of Christ, according to Paul, "so that no one might boast in the presence of God" (1 Cor. 1:29). God is the source of our wisdom, in Paul's account, and the crucified Christ "became for us wisdom from God" in order to replace our boasting in humans and our own achievements with boasting in the Lord (1 Cor. 1:29–31; cf. 1 Cor. 3:21). Fitzmyer explains:

For Paul, boasting denotes the fundamental mindset of human beings in their relation to God, manifested especially in the pursuit of their own ability and wisdom. It's an attitude with which God in the Old Testament already found fault. . . . Paul insists: humans cannot bring about their salvation by wisdom in any ordinary or natural sense through allegiance to human beings or by their accomplishments. In [1 Corinthians] 4:7 he will insist further that one's standing before God is itself a gift: "What do you have that you did not receive?" (2008, pp. 163–64)

One's "standing before God" as a gift (that is, as grace) encompasses not just one's salvation but also one's knowledge of God, in Paul's account.

Boasting in humans, according to Paul, detracts from the credit due to God alone for a divine gift, including in the area of human knowledge of God. It robs God of honor appropriate to God alone in God's self-manifesting the divine character to humans, particularly in Christ (see 2 Cor. 4:6). In doing so, it obscures human indebtedness to God for an unearned gift of divine wisdom and exaggerates the importance of humans in relation to God's gift of wisdom and power. Such human pride, being devoid of proper honor and gratitude toward God (Rom. 1:21), leads humans to trust in a false security, such as in their own thinking about God (see Niebuhr 1937, chap. 5, Stauffer 1955, pp. 88–90). In contrast, God in Christ would intervene to call for human trust in what is trustworthy: God and the divine promise of an unearned gift of the power of new life in the God relationship.

Regarding the life-giving power in the cross of Christ, Paul writes: "God proves his love for us in that while we still were sinners Christ died for us" (Rom. 5:8). Leander Keck rightly has called this theme "the heart of Paul's christology," adding: "It is the congruence between Jesus's demeanor and God's character that makes it possible for the Jesus event to be a revelation of God's righteousness, and not of God's arbitrariness or of Jesus's victimization at the hands of God" (1993, p. 36). Paul would add that the congruence depends on Jesus's being the obedient "Son of God" (see Gal. 2:20, Phil. 2:5–8) rather than an ordinary human who, contrary to Gethsemane, opts for selfish ways over God's ways.

The divine righteousness is God's perfect goodness that, climactically in Christ crucified, offers to *ungodly* people the power to be in a right relationship with God, by grace, without their earning or merit (see Rom. 3:26, 4:1–5, 5:10; cf. Käsemann 1969, 1980, pp. 105–13, 2010; Keck 1988, pp. 110–22, 2005, pp. 101–33). This right relationship, the God relationship, can be the start and the basis of one's *becoming* godly or righteous, but it does not presuppose one's being godly or righteous. It can supply to humans the guidance and the intentional power needed to cooperate with God and to conform to God's moral character, thus enabling one to exemplify God's righteousness, if imperfectly.

"Eloquent wisdom," or the wisdom of the world, can threaten or obscure the power of God's righteous love in Christ. God's self-manifesting the divine character of righteous love for humans in the death and resurrection of Christ is, if genuine, *God's* doing, and uniquely so. If God's character is uniquely one of perfect righteous love, then divine self-manifesting will be the ideal way to manifest that character, and other means will fall short. We humans should not take credit for divine self-manifesting or diminish its importance in our pride or our quest for self-achievement and self-credit, intellectual or otherwise. Whether in Jewish, Hellenistic, or other human wisdom that does not credit God's power, eloquent wisdom from humans calls attention to human thinkers and speakers in their brilliance and eloquence. It points to a human achievement in a way that would ignore or diminish the importance of what God has done for humans, particularly in Christ, the true wisdom of God. It thus would run afoul of God's unique wisdom and power.

Speculative human arguments in natural theology ignore or neglect the importance of God's unique self-manifesting of redemptive power, including the divine power of righteous love, in events of history and human experience (see Rom. 3:21–26). This is part of what makes them speculative rather than historical or experiential toward God. Such arguments, intentionally or unintentionally, call attention to human reasoners in their speculative reasoning skills, as if God's self-manifesting is somehow deficient, unreal, dubious, shameful, or embarrassing. In that respect, they focus in the wrong direction, if a perfectly good God is at issue.

Avoiding speculative arguments, Paul attributes to God a claim to self-manifesting suggested in Isaiah 65:1 (close to the Septuagint version): "I [God] have *shown myself* to those who did not ask for me" (Rom. 10:20, italics added; cf. Rom. 1:19; see Fitzmyer 1993, p. 600). The idea of God's "showing himself" to humans is central to the biblical story of God's dealings with humans (see Baillie 1956, Eichrodt 1967, Terrien 1978, Westermann 1982, pp. 25–34). It also figures in Paul's remark: "I am not ashamed of the gospel; it is the power of God for salvation to everyone who has faith, to the Jew first and also to the Greek" (Rom. 1:16). Paul thus does not try, or need to try, to mitigate any cognitive shame with speculative arguments from philosophy. Instead, he acknowledges a distinctive kind of evidence and wisdom from God's self-manifestation to humans (cf. Rom. 5:5.)

The God of Isaiah and of the crucified Christ, in Paul's portrait, aims to destroy speculative philosophical alternatives to the true wisdom of God. Such alternatives obscure and interfere with the unique power from God, who self-manifests perfect righteous love without speculative philosophy. So, to redeem humans with the power and wisdom exemplified in the crucified Christ, God would not need or desire human eloquence, the speculative arguments of philosophers, or anything else that puffs up humans. God would have the power to self-manifest the divine righteous and gracious character, climactically in Christ's death and resurrection, without relying on human achievement and pride.

Shunning misplaced pride, Paul states: "May I never boast of anything except the cross of our Lord Jesus Christ, by which the world has been crucified to me, and I to the world. For neither circumcision nor uncircumcision is anything; but a new creation is everything!" (Gal 6:14–15; cf. Gal. 5:6) God's work of making people new in Christ is the boastworthy work, in Paul's story; human achievement in eloquence or speculative argument is not. God's power of original creation would have no need to rely on humans or their power. Likewise, neither God's power of re-creation in redemption nor the human knowledge of that power would need to await help from humans in their worldly wisdom or speculative arguments, including such arguments from traditional philosophy or natural theology.

Divine Self-Revelation

Paul holds that God is self-revealed climactically in the cross and resurrection of Christ, and this view bears on how we are to understand the relevance of wisdom and philosophy to faith in God. Leander Keck has remarked on divine self-revelation:

A revelatory event . . . is one which does more than trigger an insight; it becomes part of the insight permanently because it becomes the prism through which alone the insight can be seen. A revelatory event is one to which one returns again and again because it has the capacity not only to repeat the original disclosure but to keep on unfolding its meaning into one situation after another. In this case, the relation between event and revelation is intrinsic and permanent. . . . For Paul, the gospel does not merely have its origin in the event which the cross epitomizes but has its permanent criterion and center in the cross, so that the word of the cross is the means by which that event reaches hearers as a revelation which redeems. (1983, pp. 146–47)

The revelation in question is event-centered toward the self-manifesting of divine power. It is a God-empowered episode as a series of divine events in the domain of human life, even if some humans fail to perceive the reality of the divine episode.

The "word of the cross" (1 Cor. 1:18) is the message of what God has done to self-manifest divine love in Christ crucified. It is no ordinary message, because it comes with "the power of God" for enabling cooperative humans to receive a right relationship with God, the God relationship (1 Cor. 1:18, Rom. 1:16). The message reveals God's righteousness in Christ that aims to bring all humans into a right relationship with God, even though they are ungodly and unworthy of this relationship (Rom. 3:21–26, 4:5). This righteousness is no mere talk, because it has the intentional power to manifest divine goodness and thereby to enable people to enter a new relationship with God and others. Even so, humans typically face a problem noted by Ethelbert Stauffer, following Paul: "They must make use of every device and try out their capacities to the last degree before their autonomy destroys itself by its own excess. Not till that happens will they be ready to listen to the message of the cross (Rom. 3:9ff.)" (1955, p. 89).

Keck has remarked on the connection between the cross of Christ, knowledge of God, and the world's wisdom:

It is because the story of Jesus and his cross is simultaneously the story of God's love that Paul can conclude that whoever believes this story is rightly related to the truth about God, and so redeemed from trusting a misconstrued God. Because cross/resurrection as God's act could not be integrated into what passed for knowledge of God, Paul came to see that one was forced to choose between the wisdom of the world and the foolishness of the gospel, and that if the gospel was right, the world's wisdom has been unmasked as folly in the guise of wisdom. . . . Whoever has experienced [the corrective power of God] by entrusting oneself to God as proclaimed in the gospel knows that the foolishness of God is wiser than human wisdom, and that the cross . . . is indeed stronger than human power, because, when grasped as God's deed, it has the capacity to set us right with God. (1983, pp. 148, 154)

The power of God in the cross of Christ and in the message of the cross is irreducible to affirmation or belief that something is the case. In bringing an ungodly person into a right relationship with God, this divine power frees that person from bondage to things that prevent such a relationship. One's receiving the power in question differs from mere belief that something is true, because it includes *entrusting oneself* to this personal power in submission to God. This is the heart of faith in God (as Chapter 2 noted), beyond any mere belief that something is true about God.

Even if God self-manifests in the episode of Christ crucified and resurrected, we still could lack a corresponding indication in human experience. Human evidence of God's self-manifesting, however, needs a basis in human experience if it is to be evidence of God *for a human person.* God can self-manifest in an objective event, but this will have evidential significance for a person only if the person apprehends the manifestation somehow in his or her experience. We might propose that "those who believe this word of the cross know it as both the power of God and the wisdom of God," but we cannot avoid this question: "*How* will they know this?"

Keck offers the following answer: "In a word, they have experienced the rectitude of God as rectification, the holiness of God as sanctification and the power of God as redemption because in believing the word of the cross they

know that God made Christ 'our wisdom, our righteousness and sanctification and redemption', as 1 Corinthians
1:30 puts it" (1983, p. 153). He adds: "Moreover, by adding the appositional phrase [in 1 Corinthians 1:30], Paul
clarifies the 'for us' aspect of the wisdom from God that
Christ became/was made: neither a sage whose wisdom
improves our thinking, nor a principle by which *we* interpret reality, but an event that changes our relation to the
right, the holy, and the free – i.e., to the God from whom
this wisdom came. It is because Christ is this sort of wisdom of God that he is also the power of God" (1996, p. 442).
Keck rightly asks about how people will know the message
of Christ crucified as the power of God, and he points us
in the right direction in appealing to a human experience
of God's character and power. We need, however, a more
robust answer that goes beyond talk of an "event" that
changes our relation to God.

Keck seems to think, mistakenly, that his talk of an
"event" will save us from skeptical worries. He remarks:

For [Paul] the ex post facto thinker, the event [of God at work
in the crucified and risen Christ] is a given, not a probability conceded or inferred, and as a given it admits no doubt
about its actuality. Were it otherwise, the event would be an
intriguing possibility but have no compelling power. At the
same time, because 'event' implies a tissue of meaning (and
not a 'naked fact'), [Paul] the ex post facto thinker does not
assume that one predicates meaning of the given (an act of
will as well as of cognition) but that one discerns meaning
given with the event. (1993, p. 29)

This approach is mistaken in its claim that as a given event
God's intervention in Christ "admits no doubt about its
actuality." This claim is too strong, because one can have
doubt, even plausible doubt, about what a given event is
actually an event *of*. Is it an event of God's intervention,
or, instead, is it just an event of my hopeful postulation?

The answer is not always easy, as ongoing controversy over the theological import of the New Testament story about God and Christ illustrates. Keck (1993, p. 30) claims that "believing that God had raised Jesus from the dead was the determinative datum, the given" for Paul, but this overlooks that such believing is itself subject to doubt and requires evidential support. So, we need a more resilient account.

Keck himself points in the right direction, without integrating the point. He comments: "That intrusion [of God's New Age in Christ] being the given event, the resulting new relation to God that the experience of the Spirit betokens and confirms (expressed in Romans 8:14–17 as being authorized to call God 'Abba') discloses dimensions of prior existence of which Paul had not been aware" (1993, p. 31). The key point is that the Spirit of God "betokens and confirms" the divine intervention of the self-manifesting of God in Christ. This is Paul's view, and it suggests a way to join objective divine self-manifesting with personal assurance and (appropriated) evidence from God.

As indicated, Paul offers the key theme in Romans 5:5: "hope [in God] does not disappoint us, because God's love has been poured into our hearts through the Holy Spirit that has been given to us." The removal of disappointment includes the removal of cognitive or evidential disappointment (or shame) about the basis for hope in God, courtesy of a distinctive kind of personal assurance from God. Ernst Käsemann notes that "because for Paul Christ's death has concretely manifested the love of [i.e., from] God, the basis of Christian assurance lies in it. This is why the presence of the Spirit is described in [Romans] 5:5b as the presence of God's love" (1980, p. 138). Käsemann explains:

[In Romans 5:5] the reference is to the encompassing power of God with a special orientation to [God's] being for us, as [Romans] 8:31ff. clearly indicates. . . . First, when God's love has seized us so totally and centrally, we no longer belong to ourselves; a change in existence has taken place. Secondly, since the Spirit is a down payment (Rom. 8:23, 2 Cor. 1:22), we have an 'objective' pledge that our hope will not be confounded. Finally, when the Spirit who is given us makes us constantly sure of this love, we can praise God in the midst of earthly affliction, as in [Romans] 8:37ff. (1980, pp. 135–36)

In Paul's perspective, we need to allow *God* to supply not only redemption by divine grace (as an unearned gift) but also evidence and assurance of God's genuine self-manifesting to us. This self-manifesting, given its definite qualitative contours, can set a *de re* standard for deliberations about divine reality.

Divine assurance would come courtesy of God's Spirit (that is, God in self-manifesting and self-interpreting action), but not just as a testimony. It would come by God's "pouring into our hearts," that is, our volitional centers as agents, the same love from God that was self-manifested in the crucified and risen Christ. We would need to make room, then, for *cognitive* grace in our being assured of God's reality and presence, just as we would need to make room for grace in divine salvation of humans. An epistemology for faith in God can benefit from this approach.

We should balk at Käsemann's talk of an "objective" pledge in God's Spirit. If such a pledge entails impartial certainty (as a conclusive proof) or even compelling evidence for all inquirers, it is not to be had. A more plausible approach distinguishes an objective pledge in such a demanding sense from an *intersubjective* pledge or witness, and it distinguishes certainty or compelling evidence in any impartial sense from *certitude*, which is irreducibly interpersonal in this context. Such certitude is anchored in an I–Thou interpersonal encounter of affirmation from God, and therefore differs from an "objective" proof or argument. It includes volition-sensitive evidence from an irreducible first-person perspective that is lost if objectified as an impartial proof or argument that is to convince everyone. (Chapter 5 explores the consequences of this lesson for a defense of faith in God.)

If God is able to self-manifest and self-interpret to humans, then God also is able to self-assure for humans in affirming the reality of the divine presence and character for them. This self-assuring would be an interpersonal witness from God regarding God's being with people, on God's preferred terms for them. We must allow for flexibility in exactly how God self-assures for humans, but this self-assurance would be a live option for God and an alternative to an impartial proof. (For a different approach to certitude, as subjective, see Richardson 1961, pp. 115–17.)

The Spirit of God bears witness to the reality of God's love for us, according to Paul: "You did not receive a spirit of slavery to fall back into fear, but you have received a spirit of adoption. When we cry, 'Abba!, Father!', it is that very Spirit bearing witness with our spirit that we are children of God, and if children, then heirs, heirs of God and joint heirs with Christ – if, in fact, we suffer with him so that we may also be glorified with him" (Rom. 8:15–17). This kind of interpersonal witness does not need an intervening speculative argument from philosophy. God would be adequate to the task, including the task of self-assuring humans, and arguably *only* God would be, given that God's moral character is *sui generis*. Paul remarks: "Because you are children, God has sent the Spirit of his Son into our hearts, crying, 'Abba!, Father!'" (Gal. 4:6). The Aramaic "Abba" is intended to echo Jesus in his prayers to God, and the emphasis is on the Spirit's witness to one's being in a right filial relationship as a child of God. Even so, the Spirit's witness goes beyond verbal testimony or talk of one's being a child of God.

The divine witness to God in Christ would not rest on impersonal proofs or speculative arguments. In seeking human redemption, it would go deeper, to the offered, self-manifested character traits of God. Gordon Fee has commented on the witness beyond talk in Romans 5:5:

God's love, played out to the full in Christ, is an experienced reality in the "heart" of the believer by the presence of the Spirit. *This* is what the Spirit has so richly "shed abroad in our hearts." If one is not thus overtaken by God himself at this one crucial point, then all else is lost, and one is . . . living with little real hope, and thus experiencing present sufferings as a cause for complaint and despair rather than for "boasting." What rectifies all of this for us is not simply the *fact* of God's love, . . . but that God's love has been effectively realized in the experience of the believer. (1994, pp. 496–97)

God's Spirit, in Paul's portrait, witnesses to receptive humans by offering to them and sharing with them divine self-manifested character traits, such as God's righteous love. These offered and shared traits are self-manifested evidence of God's reality and character, and they underwrite the God relationship, psychologically and cognitively.

It would be misplaced to object that "talk is cheap," because we have much more than talk in the proposed divine evidence on offer. We have the divine self-manifesting and sharing of God's unique moral character. The claims of other gods cannot copy this righteous character, because those gods do not *have* such a character to share. One cannot share what one does not have. In self-manifesting, God could witness climactically to the risen Christ as the unique representative of God, the one who manifested God's righteous love on the cross for humans needing divine forgiveness and reconciliation. (On such forgiveness and reconciliation, see Moser 2008, pp. 171–80.) The uniqueness comes from the distinctive moral character of a God of perfect, self-giving love.

Paul suggests a connection between the Spirit of God and *God in Christ*: "No one can say 'Jesus is Lord' except by the Holy Spirit" (1 Cor. 12:3). He has in mind the Jesus resurrected by God, and his talk of "saying" connotes "saying with an adequate basis," the basis provided by the self-manifesting of the Spirit of God. Käsemann adds: "The

Pauline doctrine of the Spirit is constitutively shaped by the fact that the apostle . . . is the first to relate it indissolubly to Christology. In the Spirit the risen Lord manifests his presence and lordship on earth. Conversely the absolute criterion of the divine Spirit is that he sets the community and its members in the discipleship of the Crucified, in the mutual service established thereby, and in the assault of grace on the world" (1980, p. 213). The talk of "grace" here is talk of *God's* grace, and therefore the Spirit represents the moral character of God in promoting "the discipleship of the Crucified." So, there is no conceptual circle that threatens. With the self-manifesting of divine character traits, God's Spirit would witness to the reality that Christ is God's unique agent, in agreement with God's unique character of perfect righteous love.

Alexandra R. Brown comments on the revelatory and drawing function of God's Spirit for humans: "For Paul, the Spirit not only makes accessible true knowledge of God according to the cross but pulls the knower toward a new realm of existence, namely the lordship of Christ" (1995, p. 124). Paul himself mentions the revelatory function of the Spirit: "We have received not the spirit of the world, but the Spirit that is from God, so that we may understand the gifts bestowed on us by God. And we speak of these things in words not taught by human wisdom but taught by the Spirit, interpreting spiritual things to those who are spiritual" (1 Cor. 2:12–13). Paul's use of "gifts" can include whatever comes from God's grace, including the risen Christ himself, his redemptive work for humans, and its cognitive benefits.

In Paul's perspective, human knowledge of Christ's resurrection does not come by natural means, in keeping with 1 Corinthians 12:3. Because Christ's redemptive work frees receptive humans from obstructive powers, however, the Spirit functions as not only revelatory but also liberating from spiritual and moral bondage. Hence, Paul emphasizes freedom in connection with the benefits of Christ and

God's Spirit, and the heart of this freedom is freedom to love others unselfishly as God does (see Gal. 5:1, 13–25; cf. Martyn 1997, pp. 431–66). Such freedom would be part of the humanly experienced power of God on behalf of his people, and it would aid in realizing the lordship of Christ for receptive humans. (For support for this kind of approach to freedom, see Häring 1978, pp. 121–43.)

Redeeming people by grace as an unearned gift, rather than by their merit, God would provide assurance to receptive humans on God's terms. We may prefer more control in this area, perhaps by our own speculative arguments, but the option is not ours, if God seeks to destroy human wisdom and its role for self-boasting. We should attend to the prospect of God's effort to challenge any epistemology at odds with divine wisdom, especially regarding human knowledge of God. An epistemology conformed to God's distinctive character would go deeper than philosophical speculation, as we shall see, and it would call for human participation in God's moral character and purposes.

3. PARTICIPATION AND SPECULATION

Participatory Struggle

Paul links knowing Christ, and knowing God in Christ, with existential, lived participation in the sufferings of Christ: "I want to know Christ and the power of his resurrection and the sharing of his sufferings by becoming like him in his death if somehow I may attain the resurrection from the dead" (Phil. 3:10–11). He adds: "We are . . . always carrying in the body the death of Jesus, so that the life of Jesus may also be made visible in our bodies. For while we live, we are always being given up to death for Jesus' sake, so that the life of Jesus may be made visible in our mortal flesh" (2 Cor. 4:8–11). Paul holds that in the crucified Christ (who became the risen Christ), humans can find God's wisdom and power instead of

a disappointing worldly alternative. Human appropriation of this wisdom and power through faith in God is
demanding, because it requires dying to anti-God ways
in order to live cooperatively in *koinonia* with God in
Christ, as Christ cooperated with God in Gethsemane. It
thus requires one's struggling against some of one's own
tendencies, particularly selfish tendencies, in order to be
conformed to the God relationship in Christ.

J. Louis Martyn links knowing by the cross of Christ with
the human dying in daily discipleship toward Christ:

Together with the community that is being formed in him,
Christ defines the difference between the [old and new] ways
of knowing, doing that precisely in his cross. The cross of
Christ means that the marks of the new age are at present hidden *in* the old age (2 Cor. 6:3–10). Thus, at the juncture of the
ages the marks of the resurrection are hidden and revealed in
the cross of the disciple's daily death, and *only* there (2 Cor.
5:14–15). (1967/1997, p. 110)

Citing Galatians 3:13–14, Charles Cosgrove strikes a similar note: "For Paul, participation in the crucifixion of Christ
is the sole condition for ongoing life in the Spirit" (1988,
p. 172; cf. pp. 178, 184). Participation in this death signals
what Cosgrove calls a "disruption" of the life in this world
for the sake of new life in Christ. We should be uneasy,
however, about putting participation in Christ in such
monolithic terms, given that we are talking about participation in the *resurrected* Christ. Cosgrove rightly notes, in a
more accurate formulation: "dying and rising with Christ
belong together in Christian experience" (1988, p. 187; cf.
Gorman 2009, pp. 129–60).

Paul endorses the inextricable connection between dying
and rising with Christ:

We have been buried with him by baptism into death, so
that, just as Christ was raised from the dead by the glory of

the Father, so we too might walk in newness of life. . . . So you also must consider yourselves dead to sin and alive to God in Christ Jesus. No longer present your members to sin as instruments of wickedness, but present yourselves to God as those who have been brought from death to life, and present your members to God as instruments of righteousness. (Rom. 6:4, 11, 13)

Paul speaks of those who, having died with Christ, "have been brought from death to life," and he adds that this is "just as Christ was raised from the dead by the glory of the Father."

Paul does not have bodily resurrection in mind, but a kind of spiritual resurrection in the present fits with Paul's statement. This theme is widely neglected in discussions of Paul, even among New Testament scholars, but it becomes explicit in later Pauline writings (see Col. 3:1, Eph. 2:5–6). The theme is important, because, as Michael Gorman notes (2009, p. 71), "as an experience of the risen or resurrected Christ, co-crucifixion is not merely a metaphor but an apt description of an encounter with a living person whose presence transforms and animates believers (Gal. 2:20)." In Paul's perspective, one's rising now with Christ is thus experiential, courtesy of God's self-manifesting Spirit, the Spirit of the risen Christ, and it is anchored in the divine righteous love poured into one's heart (Rom. 5:5).

The Spirit of God would enable cooperative people to apprehend God's presence in the (preached) cross of Christ. Brown notes, in the light of 1 Corinthians 2:10: "The wisdom of the cross Paul preaches finds its way into the heart only by the agency of God's Spirit who alone has the power to claim for God the hearts of 'those who love God' (1 Cor. 2:9)" (1995, p. 165). The redemptive claiming of the Spirit would not be coercive toward humans; it would be sensitive to the volitional receptivity of human agents, and thus would not vacate their being genuine intentional agents. If their intentional agency were eclipsed, divine redemption would not be genuinely interpersonal. It would not be the redemption of authentic agents who freely exercise *their wills* toward God.

Following the pattern set by Abraham (Rom. 4:16), a human faith-commitment of self-entrustment to God would be needed as a free response to God's self-manifesting to humans (see Cosgrove 1988, p. 176). This kind of response would not earn or merit God's offer of redemption and its benefits, and therefore it would fit with God's redeeming humans by grace on the basis of the promise to Abraham (Rom. 4:4–5, 13–14). Such redeeming by divine grace would allow humans to be genuine agents rather than pawns of God, and this entails that humans could reject God's offer, however unwisely.

Chapter 2 noted Paul's following remark on the role of human weakness, or impotence, in relation to God's power: "We have this treasure [of redemption from God] in clay jars, *so that* it may be made clear that this extraordinary power belongs to God and does not belong to us" (2 Cor. 4:7, italics added; cf. Fitzgerald 1988, Savage 1996, Brown 1998, Gorman 2001, pp. 268–303). The power and wisdom needed by humans, according to Paul, must come from God, because God alone has such power and wisdom. Paul describes the relevant power and wisdom:

We have not ceased praying for you and asking that you may be filled with the knowledge of God's will in all *spiritual wisdom* and understanding, so that you may lead lives worthy of the Lord, fully pleasing to him, as you bear fruit in every good work and as you grow in the knowledge of God. May you be made strong [= empowered] with all the strength [= power, *dunamis*] that comes from his glorious power, and may you be prepared to endure everything with patience, while joyfully giving thanks to the Father. (Col. 1:9–12, italics added)

Paul's "spiritual wisdom" is not mere knowledge that a claim is true. It is directed toward "lead[ing] lives worthy of the Lord, fully pleasing to him."

We have a sharp contrast between "spiritual wisdom" and mere factual knowledge and even any kind of "human wisdom." Exceeding mere factual knowledge, spiritual wisdom sympathetically *cooperates with* God's power, including the power of *agapē*, for the sake of living a lasting good life, pleasing to God (or, "worthy of the Lord"). Such wisdom is participatory in God's character and redemptive purposes, and hence cannot be reduced to armchair reflection or speculation. So, it does not sit well with traditional speculative philosophy. It resists separation from obedient cooperation with God, because it is inherently volitional and active toward God. This fits with a God relationship that is similarly volitional and active. As Chapters 1 and 2 suggested, we must allow for this option in connection with the notion of a perfectly redemptive God, to avoid misleading bias in inquiry. We should not exclude at the start God's seeking an interpersonal relationship with humans where faith, evidence, knowledge, wisdom, and meaning regarding God are appropriated in sympathetic cooperation with God's will. The ethics for inquiry about God requires as much.

Paul anchors spiritual wisdom not in an abstract or a speculative principle or even in a Platonic Form, but instead in a personal agent who manifests God's power without defect. As suggested, he refers to "Christ the power of God and the wisdom of God" (1 Cor. 1:24) and to "Christ Jesus who became for us wisdom from God . . . and redemption" (1 Cor. 1:30). A question concerns what particular features of the person Jesus Christ constitute his being the power and the wisdom of God.

Paul's answer includes the following: "Christ Jesus, who, though he was in the form of God, did not regard equality with God as something to be exploited, but emptied himself, taking the form of a slave, being born in human likeness. And being found in human form, he humbled himself and became obedient to the point of death – even death on a cross" (Phil. 2:5–8). A key feature is the willing conformity of Jesus to God's will, even when the result is self-sacrificial death on behalf of others. Paul introduces the idea of Jesus's *humble obedience* to God to capture this feature. This obedience differs from grudging obedience and even mere obedience. It ultimately welcomes God's perfect will, even if one is initially ambivalent and faces rigorous consequences, as in the case of Jesus in Gethsemane.

In his conformity to God's character and will, Jesus exemplifies the power and wisdom of God as an agent humbly and sympathetically cooperating with God on the basis of God's power and wisdom, including the power of self-sacrificial *agapē*. In being redemptive toward humans, God would challenge other humans to participate in the same divine wisdom, as they participate obediently in dying and rising with Christ. In doing so, humans would entrust themselves to God and thereby exemplify faith in God. They thus would live as adopted children of God, with God as their Father. Paul notes, "If anyone is in Christ, there is a new creation: everything old has passed away; see, everything has become new!" (2 Cor. 5:17; cf. Hubbard 2002). Such new creation changes the standard for philosophy, at least in a Christian context, owing to the standard set by divine self-manifestation to humans.

Philosophy Recast

Philosophers conformed to Christ are philosophers conformed to a new life of dying and rising with Christ, in the power of self-sacrificial *agapē*. This point involves *philosophers* conformed to Christ, because human agents (rather than philosophical views) undergo the dying and rising in question. Going beyond philosophers, the conforming of philosophical *content* to Christ can take two forms. One form, *the strict-content form*, entails philosophy that is explicitly Christian in substantive conceptual content, involving positive claims regarding Jesus Christ, the Spirit of Christ, forgiveness from God, reconciliation to God in

Christ, inward transformation by Christ, and so on. This form will be significantly narrowing toward philosophy if one uses it to exclude all other forms of philosophy, but it need not be used in that exclusive manner. It can be combined with a different form of philosophy.

A second form of content conforming to Christ, *the kingdom-enhancement form*, requires philosophy (whatever its substantive content) to *contribute positively* to a philosophy that (a) is Christian in substantive content *and* (b) enhances God's redemptive kingdom under the good news of God in Christ and its divine love commands. In thus contributing positively, this form does *not* require philosophy conformed to Christ to be explicitly Christian in substantive conceptual content. Such contributing can be genuine without itself offering explicitly Christian content, such as when a philosophical contribution illuminates an I–Thou interaction between humans and God without offering explicitly Christian content (see Buber 1923).

The relevant kingdom-enhancement can contribute either to new human reconciliation to God or to deepened reconciliation with God, including a deepened appreciative understanding of God's redemptive ways. Given that the desired reconciliation proceeds by divine *agapē* and its love commands, we may understand kingdom-enhancement in terms of the expansion or the deepening of God's kingdom of *agapē*. Such kingdom-enhancement depends on the power of divine *agapē*, which can exist and work apart from explicit Christian content. Otherwise, the Spirit of God would be unable to prepare people in advance of their coming to consider and to receive Christian conceptual content. Even so, we may think of the relevant kingdom-enhancement as being conformed to Christ, at least in a broad sense, if we accept the New Testament view that Christ is the focal center, at least *de re*, of the kingdom (see Mark 1:14–15, Luke 11:20, Matt. 12:28, 25:31–42, Col. 1:13–14).

It would be unduly exclusive and short-sighted to prohibit doing philosophy in the kingdom-enhancement form for the sake of just the strict-content form. Such narrowness conflicts with the way various contributors of wisdom literature in the Jewish Bible engaged with, and borrowed from, non-Hebraic wisdom traditions. If God is the ultimate ground and sustainer of all wisdom, then genuine wisdom is valuable wherever it emerges, even outside the people of God. So, we should not expect or advocate for an explicitly Christian ghetto with a monopoly on wisdom.

It does not follow either that "anything goes" in philosophy conformed to Christ or that all philosophical truth or sound argument is intrinsically valuable or even worthy of human pursuit. The kingdom-enhancement requirement for philosophy conformed to Christ sets a definite boundary with this standard: enhancing God's redemptive kingdom under the good news of God in Christ and its divine love commands. Mere truth-acquisition, even for philosophical truth, does not meet this standard. Some philosophical truths contribute to kingdom-enhancement; others (such as the metaphysics of celestial time-travel for angels or demons) do not. That much is clear, even if some cases call for patience in careful discernment, and even if some cases are disputable. We need not digress, however, to pursue a full list of cases.

We humans have finite resources, including finite time, in this life under the divine love commands. We thus should adopt a triage approach to the matters we pursue in philosophy conformed to Christ (as in Christian life generally). We should distinguish between (a) the philosophical questions we may engage, if only briefly, to find out their positive relevance or the lack thereof to kingdom-enhancement and (b) the questions we may pursue as a research focus in a Christian life, as an evident means of kingdom-enhancement. Any new question may be fair game for category (a), but (b) is more demanding. As a research focus, philosophy conformed to Christ (and Christian inquiry in general) should be attentive to (b) in a manner that is often neglected, owing perhaps to the dubious assumption that any philosophical inquiry or truth is intrinsically valuable or otherwise worthy of human pursuit. We have no good reason to accept the latter assumption, even if the field of options can raise some epistemic problems regarding which truths are actually kingdom-enhancing.

If God in Christ is worthy of worship, then this God is morally impeccable, altogether without moral defect. Otherwise, we would have a false god. This is an implication of the maximally exalted title "God." The speculative arguments of philosophy, found in traditional natural theology, will not take us to such a God, even if they yield lesser gods who fall short of worthiness of worship (see Moser 2010, chap. 3). God's self-manifesting alone would take us to God as *sui generis*, courtesy of the divine character-manifesting of God's Spirit, as identified in Romans 5:5. Stauffer remarks: "The word of the cross marks the end of all the false attempts which are summed up in the concept of natural theology" (1955, p. 90). It does so, because it purports to bring God near to humans in the power of the message of Christ crucified, rather than in speculative arguments from philosophy. It provides for a direct manifesting of God's character of perfect righteous love, courtesy of God's Spirit, without any need for speculative arguments.

An appeal to speculative philosophy to know God is often analogous to the mistake of certain opponents of Paul to "seek to establish their own righteousness" before God (Rom. 10:2; cf. Gal. 2:16, Phil. 3:8–9). The analogous mistake is to "seek to establish one's own avenue to knowing God," in direct conflict with the lesson of 1 Corinthians 1:21, 2:4. Humans have this tendency to make room for self-credit, including in the area of knowing God, but God's self-manifesting the divine character would have no need for it and set it aside as misguided. From a Christian point of view, speculative philosophy goes awry in not giving a primary, irreplaceable role to God's self-manifesting the divine moral character, including righteous love, particularly in the message of Christ crucified. This message enables God's presence and character to be confirmed and witnessed to by God's unique Spirit, with no need of speculative arguments from philosophy. It enables God to give the needed assurance to receptive humans by a self-manifesting of God's unique character of righteous love. We see the abiding importance of this message throughout the New Testament. (For recurring components of the message, see Lemcio 1991, pp. 115–31; cf. Dodd 1936, Piper 1959.)

Speculative philosophy assumes that, at least for some people, God's self-manifesting in the message of the cross would not, or at least does not, adequately witness to God's presence and reality. It thus goes speculative in search of different, "natural" sources of potential evidence for God. This is the big mistake of speculative philosophy and traditional natural theology, at least according to Paul's epistemology for knowing God. They thus have the same defect of worldly wisdom: the neglect of God's unique and irreplaceable self-manifesting via God's Spirit, climactically through (the message of) Christ crucified. It is here, according to Paul, that God chooses to self-manifest climactically, in order to bring the highest honor to God's crucified Son, and alternative human preferences will not change this. Just as we would not be in a position to set God's plans for creation, we would not be in a position to dictate God's plans for re-creation in redemption, including God's plan for supplying evidence by self-manifesting the divine character for the sake of a *koinonia* relationship with humans.

The neglect of the prospect of divine self-manifesting can obscure the directness of evidence for God via God's Spirit in the message of the cross. Alluding to passages in Deuteronomy, Paul remarks: "Do not say in your heart, 'Who will ascend into heaven?' (that is, to bring Christ down) or 'Who will descend into the abyss?' (that is, to bring Christ up from the dead). But what does it say? 'The word is near you, on your lips and in your heart' (that is, the word of faith that we proclaim)" (Rom. 10:6–8). Speculative philosophy that includes traditional natural theology aims to find evidence of God's reality outside the self-manifesting of divine righteous love. Instead, it obscures with philosophical complexity and controversy the key role of God's self-manifesting. It leaves the matter obscure and controversial at best, and falls short of offering the reality and power of a God of perfect love who is worthy of worship. It ends up with lesser gods at best, despite what may be good intentions.

As noted, the New Testament writers do not appeal to speculative arguments to offer evidence for God's reality or presence. Paul could have done so, but he acknowledges that God self-manifests instead with a personal witness, climactically the witness of God's Spirit via (the message of) the cross. It is implausible, then, for some writers to suggest that in Romans 1:18–20 Paul is suggesting an argument of natural theology based on creation. This is not natural theology at all, because Paul reports that *God* has shown God's reality to people: "For what can be known about God is plain to them, because God has shown it to them" (Rom. 1:19). God can self-manifest to humans "through creation," but this would not entail that creation *by itself* shows or otherwise establishes God's reality. So, we do not have a basis for an argument of natural theology here. Some people try to read such a basis into Romans 1, but Paul is clear: *God* is doing the showing of God, and creation by itself is not. This lesson fits with Paul's other acknowledgments of God's self-manifesting to some humans (e.g., Rom. 10:20).

Paul uses arguments in his letters, but it does not follow that he uses speculative philosophy or arguments of natural theology. He also seeks to destroy certain arguments: "We destroy arguments and every proud obstacle raised up against the knowledge of God, and we take every thought captive to obey Christ" (2 Cor. 10:4–5). Destroying arguments, however, does not require any endorsement of speculative philosophy or arguments of natural theology.

One can destroy arguments by identifying why they fail to deliver their promised conclusions. Many philosophers have contributed to doing this for the traditional arguments of natural theology (see Hick 1971, Martin 2007). Such arguments thus become little more than an intellectual distraction, at least from the standpoint of various New Testament writers. Paul offers a more resilient approach that takes seriously the evidential role of God's own Spirit in self-manifesting God to humans. He thus embraces cognitive grace, and disowns cognitive earning or self-crediting before God.

The arguments of traditional natural theology do not sit well with the recurring biblical theme that God is elusive and hides divine existence from some people at times. According to this theme, God does not offer divine existence as ever-transparent for all inquirers, in part because some people are not ready to face God's reality (see Chapter 3, and Moser 2008 for some relevant biblical passages; cf. Terrien 1978, Balentine 1983). A perfectly good God would not force salient evidence of divine reality on humans (as Chapter 1 noted), and we should not try to do so either, especially with arguments that fall short of a God worthy of worship. Even if one gets to the reality of a lesser god by some speculative argument (which is doubtful), one still would face the debilitating question of how one gets from the lesser god to a God worthy of worship. One will need some kind of account or argument, and if one has such an account or argument, it will be doubtful that one will need the original argument for the lesser god. In that case, the speculative argument in question would be dispensable. We then would have no real need of it.

A proponent of an argument of natural theology might retreat to a distinction between "knowing that God exists" and "knowing God." The claim would be that the preferred argument supports the former knowing but not necessarily the latter. This would be no surprise if "knowing God" requires some kind of direct personal interaction between a human and God. A speculative argument of natural theology does not require any such interaction. Even so, it is unclear that a redemptive God would want ideally to separate the two kinds of knowing, because merely knowing that God exists could be accompanied by human hate toward God. Such knowing thus would be very thin relative to God's desire to redeem people in a cooperative relationship with God. Some version of this concern perhaps underlies the following deflationary remark in James 2:19: "You believe that God is one; you do well. Even the demons believe – and shudder." Ideally, God would want to promote "knowing that God exists" only as it figures in "knowing God" in a cooperative manner. A perfectly good God thus would seek to be cognitively redemptive.

Perhaps much of speculative philosophy about God and natural theology stems from a failure to trust God in an evidential role. Part of the problem is that we cannot predict whether God will self-manifest to humans at a certain time. Jesus suggests this kind of inability in John's Gospel (see John 3:8), and I see no reason to try to overcome it with arguments that only create more problems for, and divert attention from, what would be the genuine evidence for God. I recommend, then, that we focus instead on the more fitting kind of evidence in the divine self-manifesting of God's character. The latter evidence would be experiential and not speculative, and it would fit with God's unique character as a personal agent with perfect love for all concerned, even enemies. In that case, we would not be talking about a god who falls short of worthiness of worship. Philosophy conformed to God in Christ should retain the centrality of the perfect moral character of a God worthy of worship. It thus would conform to the Christ who represents this God perfectly and set aside efforts toward knowledge of God that fall short of a God worthy of worship.

Philosophy conformed to God in Christ portrays philosophy under, or aligned with, God in Christ, and this involves a distinctive kind of wisdom: God's wisdom in Christ. If philosophy is the love and pursuit of wisdom of a special kind, philosophy conformed to Christ is the love and pursuit of God's wisdom under divine authority in Christ. Such wisdom would call for an ongoing volitional union with Christ, including one's belonging to God in Christ. It contrasts with what Paul calls "human wisdom." If someone finds this approach to philosophy too demanding, a question arises: Too demanding *for what?*

The fact that my suggested approach challenges business as usual among professional philosophers is no reason against this approach. We should expect such a challenge given the transformative and redemptive kind of divine wisdom that would be found in God in Christ. Responsible inquiry about this God, as suggested, requires that we allow for the human appropriation of divine wisdom in a context of the God relationship, where humans cooperate sympathetically with God's will. A responsible approach to philosophical inquiry should allow for this option.

The perspective on offer acknowledges the importance of being *Christ-shaped* with regard to the mode and the ultimate purpose of Christian philosophy (and other truth-seeking disciplines submitted to God in Christ). Here we can find a trustworthy criterion, in being Christ-shaped, for separating the good from the bad in professional philosophy, at least for the sake of distinctively Christian philosophy. This criterion calls for a detailed explanation beyond the scope of this book, but it does point us in the right direction for Christian philosophy. I suggest, for instance, that doing mathematics via the received power of God in Christ, *with the accompanying fruit of God's Spirit* (e.g., love, joy, peace, kindness, patience), and *for the ultimate honor of God in Christ*, will look different in a personal and an interpersonal mode (even if not in content) from doing mathematics otherwise. I submit that the same is true for philosophy, in terms of a personal and an interpersonal mode. By way of contrast, we often see a harshly competitive interpersonal mode in academic pursuits. The criterion of being Christ-shaped in inquiry would prohibit such a mode.

A philosophy will not be Christ-shaped just because it includes truths and sound arguments that are philosophical. Something more is needed to satisfy the exalted normative character of being *Christ-shaped*. We might say that a philosophical argument is (objectively) good because it is sound. It does not follow, however, that it is good in a different, redemptively significant manner: particularly, in virtue of being a central component of a Christ-shaped philosophy. Philosophy done for the redemptive purpose of the honor of God in Christ differs, at least in intention, from philosophy done just to accumulate truths and sound arguments (and avoid falsehoods and bad arguments) in philosophy. Not all truths and sound arguments in philosophy are redemptively significant, from a Christian point of view, even if we have a hard time discerning relevant differences in some cases.

Redemptive significance according to the Christian good news depends on God's plan of redemption as reconciliation to God in Christ (*de re* if not *de dicto*). Paul remarks: "Through him [= Christ] God was pleased to reconcile to himself all things, whether on earth or in heaven" (Col. 1:20). (For a *de re* illustration, in the absence of Christian *de dicto* content, see Matthew 25:35–42.) The general mission of the body of Christ, the church, is to exemplify and to extend such divinely empowered reconciliation to all people willing to consider it. The demonstration of God's *agapē* in the self-sacrificial cross of Christ is at the center of this redemptive plan, but this does not exhaust the plan. The convicting and edifying work of God's Spirit is also crucial to the plan, as Paul suggests in Romans 5:5. Even so, humans must cooperate with God's Spirit to make the redemption as reconciliation to God *actual* for themselves. Humans thus must share the response of Jesus to God in Gethsemane (on which, see Chapter 2).

In Christ-shaped inquiry, including philosophy, a key question is: *How* are we to pursue the questions (including philosophical questions) that attract our attention? God, being morally perfect, would care about this, even if we do not. Will we pursue the questions to the neglect or the disadvantage of other people? Will we thereby exclude ourselves from the divine love commands? *How* we pursue questions is not an ethically neutral matter, as if God would not care. We need not exclude any profound or important philosophical question from Christian philosophy, as long as the question is pursued in keeping with the love commands and contributes positively to the redemptive project of God in Christ. As indicated, we do not need a complete list now of what would thus contribute in order to use the proposed criterion, just as we do not need a full list of foods to recommend that people eat food.

A philosophy will be Christ-shaped only if it is an integral part of God's redemptive movement grounded in Christ. From a Christian perspective, a philosophy with no positive contribution to that movement will amount to fiddling while Rome burns. The redemptive task in question requires self-giving trust in God as part of its mode. So, Paul states that "whatever does not proceed from faith [in God] is sin," where sin includes alienation from God and God's redemptive mission (Rom. 14:23). Following Paul, we should expect two contrasting kinds of philosophy and wisdom: philosophy and wisdom integral to God's redemptive effort in Christ, and "human" philosophy and wisdom that are not thus integral (for some details, see 1 Corinthians 1 and 2).

4. MEANING, PURPOSE, AND WILL

The God relationship would disclose wisdom from God, and that wisdom, in turn, would disclose meaning for human life. One question concerns how such meaning would be disclosed to humans and appropriated by them.

Philosophical reflections about "the meaning of life" or, less ambitiously, "the meaning in life" include questions about whether there is an overarching, all-inclusive purpose for human life. These questions do not concern whether everyone *knowingly* has such a purpose, because it is clear that not everyone does. The questions concern whether such a purpose is available to be known by humans and thereby to guide human lives.

Many philosophers have overlooked an important option: the *affective Gethsemane option* that directly involves a human's will and affections relative to God's will and affections. Meaning from God may be sensitive to a human's will and affections in a manner that makes the recognition of such meaning variable and elusive. Such meaning thus would fit with the elusiveness of a God worthy of worship. It would fit with God's aim to encourage humans to cooperate in the God relationship of *koinonia*.

Most philosophers have no objection to ordinary talk of the meaning *in life*, given that humans typically have various purposes or intentions in life. Those purposes can yield meaning in life, at least for the people with the purposes. I can intend to become the world's best photographer of abandoned American farms, for example, and that can give meaning in my life, at least for me. The plot thickens regarding the meaning *of life*, because it is unclear to many people that there is any such thing as "the purpose of life." It is unclear, in particular, that there is any intentional *source* for such a singular overarching purpose.

A key question is: *Whose* intention or will is to supply "the purpose of life"? No merely human intention will serve, because such an intention by itself will not automatically be normative for all other human agents. Merely human intentions, in addition, are transient in that they do not endure without end, and thus they can fail to bear on some human agents. They also can be distorted and misguided relative to what is genuinely good for humans, and hence can be harmful. We shall ask whether something that transcends merely human purposes could provide "the purpose," and hence "the meaning," of human life.

If God is perfectly good and thus compassionately redemptive toward humans, the will of God could underwrite an enduring purpose for humans, even if humans are unaware of this will and their own purposes conflict with it. Perhaps God allows human wills to obstruct God's perfect will to some extent. In that case, God could hide the divine will from some humans when such hiding is best for them, such as when they would only deride it or otherwise diminish its significance. The meaning of human life as represented in God's will thus could be hidden from them, at least for a time. So, humans may need to seek for this meaning and discern it in some careful way.

In keeping with the God relationship, we shall consider that a certain kind of *affective Gethsemane resolution* is needed not only to bring human wills, purposes, and affections in line with God's will, purposes, and affections, but also to reveal, in a well-founded manner, God's will and affections to humans and hence any overarching meaning for human life. In this perspective, suitably well-founded human discernment of God's will and affections requires a Gethsemane resolution that includes sympathetic human cooperation with the attitude of Jesus toward God in Gethsemane: Not what I will, but what you, God, will (see Mark 14:36). The Gethsemane resolution demands that humans die to what they themselves will apart from God's will, in order to live by what God wills. Humans thus must die into God's purpose, meaning, and life for the sake of lasting life in sympathetic cooperation with God, that is, in *koinonia*.

Because God's will would include compassion for people, including enemies, it would be irreducibly affective. (On God's affective character, see Heschel 1962, Moltmann 1981, Fiddes 1988, and Moser 2018b.) The meaning of life, then, could be hidden at times from humans, but would be available to them in a Gethsemane resolution relative to God's will and affections. Just as God would hide for redemptive purposes, so also the meaning of life, which depends on God's will and affections, would be elusive and even hidden at times from some humans for redemptive purposes.

Although a purely *de dicto* statement representing the meaning of life could be made to people in general, it would lack, for many people, the distinctive kind of *de re* evidential base available only from a first-person affective Gethsemane perspective. We shall consider a first-person *de re* component that is crucial to the needed supporting evidence, but this component does not rule out a purely *de dicto* statement that represents the meaning without the needed first-person evidence. The merely stated meaning will lack an evidential motivation for people in the absence of the supporting first-person evidence. The *de re* meaning of life thus could be evidentially hidden from many people, in the way that God would sometimes be hidden. God would intend this result in order to uphold the value of the compassionate and hence sympathetic component in divine self-manifesting, and to discourage people from a final rejection of God's offered redemption without a sympathetic first-person assessment of it.

Many defenders of Christian belief assume that God's purpose for human life can be identified simply on intellectual grounds, on the basis of the historical evidence now available to everyone. They sometimes look to the history of Jesus in the New Testament and infer that this history reveals God's purpose for human life for all humans. The rough idea is that this history indicates that God's purpose for human life is for humans to trust, obey, and love God in Christ and thereby to love all other persons, even enemies. This rough idea may be correct as far as it goes, but it lacks something from the standpoint of meaning that motivates a person to act in meaningful ways. It can strike a person as just another objective truth that fails to prompt one to act and to live one's life accordingly. It thus can seem abstract and devoid of motivating significance. Even if it offers the *de dicto* meaning of human life, it does not offer *lived, experienced,* or *felt* meaning, at least for many people. Something is missing, and we need to identify the missing piece.

A human must be motivationally connected to any objective meaning or purpose for the latter to become *lived* meaning for that human. Otherwise, the meaning will float free of what moves the person to live one kind of life rather than another. In that case, the meaning will be life-indifferent for that person, in the way that an abstract truth of mathematics (say, the Pythagorean Theorem) can be motivationally irrelevant to one's life. It would be odd to hold that a perfectly redemptive God supplies the meaning of life for humans, but that this meaning is motivationally irrelevant to their lives. Such a position would make the meaning of life irrelevant to the redemption of actual lives. A perfectly redemptive God would supply the needed opportunity for motivation for the sake of actually redeeming human lives in the God relationship.

We can distinguish between a lived meaning *in life* and a lived meaning *of life,* the latter being broader in scope than the former, and more controversial too. A lived meaning in life for me will depend on an actual intention or purpose I have in my life. My intention to revive an abandoned farm town in North Dakota could give me a lived meaning in my life, complete with frigid winters and hot summers. This meaning would be limited to considerations regarding my reviving the abandoned town. In contrast, a lived meaning of life for me would bear on the meaning of my life *as a whole*; it would not be limited to considerations regarding a particular project in my life. This meaning of life for me would ideally guide all of the particular purposes in life for me. It thus would function as an umbrella norm for meaning in life for me. Even so, a lived meaning of life for me would have a basis in what I intend for the meaning of life for me. It would be motivating for me and hence would be a lived meaning for me.

Although many philosophers refrain from acknowledging an overarching meaning of life for a person, we should give the idea of such meaning careful attention. One problem is that the idea is often tied up with a notion of God, and many philosophers doubt that the latter notion picks out an actual personal agent with causal powers. Nonetheless, we need to give the idea of such meaning a cautious hearing, because it suggests something that would be important for human life: a kind of overarching meaning that integrates and sustains, at least ideally, the various meanings in human life. Such integration and sustenance would unify a human life in important ways, and perhaps even add to its resilience in the face of obstacles and failures.

If a meaning of human life depends on a divine agent's will that is normative for humans, we face a question about the relevance of God's will. As suggested, we may think of the term "God" as a maximally exalted title for a being who is worthy of worship and hence morally perfect. Being thus perfect, God would want what is best, all things considered, for all agents, even enemies of God, and God's affections, particularly God's compassion, would follow suit. God would be perfectly compassionate in a way that seeks the redemption of all humans in reconciliation to God in *koinonia*. This sets a high standard for God, but we should expect that kind of standard for a God worthy of worship.

If God wants what is best for humans, all things considered, we do well to consider the following result by Blaise Pascal, noted previously: "God wants to motivate the will more than the mind. Absolute clarity would be more use to the mind and would not help the will. Humble their pride" (1662, sec. 234; cf. Moser 2018a). God would want to move human wills toward sympathetic cooperation with God's perfect will, to reconcile humans to God in *koinonia*. This would include a challenge to human pride, or presumed self-sufficiency, because God's perfect will would have moral priority over human wills and seek to be convicting and corrective toward them. God would want to move human wills in a manner that does not coerce them and thereby extinguish human agency. The divine redemption of human persons would fail if it destroyed the persons needing redemption by removing their volitional agency. So, God would seek to woo people by self-manifesting divine love without coercion. The aim would be to encourage human wills to yield to, and sympathetically cooperate with, God's perfect will in the God relationship, for the good of humans.

John's Gospel identifies an important role for a human will relative to God's will: "Anyone who resolves [= wills] to do the will of God will know whether the teaching is from God or whether I [Jesus] am speaking on my own" (John 7:17). Resolving to do the will of God goes beyond reflection on God's will. It includes an exercise of the human will to cooperate with God's will, in a manner that involves obedient action. Thinking about God's will need not include, or even lead to, obeying God's will or even resolving to obey God's will. In fact, a person can think about God's will but hate it and resolutely disobey it. In that case, one will be, in effect, an enemy of God, and one then will not be reconciled to God (at the time of being an enemy). Such a volitional problem would be central to God's dealings with humans, because God would want to include all humans in a relationship of sympathetic cooperation with the divine will, for their own good.

God would pursue humans in various ways (before humans pursued God) to offer them reconciliation to God as the center of a renewed life. We have no reason to acknowledge a narrowly singular way for God to pursue humans throughout history; nor should we expect one, given significant human differences across time and cultures. We do have, however, some striking cases that arguably include God's pursuit of humans. Perhaps the most striking is the life of Jesus. Our best evidence indicates that Jesus regarded his life as a call from God to humans to receive the good news of God's offer of reconciliation in the God relationship (see, for a sample, Mark 1:14–15, Luke 11:20, Mark 14:22–24, Luke 15:3–7). This call includes a call to faith, including trust, in God, and it extends to anyone who would sincerely listen to God, regardless of social or religious affiliation. It is thus the kind of call one would expect of a God who perfectly loves all people, and not just a select group.

A distinctive feature of the call from the life of Jesus is its emphasis on God's offer of forgiveness to humans. In one context, Jesus asked the following: "Which is easier, to say to the paralytic, 'Your sins are forgiven,' or to say, 'Stand up and take your mat and walk'? But so that you may know that the Son of Man has authority on earth to forgive sins – he said to the paralytic – 'I say to you, stand up, take your mat and go to your home'" (Mark 2:9–11). Jesus used the example of physical healing to lend credibility to what he deemed more important: his authority from God to offer forgiveness to humans for the sake of their being reconciled to God in *koinonia*.

As Chapter 3 noted, Jesus presented himself as a physician for human problems, in relation to God, that concern sin and righteousness: "Jesus . . . said to them, 'Those who are well have no need of a physician, but those who are sick; I have come to call not the righteous but sinners'" (Mark 2:17). He offered a divine relational cure for spiritual illness, and it includes forgiveness from God. He did not think that some humans are actually righteous on their own. Instead, he acknowledged that some humans presume to be self-sufficiently righteous and hence in no need of God's cure. One might say that, in his perspective, they are in serious denial.

The Gospel of Luke offers a concluding summary by Jesus that puts forgiveness at the center of his mission: "[Jesus] said to them, 'Thus it is written, that the Messiah is to suffer and to rise from the dead on the third day, and that repentance and forgiveness of sins is to be proclaimed in his name to all nations'" (Luke 24:46–47).

Luke portrays Jesus as having come to offer God's forgiveness to humans, even at the cost of his own life. So,
Luke is aware that people do not universally receive the
forgiveness on offer, and that some people oppose the
offer vigorously and even violently. He represents Jesus
as commenting thus: "I tell you, her sins, which were
many, have been forgiven; hence she has shown great
love. But the one to whom little is forgiven, loves little"
(Luke 7:47). "The one to whom little is forgiven" is the
one who does not receive the forgiveness on offer and
perhaps even denies his or her need of it. So, the divine
offer of forgiveness can generate conflict and controversy
among humans. (For discussion, see Mackintosh 1927,
pp. 77–102, Fiddes 1989, pp. 171–89.)

The divine offer of forgiveness would not be an end in
itself. It would be an intended means to the reconciliation
of humans to God and to other humans in a relationship
of *koinonia*. God would offer reconciliation, including forgiveness, to humans, who may or may not receive what
is being offered. Forgiveness, at its core, is a release from
condemnation, hostility, and ill will from the one who forgives. When forgiveness is received, the person forgiven is
ideally released from fear of condemnation, hostility, and
ill will from the one who forgives. This kind of release can
enhance the prospect of reconciliation, because it removes
the fear that often hinders reconciliation.

Divine reconciliation would include interpersonal relationships that are peaceful, friendly, and good for the
person reconciled to God and to other persons. Ideally,
it would remove enmity, avoidance, and resistance from
humans in relating to God and to other humans. It would
replace those obstacles with sympathetic and harmonious cooperation with God by the reconciled humans. God
would seek and empower a good, peaceful community of
all cooperative persons. So, reconciliation to God, as one
whose goodness is authoritative for all persons, would be a
priority for God relative to humans. As a priority, it would

figure centrally in the divine effort to restore humans to a cooperative relationship with God in *koinonia*.

Humans would be able to opt out of divine forgiveness and reconciliation, as we see from the resolute opponents of Jesus in the New Testament. This would amount to choosing death over life, if life is sustained by God. The human will, then, would be crucial to the human reception of divine forgiveness and reconciliation, even if God's will always favors this reception. So, this reception is not a matter of divine coercion. It depends on the cooperation of humans with God's will, and such cooperation depends on the human experience of God's will.

5. EXPERIENCING GOD'S WILL

The human recognition of God or God's will in experience would not be a casual, spectator sport. God would be too morally profound and serious for that kind of superficiality. Humans would need to discern the reality of God or God's will in their experience, with due attentiveness, given God's purpose of reconciliation for humans. God's will would include a divine purpose of reconciliation, and humans would need to discern this purpose in their experience. So, they would need to avoid being "out of focus" with God's reality and will. Herbert H. Farmer has remarked: "Many questions are answered wrongly, not because the evidence is contradictory or inadequate, but because the mind through its fundamental dispositions and presuppositions is out of focus with the only kind of evidence which is really available" (1927, Preface). Humans can overlook the reality of God's will in their experience if they are out of focus with it, say, in a situation where they focus only on their own will and its selfish tendencies. They thus may settle for agnosticism or atheism, and deny any role to God in reality or in life's meaning.

God's morally perfect will would not be fully continuous with an imperfect human will. In experiencing God's will, with due attention, an imperfect human would notice a fracture in conscience at some point between his or her own will and God's will. One's own will thus would not line up fully with God's perfect will. God's will would involve a challenge and perhaps even a conviction in human conscience, to conform to God's will, and this challenge at some point would manifest the shortcoming of an imperfect human will relative to God's perfect will. A human can experience such a challenge in conscience, if only by a *de re* presentation of God's will, without acknowledging or recognizing that it is a challenge *from God*. The character of God's will could manifest the falling short of a human will, via a sharp contrast. One might attribute this to such an influence as one's parents, one's peers, or even one's reflective self. So, the role of God in conscience would not bind a person to acknowledge God through coercion. Alternative interpretations are typically live options for a person, and many people favor an alternative independent of acknowledging God.

Why should one suppose that there is a divine will at all? (Chapter 5 returns to this question, and offers an answer.) The question is appropriate, but it may be that one should *not* acknowledge a divine will, if one lacks the needed evidence. We would need, in any case, to discern God's reality via God's will and God's moral character revealed in that will. We could not apprehend God as if God were a scientific object or a household object. Specifically, we could not approach God as if the attitude of the inquirers, including our own attitude, did not matter, because God would have a redemptive aim for humans even in their inquiring about and knowing God. As suggested, God would intend that humans have an attitude of sympathetic cooperation toward God, for the sake of their redemption in reconciliation to God. This lesson, as Chapter 2 noted, figures in the ethics for inquiry about God.

Just as God could hide God's reality and will from a person, perhaps owing to that person's uncooperative attitude toward God, so also God could hide the meaning of human life, anchored in God's will. The elusive meaning would be the purpose of God for human life found in God's will, particularly in sympathetic cooperation with God's will. At the heart of this purpose or meaning would be the God relationship itself, because this relationship would be the divinely appointed focus of human redemption as reconciliation with God. In addition, the God relationship would be the means of suitable appropriation and discernment of God's purpose for human life, because that relationship would give one direct awareness of the purpose. People do not usually think of the meaning of human life in terms of an interpersonal relationship (with God), but a perfectly good God would have an authoritative say in this direction, in keeping with God's perfect moral character.

As Chapter 3 suggested, given God's unique character and its evidential significance, God would seek for one to know God directly, or person-to-person, at least at times. Otherwise, one would lack direct acquaintance or encounter with God's unique moral character, which can set an epistemic standard for genuine knowledge of God. We humans have a hard time, and even resist, depending on or holding on to God and God's will only or even primarily. We find substitutes more convenient, if only because they are less challenging to us. In presenting us with a new standard in God's moral character, direct interaction with God can upset our lives, including our personal agendas, our peer networks, and our self-indulgent ways. So, we tend to neglect, avoid, and shy away from direct interaction with God, including any intentional power in our experience that offers such interaction. (For discussion, in connection with New Testament interpretation, see Crump 2013.)

A familiar alternative to direct interaction with God occurs in natural theology that relies on versions of the traditional arguments for God's existence: including ontological, cosmological, design, fine-tuning, and moral arguments. As suggested, people using those arguments

typically assume that direct interaction with God is cognitively inadequate, at least for many people, and that
therefore an argument from natural theology is needed.
The arguments offered are rarely compelling for people
without an antecedent commitment to God's existence,
and, bracketing ontological arguments, the arguments fail
to yield a God who is worthy of worship and hence self-
sufficiently morally perfect. The latter defect raises the difficult question of how one reasonably can proceed further,
to a God worthy of worship. If one appeals at some point to
direct experience of such a God, the question will arise as
to whether the arguments of natural theology then become
dispensable. If direct experience is ultimately doing the
work for needed access to God, the arguments in question will seem superfluous, especially if they fail to yield a
God worthy of worship. (For detailed argument, see Moser
2010, pp. 142–84, 2013, pp. 120–37.)

Another common alternative to direct interaction with
God emerges from religious rituals of various sorts. I can
attend religious services every week or even every day and
participate in all of the rituals offered, such as a communion ceremony, a candlelight event, or a sacred procession.
Even so, I could fail to have a direct experience of God, and
even acknowledge this failure. I might come to prefer the
religious rituals to a direct experience of God, because the
rituals do not require me to change my life toward cooperating with God's will. I could use the rituals to replace
the hard redemptive work of cooperating with God's will,
including the demand to forgive and love others, even my
enemies. In addition, I could use the rituals to divert my
attention from a direct interaction or encounter with God.
This may be a misuse of the rituals, but many people have
confessed to such a misuse.

We have a kind of control over arguments and rituals
that we would not have over God's will. I cannot control
what God wills, including when God wills to offer divine
self-manifesting to a person, although I can do things that

would obstruct my discernment of God's will and self-manifesting. I can divert my attention from God, perhaps out of either fear of divine challenge to me or a desire to maintain control for myself. The resulting lack of direct interaction with God would entail a lack of direct evidence of both God and meaning from God. We see an example in the Jewish Bible of human avoidance of God in the demand for a human king as an alternative to God as king (see 1 Sam. 8:1–22).

In diverting my attention from God, I would look away from any experience in my conscience of my will's being challenged by God. The latter experience would include an event of attention-attraction from God that makes me aware of an alternative to my will, that is, an alternative in God's perfect will. For instance, I could be convicted (by God) in conscience to forgive and to love my enemies, including one who is currently harming me. I could not give this experience of attention-attraction and conviction to others, but I could report it to others. The key point, however, is that I would need to decide how to respond to the volitional challenge at hand: I could ignore it, reject it, or yield to it.

I could live in sympathetic cooperation with the divine will in question, and, in doing so, I myself could become indirect evidence for others of God's unique will. This would be human personifying evidence of God, owing to God's will being reflected, if imperfectly, in a cooperative human life (see Moser 2010, pp. 209–30). A distinctive feature of God's will would be its demand for forgiveness and love of one's enemies, even toward those who are now harming one. A god who failed to make this demand would fall short of moral perfection and hence worthiness of worship. We have, then, a way to identify false gods. We also would have a way to let God be supremely authoritative for our lives, in our yielding to the divine will self-manifested to us.

One's experience of God's will in conscience should prompt a question: What does this mean? (See Acts 2:12.)

Perhaps such an experience would be dismissed by many, just as the distinctive experience of Acts 2 was disregarded by some people in its original setting. Some people, however, would discern something important in an experience of God's will in conscience, and make themselves available to God by way of a cooperative response. So, they might ask: What is this? A new teaching? (See Mark 1:27.) An informative answer could bring illumination to one's experience by making some sense of it. (Chapter 5 returns to the matter of explanation in a defense of faith in God.)

In making themselves cooperatively available to God, people would be willing to be apprehended and known by God, and not just to apprehend and know God (see Gal. 4:9, 1 Cor. 8:3). They would defer to God by allowing God to have authority over themselves and their lives. They would sincerely resolve to let God alone be supremely authoritative over who they are and what they do. Such resolve would be irreducible to factual knowledge (that something is the case), because it would put one in a relation of volitional submission toward God. One's sincere resolve to submit to God may be imperfect, but it would not be empty; it would have definite implications for how one responds to God. We need to link such resolve to faith in God and meaning from God.

6. FAITH AND FELT MEANING

People do not ordinarily acknowledge that one's apprehending meaning from God for human life depends on one's having faith in God. Perhaps this fact results from widespread misunderstanding of what faith in God is. One common misunderstanding is that faith in God is the same as belief that God exists. As Chapter 2 suggested, one can believe that God exists, but refrain from trusting God at all and hence from having faith in God. Because faith in God requires trust in God, belief that God exists falls short of faith in God. Faith in God has a directness toward God that removes the need for substitutes for God. It is prompted, in genuine faith, by a direct acquaintance with God's will, to which one responds with a resolve (if only *de re*) to trust and cooperate with God. Faith in God, then, is a response to an experience of God, perhaps in conscience, and therefore it is irreducible to wishful thinking or guesswork about God. (For details, see Chapter 2, and Moser 2010, pp. 90–125, 2013, pp. 115–20, 144–59.)

Faith in God is anchored in experiential evidence, because it is a response to a direct experience of God and God's will. A direct experience of God that is pertinent to life's meaning would be a direct experience of God's will, and a direct experience of God's will that is pertinent to life's meaning would be a direct experience of God. Meaning for human life requires purpose for human life, and God's purpose for human life would be in God's perfect will. God would be the ultimate source of God's purpose, and this purpose would cohere with God's morally perfect character, a character worthy of worship that self-manifests for the sake of redeeming humans. God's purpose would include the realization of the God relationship among humans for the sake of human reconciliation to God in *koinonia*.

Faith in God would be the suitable avenue to God's purpose or meaning, because faith in God would be positively responsive and sympathetic toward God in a way that makes one available to understand God's compassionate redemptive purpose to some extent. Faith in God excludes the kind of volitional or affective resistance to God that impedes one's understanding of God's purpose or meaning. The understanding and meaning in question would be *felt*, affective understanding and meaning, not merely intellectual understanding and meaning. They thus would depend on the feelings or affections of an agent. God's redemptive purpose would not be merely intellectual, but would be a felt purpose, given its anchor in the kind of *agapē* that includes perfect compassion as sympathy, even toward enemies. The same holds for God's will: It would be affective owing to its inclusion of felt compassion, and not just a notion of compassion. We no longer have God's will if we divorce it from felt compassion for others, because we then divorce it from perfect *agapē*.

God's purpose would be subtle, elusive, and affective in a way that calls for an affectively sympathetic response from humans if they are to understand it suitably, that is, in the manner intended by God. God would intend that humans have this kind of sympathetic response and could reasonably hide from humans in the absence of it, in order to preserve the redemptive value of God's *agapē*-centered purpose for human life. The intended response would include one's feeling compassion with God, or better, one's *sharing in* God's feeling of compassion in God's redemptive purpose. In the absence of such a response, humans will be left with vague glimmers at best of God's purpose, because they will not be available to understand suitably the kind of purpose God would offer. Their understanding might then be intellectual, but that would fall short of what God intends in affective and volitional understanding for the sake of compassionate *agapē* in relationships, including the God relationship.

God's purpose would encompass affective enemy-love, including enemy-compassion, as a central part of its affective content. So, a human failure to apprehend such love and compassion affectively would inhibit suitable understanding of them and the corresponding divine purpose. It also would obstruct one's knowing God, whose character includes perfect compassion toward all other agents. As the writer of 1 John states: "Whoever does not love does not know God, for God is love" (1 John 4:8). I take this to imply that whoever does not receive and exemplify God's kind of love does not know God, because God is inherently loving and is known in one's exemplifying divine love. The love in question is affective and volitional, not just intellectual, because it is compassionate in seeking the good of others.

Without receiving God's kind of affective compassion (knowingly or unknowingly), even for enemies, humans will lack a source and a model for divine felt compassion. It is doubtful that humans can create it by themselves in a manner that captures what would be God's perfect compassion. Here, again, we should consider the following from the writer of 1 John: "love is from God" (1 John 4:7). It is doubtful that humans on their own can produce and sustain the kind of affective volitional love that would be characteristic of God, even if they can share in that love. We see a kind of enemy-love in memorable cases where a person forgives with compassion another person who has intentionally brought great harm to the former person. These are arguably cases of sharing in God's unique love, even if one is unaware of doing so. When humans take credit for such love, they exaggerate what they produce on their own and take the risk of dishonoring the divine source of this love.

We should highlight the idea of understanding God's purpose or meaning of human life *to some extent*. One can have faith in God that includes volitional and affective sympathy with God's will, but still have meaning for human life from God that is incomplete and puzzling. Gaps in God's revealed will would leave humans with incomplete meaning and understanding regarding human life. The book of Job illustrates this lesson: Job is left with unanswered questions about God's purposes in allowing evil and in creating the world. We overreach if we now expect a perfectly complete system of meaning for human life from God, especially a complete theodicy that explains all of God's purposes in allowing evil in human life. If the meaning of life for humans depends on God's redemptive purpose for human life, and God has not revealed the latter purpose fully to humans, we will not fully comprehend the meaning of human life. We evidently are now in a situation of possessing incomplete meaning, for better or worse. This should be no surprise, if only because we humans seem not to be in a position now to understand God's redemptive purpose fully.

The incompleteness of the meaning we apprehend does not challenge the reality or the value of that meaning. It does call, however, for modesty regarding how much we understand about the meaning of human life. We might come to know that God wants us to learn to love others as God loves others in the God relationship, but this lesson can leave unanswered many of our questions about God's purposes in redemption. In this regard, humans now live with fragmentary meaning at best. Perhaps this limitation helps to save us from unbridled arrogance about our explanatory resources in connection with life's meaning. Perhaps, too, this is part of God's purpose for human life, given the relational harm done by human arrogance.

It is doubtful that our having an incomplete understanding of the meaning of life would interfere with God's purpose to have us learn to love others as God does in the God relationship. We still could grow in the kind of affective and volitional love characteristic of a God worthy of worship. Such love does not require that we fully understand God's purpose for human life. As one sympathetically cooperates with divine love more deeply, however, one could understand God's redemptive purpose more deeply.

If we apprehend meaning for human life from God by sympathetic faith in God, we will face considerable variability in human perception of the meaning of life. We have similar variability in human recognition of the reality of God; hence the existence of theists, atheists, and agnostics. Just as the reality of God appears to be hidden from some people, so also does the meaning from God for human life. (We may say the same for grounded hope in lasting meaning for human life.) So, we should not expect to have a cogent argument for the meaning of human life that convinces all inquirers, just as we should not expect to have such an argument for God's reality that is, or should be, acknowledged by all inquirers.

Many agnostics about divine meaning for human life, like many agnostics about God's existence, can reasonably be agnostics, given their (available) evidence. In that case, if I am a theist, I should not expect to silence all dissenters with an argument. The relevant evidence (involving relevant experience) is too variable among persons for such an expectation. Perhaps this fact will discourage us from misplaced arrogance about the scope of our evidence for God and the meaning of human life. Perhaps it also is part of God's purpose for cognitive modesty in human life, especially for those who presume to have knowledge of God or even good evidence of God's reality and character. In any case, ambitious apologetic purposes can lead one to be overconfident, if not dogmatic, about the reach and the cogency of the evidence for God's reality. (Chapter 5 returns to this matter.)

Perhaps the meaning from God for human life has normative value, in that it would be good, all things considered, for all people to embrace. Even if it has such value, it does not follow that all people are in an evidential or psychological position to embrace that meaning now. Many people may not be prepared now to embrace the meaning from God, for one reason or another. This consideration, however, does not challenge the normative value of meaning from God. Instead, it challenges a claim that all people are now motivated, or otherwise ready, to recognize such meaning. So, God may hide such meaning from some people, to protect its value for a future redemptive purpose, say, by avoiding their detesting, trivializing, or finally rejecting it now.

God would reveal meaning for life to humans in ways that suit God's redemptive purposes, and God would know that some people are not ready now to satisfy, or even to take seriously, those purposes. God thus would be able to delay self-manifesting and the corresponding revelation of divine meaning for life until an opportune time for such people. It does not follow, however, that we have a complete account of the purposes for divine hiding at times. As suggested, I doubt that a complete account is now available to us (see Chapter 3, and Moser 2008, pp. 105–13, 140–43, 2010, pp. 254–62). Proponents of theism sometimes overreach by neglecting the kinds of variability just outlined, and that makes their theism appear to depend on special pleading in a way that disregards evidence. Such neglect also can repel people from theism as a well-founded option. (Chapter 5 returns to this idea in connection with a defense of faith in God.)

7. MEANING IN DEATH

If God wants to build a good community of *koinonia* among humans for their redemption, a serious obstacle emerges: death. Death interrupts such a community and development toward it. Would a redemptive God who seeks to give meaning to human life allow for such an obstacle? If so, why? These questions confront any account of meaning for human life from God, and we do not have complete answers. As suggested, we humans should not expect to have now a complete understanding of God's purposes in allowing the difficulties of human life. If the book of Job is right, God has not seen fit to reveal all of those purposes, and we have no reason to think that we can identify them on our own. So, cognitive modesty is in order, as is usual with explanations regarding God's ways toward human life.

We sometimes portray a divine redemption of humans as a continuous development from the life we now have: It is more of the same, but better. This, however, may be an uncritical portrayal. Perhaps divine redemption is not, at center, a development from this life, but is instead a break from it, with a new beginning. Some of the New Testament writers suggest as much, and we should consider this possibility. Paul remarks: "If anyone is in Christ, there is a new creation: everything old has passed away; see, everything has become new" (2 Cor. 5:17). In John's Gospel, Jesus suggests that redemption in God's kingdom is a matter of being "born again, from above" (John 3:3, 7). In this portrait of divine redemption, we have something other than a continuous development from the life we now live. We have a new beginning, a new "creation." The theme of new creation looms large in the New Testament story of divine redemption (see Minear 1994 and Hubbard 2002), and it bears on the problem of death and meaning for humans.

We can understand death in the New Testament in terms of its symbolic value: as signifying the need for a new beginning with God as supremely authoritative. This new beginning is not life as usual, because it includes a new center of authority, power, wisdom, and meaning: namely, God (see Harrisville 2006, pp. 98–102). Even our knowing other people becomes new, in Paul's thought. He remarks: "From now on, therefore, we regard no one from a human point of view; even though we once knew Christ from a human point of view, we know him no longer in that way" (2 Cor. 5:16; see also Martyn 1967/1997, Brown 1995). Paul thought of this new way of knowing as guided by what God has done for humans in the death of Christ; as suggested: "God proves his love for us in that while we still were sinners Christ died for us" (Rom. 5:8). The death of Christ, as God's beloved Son, becomes the demonstration of God's self-giving love for humans. It manifests that God gives God's very best to call humans out of alienation from God into reconciliation with God.

In Paul's good news, God raises Christ from death, thereby validating Christ's self-giving love on behalf of God for humans. So, God's manifesting self-giving love in the death of Christ is not made futile by death, because God overcomes death in the resurrection of Christ. This act of God can open the door to lasting meaning from God for human life, because death no longer would be a final threat. We humans cannot by ourselves supply lasting meaning, in contrast with temporary meaning, because we do not, and cannot, last by ourselves. Lasting meaning for us would require that we cooperate with, and share in, the intentional power of one who does last and can supply lasting meaning. Otherwise, the death of humans will be the end of meaning for humans (see Russell 1903 for candor here, along with misplaced edification).

Some humans claim to have no objection to being without lasting meaning for life, on the assumption that this life is enough. Others, however, hope for lasting life and lasting meaning from God. I suggest that we not lower the bar for desired meaning for life in advance of a search for lasting meaning (including lasting meaning from God) that is not only intellectual but also affective and volitional. Philosophers often assume that the search is simply intellectual, relative to the evidence one now has, but this assumption is too narrow. (Chapter 3 offered an analogous lesson regarding the evidence for God's reality.)

The search should be sincerely open to finding a meaningful life for humans that is lasting. In Matthew's Gospel, Jesus remarks: "Those who find their life will lose it, and those who lose their life for my sake will find it" (Matt. 10:39; cf. Luke 9:24). This claim seems enigmatic at best, but we can make sense of it if we relate it to the self-giving life of Jesus himself. The idea is: Those humans who seek to find a lasting meaningful life on their own terms and power will fail, owing to the impending demise of their lives; but those who rely on God, volitionally and affectively, for the meaning of their lives can enjoy lasting meaning for their lives, courtesy of God's power and purpose. The contrast is between a human life limited to human power and purposes and a human life that cooperates sympathetically with God's lasting power and purposes for human life. The merely human power and purposes will not last, but the divine power and purposes offer viable candidates for lasting meaning for human life.

Perhaps death is to serve as a wake-up call for humans who tend to overlook that the value, purpose, and meaning of human life are fragile and at risk. If human life has a final demise, its value, purpose, and meaning will go with it. Everything merely human will then be lost. Death may be a signal that something beyond human power is needed to avoid a final demise. Paul suggests as much in a remark already noted: "We have this treasure [of God's power and good news] in clay jars [subject to physical destruction], so that it may be made clear that this extraordinary power [of new, lasting life] belongs to God and does not come from us" (2 Cor. 4:7). Paul holds that only God's power can solve the human predicament of death and that this power must not be confused with human power. A lasting good life, in his perspective, cannot make do with human power, but must rest on God's unique intentional power.

Death may be the suggested signal even if some humans have no desire to avoid a final demise. This lack of desire is disconcerting if it bears on people generally. Even if one has no concern for lasting life in one's own case, one might consider that some other people do prefer lasting good life in a good community. It would be puzzling for one to desire that the lives of these other people also have a final demise. It seems more charitable and less grudging to endorse their desire for lasting life for themselves at least, even if one excludes oneself from such a desire. A lasting human life under the power and purpose of a morally perfect God seems to be a plausible candidate for a good life. We should not dismiss it as a bad thing, even if one thinks that the supporting evidence for its reality is thin.

In suggesting that death may be a wake-up call, I am suggesting that it could have existential value. It could prompt people to evaluate the direction of their lives and their options for redirecting their lives if appropriate. It thus could figure in the kind of moral overwhelming by God outlined in Chapter 2. The undertaking of such an evaluation is no small project. It may be hard work, and it may take a lifetime. Some people may not want to be bothered by it, but that omission could result in a missed opportunity that is important and meaningful for human life. I see no reason to exclude the opportunity in question.

The undertaking in question should not be merely intellectual, but should attend to affective and volitional considerations about inquirers in relation to God. The inquirers should be prepared to share in God's affective and volitional states. They should be open to feeling and willing what God feels and wills, as a way to be in a position to receive salient evidence of God's reality and will. Perhaps the best way to know God is to share in God's affections and will. That sharing also may be the best way to receive meaning for human life from God. Indeed, that may be the *locus* of meaning for human life from God, in one's sharing in God's affective and volitional character, that is, in one's sharing in the God relationship.

8. CONCLUSION

Humans typically fail to love others as God would love others, and this failure would alienate them from God. If God's compassionate love is inherent to, and characteristic of, who God is, then one's being out of step with it will entail one's being out of step with God. Humans often are out of step with God in that regard, as human interactions with other humans show. Our affective and volitional set strays from what would be God's moral character, and this would obstruct our receiving good things from God, such as evidence, wisdom, purpose, and meaning. A practical issue for humans becomes: Are we willing to redirect our affections and wills toward God's?

The issue has us face this question: Are we willing to forgive and love with compassion toward our enemies, even enemies now harmful to us, in the way that God would? The track record of humans is not encouraging on this front. We are familiar with harmful conflicts with others that seem not to go away. It is rare when such conflicts end in forgiveness and reconciliation. When they do end thus, they often end in stories of exceptional, rather than normal, human behavior.

The problem is not merely intellectual, and hence is not solved just by thinking harder or more clearly. It concerns how we feel and will toward others, including our enemies. We often refrain from willing what is best for them, and we sometimes will that they suffer condemnation, often on the assumption that they deserve it. In addition, we often harbor destructive feelings toward our enemies and do nothing to counter those feelings. Compassion is not among those feelings, but animosity often is. We end up, then, out of step with what God would will and feel toward the people in question. We thus become out of step with God, at odds with the God relationship.

Is there a solution in our sympathetically cooperating with God, in the divine purpose for redemption? Evidence from my experience suggests an affirmative answer, but I cannot presume that all others have the same evidence. So, I have not assumed that God's existence or redemptive power is indicated by the experience or evidence of all others. I have talked of what God *would* do or *would* be like, to avoid begging key questions. I can recommend, however, that inquirers make the effort to inquire responsibly about God, in keeping with the ethics for inquiry about God, and thereby put themselves in a position to receive salient evidence and meaning from God. That effort could change the direction of a person's life, for the better, if the relevant evidence and meaning are found. In that case, lasting meaning will eclipse despair, and one's will and affections will be renewed by the unique, self-manifested character of God. Life then could begin again, for the better, with new purpose and meaning. The relationship theism of this book nods in this direction. We turn, finally, to the place of *koinonia* and defense in such theism.

5

~

The God Relationship, *Koinonia*, and Defense

Genuine faith in God, according to Chapter 2, is sympathetically cooperative with God in a God relationship that
makes some humans co-workers with God. Faith in God
thus includes a kind of fellowship or companionship as *koinonia* with God. This chapter explores the role of companionship as *koinonia* in the God relationship and identifies
the bearing of this role on a defense of faith in a redemptive
God who self-manifests to humans. This effort will illuminate an important feature of responsible inquiry about God
and put the defense of faith in God in a new perspective. It
suggests that the ethics of companionship may bear on the
ethics for inquiry about God.

1. VIRTUES AND VOLITIONS

A neglected kind of virtue calls for special attention in an
understanding of faith in God: *interpersonal reciprocating
virtue*, or "reciprocating virtue," for short. A virtue can be
good-conferring, even truth-supplying in a worthwhile
manner, but fail to include one person's intentionally giving something good to another person. In contrast, reciprocating virtues require one person's intentionally giving
something good to another person, and they require intentional reciprocation, mutuality, or interchange in such giving between persons. We shall clarify the importance of one

such virtue for human faith in God, because philosophers and theologians have neglected its importance.

A reciprocating virtue akin to human companionship (properly understood) is crucial to human faith in God, and it yields a distinctive *agonic*, or struggle-oriented, character for such faith. This view is implicit in the Gospel of John (see John 15:12–17), but philosophers and theologians have not given it due attention. We have identified the central role of *interpersonal interaction* of a direct, second-person sort. Such interpersonality, as Chapter 1 noted, is *de re*, or more accurately *de te* (from the Latin "*tu*" = "you"), involving the direct acquaintance, encounter, or meeting of one personal agent with another personal agent in the second person, beyond any *de dicto* (conceptual or notional) relation involving concepts or ideas (at least of a non-ostensive sort). We will identify a key role for interpersonal *companionship* and *struggle* for the shared good in the relevant faith relationship. We shall see that communion with God figures centrally in the kind of companionship to be portrayed. The result will be an existentially and morally robust approach to faith in God and knowledge of God, in contrast to a primarily intellectual or emotional approach.

Some virtues, including some intellectual virtues, fail to be personally reciprocating or interpersonal at all. Consider either a moral virtue of self-control in action or an intellectual virtue of belief compliance with one's evidence. Neither such virtue requires responsiveness between persons or any intentional interaction between persons. I can manifest a moral virtue of self-control but sustain no reciprocity in intentional action with another person. The same holds for my intellectual virtue of belief compliance with my evidence. It does not require interaction with another person; I could have this virtue even if no other person existed. Such non-interpersonal virtues are thus thin in comparison with reciprocating virtues, with regard to interpersonal exchange.

Reciprocating virtues are more demanding interpersonally than simple, non-interpersonal virtues, because they are, by nature, mutually responsive between persons. They demand the interpersonal giving of something good to another person, but non-interpersonal virtues do not. We will consider the reciprocating virtue known as unmerited *companionship*. This virtue exceeds one's *offering* companionship to another person, because actual companionship is reciprocal between persons and is thus no mere offer from a person. So, actual companionship is not just an offer of companionship. It includes an interpersonal mutuality or interchange of intended good between persons.

Unmerited companionship exemplifies mutual self-giving between willing persons for the unmerited good of the people involved. We may call this *gracious companionship*. Some philosophers, including Aristotle, have suggested that a companion must be worthy of companionship, but I see no reason to endorse that demanding line. Instead, I shall focus on gracious companionship that does not require companions to be worthy of companionship. This focus allows companionship to be an *unmerited* gift, and hence allows for a broad pool of candidates for companions, including imperfect humans as companions of a God who is perfectly gracious. It also accommodates the etymology (from classical Latin) of "companion" as "one who breaks bread with another." One need not be worthy to eat with another person, in the typical case.

I have mentioned, as a key feature of gracious companionship, "mutual self-giving between willing persons for the unmerited good of the people involved." Such companionship is freely given and cooperatively received by some agents; it is not coerced. I cannot force another person to be my companion in this sense, against that person's will: the other person must be willing to cooperate. The use of force would interfere with the free exercise of that person's will in participating in the companionship. It would preclude the person's being a genuine agent with respect to participating in the companionship. This force would undermine the freely given mutuality or interchange needed for a genuine companionship. We can clarify this point in connection with a redemptive God who would seek a distinctive kind of companionship with humans.

Philosophers of religion and theologians have not given due consideration to the interpersonal virtue of unmerited companionship from God, and thereby from humans, as central to the divine redemption of humans. This virtue plays a role in various narratives in the Jewish Bible and the New Testament (see, for instance, Exod. 33:11, Isa. 41:8, 2 Chron. 20:7, Mark 2:19, John 15:14–15, Jas. 2:23). The neglect in question has led to widespread misunderstanding regarding what would be God's key purpose (and the corresponding evidence thereof) in the redemption of humans. A central part of God's redemptive aim would be for humans freely to appropriate and to manifest the power of divine companionship, even toward their enemies.

The previous chapters have considered a God who is worthy of worship (including full, unqualified adherence) and hence is self-sufficiently morally perfect, altogether free of any moral defect or inadequacy. They use the term "God" as a perfectionist title that connotes such a being, even if it does not denote, or refer to, an actual being. This kind of God would have perfect love toward all people, even enemies of God, and therefore would seek what is morally and spiritually best for all other persons. Anything less would leave us with a god who is morally imperfect and therefore unworthy of worship and of the normative title "God."

The perfectionist title "God" does not allow for mere moral goodness in a viable candidate: it requires perfect moral goodness, and this includes perfect goodness toward all other agents, including God's enemies. So, the list of viable candidates for this title quickly becomes short. Some people hold that the list is empty, but this seems premature. We should ask why a morally perfect God would seek companionship with humans. A general answer is: In order to flourish lastingly, humans need to be interactively sustained and empowered by God over time in a manner that preserves human freedom and cooperation with God. Companionship from and with God would provide for this need via God's life-giving power, as no alternative would. The power of divine companionship could supply lastingly good life for cooperative humans, and God, as perfectly loving, would desire and seek such life, even if the process is long and difficult.

2. REDEMPTIVE *KOINONIA*

Being morally perfect, God would seek what is morally and spiritually best for people, in keeping with God's being morally good without defect. This goal would include our freely being acquainted with and participating in God's self-manifested moral character, in cooperation with God. Such cooperative acquaintance and participation would have a basis in gracious companionship from God, including God's self-manifesting the divine moral character to humans willing to cooperate with God. Direct acquaintance with God's moral character could anchor human companionship with God in a salient experience (of divine moral perfection, including divine *agapē*) and thereby contrast such companionship with mere wishful thinking or fabrication. Such acquaintance, as Chapter 3 explained, could supply humans with a distinctive kind of evidence of God's reality.

Humans would not have companionship with God just in virtue of being human or even just in virtue of being morally accountable agents. Given freedom of will, at least to some extent, humans could be alienated from (companionship with) God in virtue of their either ignoring or resisting God's will for humans. (For now we can bracket nonculpable ignorance of God's will, such as that arising from developmental immaturity or serious mental disability.)

Gracious companionship with God for alienated humans would include God's reconciling humans to God via inviting them to resolve to cooperate sympathetically with God in an ongoing good relationship. This would be a relationally curative effort anchored in divine grace, and it would enable humans to start anew in how they relate to God, without condemnation or despair.

Divine reconciling of humans would require God's forgiving humans, and hence releasing them from divine condemnation for their culpably neglecting or opposing God's status as worthy of worship, honor, and obedience. This forgiving would rest on God's unearned mercy toward humans, and not on human merit, at least for humans who fall short of perfectly obeying God. For such humans, their being reconciled to God would not be something they earn or merit. We should expect divine companionship with humans like us, in our moral imperfection, to require forgiveness, even in an ongoing manner. We also should expect it to bring a kind of peace with God, owing to new experience of sympathetic cooperation with God and freedom from condemnation and shame before God. (On the relevant kind of forgiveness, and human experience of it, see Mackintosh 1927.)

A morally perfect God – the only kind worthy of worship – would need to seek the reconciliation of alienated humans to God, at least humans potentially agreeable to it. This reconciliation would be a first step toward companionship with God, but God would seek, in addition, a lasting good relationship with humans, anchored in sympathetic cooperation. In doing so, God would seek to befriend such humans, for the sake of their good life in ongoing cooperation with God. Failure to seek such reconciliation and companionship would entail moral imperfection in a candidate for God, owing to a deficiency in moral goodness, and therefore would block this candidate from worthiness of worship and actually being God.

Given divine moral perfection, God's forgiving humans would not include condoning any human wrongdoing.

God would not lapse into moral imperfection, such as a corrupt moral character, for the sake of redeeming humans through forgiveness and reconciliation. That kind of lapse would disqualify one as the God worthy of worship and thereby as the divine source of human redemption. Given such a lapse, the kind of redemption and redemptive companionship in question would be lost as a real option for humans, because at most a morally inferior alternative would be available. A morally perfect God would need, then, to extend forgiveness, reconciliation, and companionship to wayward humans in a manner that preserves God's morally perfect status. In this respect, divine companionship with humans would be irreducible to what many people regard to be friendship. (See Mackintosh 1929, pp. 56–68.)

Being worthy of worship, God would need to emerge as perfectly just or righteous and as the perfect justifier of morally imperfect humans who are sympathetically cooperative with divine redemption (see Rom. 3:26). Being thus cooperative entails sincere human willingness to cooperate with God's perfect will. We should not, however, ascribe standards of justice to God that are at odds with God's perfectly gracious and merciful character. Otherwise, we risk portraying God as defective in grace and mercy toward others, and hence as unworthy of worship (on which see Moser 2018a). God, then, would exemplify a kind of justice or righteousness that fits with perfect grace and mercy toward all people. (This is part of Paul's main point in Romans 3–4.) Such justice would enable God to be worthy of worship, and hence above moral reproach in the redemption of humans by grace, given that God would meet the other standards for self-sufficient moral perfection.

In cooperatively receiving divine forgiveness, humans would be released from divine punishment, guilt, and shame for their culpable relational failures, in order to enter into redemptive companionship with God. Their cooperative reception of divine forgiveness, reconciliation, and companionship as an unearned gift would itself be part of human cooperation with the God who seeks the gracious redemption of humans. The need for human cooperation with God would allow humans to be potential co-creators of their relationship with God, rather than merely passive objects. Such cooperation, when realized freely, would enable human lives to be profoundly meaningful in virtue of having a deep participatory purpose: the purpose of sharing freely and sympathetically in God's redemptive life and power. Sincere human cooperation with this purpose could bring integrity, adventure, and depth to human lives, even lastingly. God, as worthy of worship, would underwrite and advance the participatory purpose in question by self-identifying with humans in their predicament.

The need for human faith, including trust, in God reflects the need for deep-seated human cooperation with God in the divine redemption of humans. Such faith, we have seen, will involve one's will and one's affections, including one's sympathy, in agreement with God. It will include the human cooperative receiving of God's self-manifestation, forgiveness, and authority, and therefore is not to be confused with either mere assent to a proposition or a wishful "leap in the dark." Belief that a claim is true can be merely wishful believing and can be motivationally superficial in one's life. Genuine faith in God, however, differs from such belief, because it is an affirmative response of sympathetic self-entrustment to the God who intervenes personally in one's experience with divine self-manifesting.

In sympathetically receiving divine self-manifesting, faith in God includes one's cooperatively receiving God's gracious companionship and *agapē* via one's self-entrustment to God. In that case, a human would be relationally justified or approved before God, and reconciled to God, via cooperatively receiving, in self-entrustment to God, divine authority and companionship. In thus receiving, a human would not initiate the companionship in question; instead, God, being the source of redemption, would initiate this for the benefit of humans. So, a human would find no basis for self-righteousness about companionship with God, even if the attitudes of some misguided religious people suggest otherwise.

Cooperative human receiving from God can entail an ongoing struggle of self-entrustment to God, given human moral difficulties in becoming companions of God. Such struggle in self-entrustment does not (attempt to) earn or merit divine approval, even if it requires sympathetic cooperation toward God's motives. Human struggling to receive the divine redemption on offer does not entail obligating God to supply that redemption on the basis of human merit. So, we can avoid any Pelagian approach to meriting redemption or approval by God. We also can allow that cooperative human receiving toward God need not be perfect, given human weaknesses of various sorts. One can be on the whole sympathetically cooperative with God's will even though one falters at times, say as a result of weakness of will. The main test is whether one's will is on the whole sympathetically cooperative with God's will presented to one.

The gracious companionship in question is *redemptive* companionship from God, and therefore is more demanding of humans than companionship as often understood. Many "companionships" have little, if anything, to do with the personal redemption of the companions involved. Sometimes they are just "companionships of convenience" or even partnerships in wrongdoing or crime. Redemptive companionship from God, however, would have a definite purpose that includes human companions of God in freely sharing, if imperfectly, in God's perfect moral character. Because God would perfectly love all other agents, in keeping with God's morally perfect character, humans in companionship with God would need to learn to love others similarly, even their enemies. This is no small task for typical humans, but we should expect morally imperfect humans to need to struggle to receive cooperatively a gift of companionship from a morally perfect God. Humans typically fall short of a divine character of moral perfection, and such a character would not come "naturally" to humans, if it comes at all.

Divine companionship would be an effective means of sharing God's moral character and redemptive power with humans who cooperate with God's will as they conform to God's moral character. Via the power of companionship, God would extend to humans (an offer of) human life in cooperation with God, and empower human lives accordingly, upon human cooperation with God. Uncoercive empowering by God would enable humans to share God's moral character in salient ways, not selfishly but for the good of all involved. This sharing of God's moral character with humans would come via something that involves humans as responsible agents, in terms of who they are and what they value. It would come via the human response (to a divine intervention) of self-entrustment to God. Such a response is at the core of human faith in God, but can be absent from belief that God exists.

Faith in God, as indicated, is not reducible to anything merely intellectual. Like companionship, the faith in question has an irreducible volitional component that involves an agent as a responsible self, in this case a self accountable to God and capable of self-entrustment to God. Such faith is at the center of human reciprocating toward what would be God's offer of redemptive companionship.

3. KOINONIA IN DIVINE AGAPĒ

Faith in God, I have suggested, requires a sympathetic response (to God) of self-entrustment to God, and God would take the initiative by offering redemptive companionship to humans. This offer would come in various forms, owing to what would be God's different ways of self-manifesting to people of different psychological temperaments, intellectual capacities, and social backgrounds.

It is doubtful that we can list all of the potential ways of God's self-manifesting to humans. Even so, we can identify some common features of the potential ways, given that the self-manifesting would represent the morally perfect character of a God worthy of worship.

Walter Burghardt has suggested that an encounter with God will leave a suitably cooperative person with identifiable features of experience.

(1) You will find yourself absorbed by a *living* presence, a divine activity more real than your physical surroundings. (2) You will be aware of a *holy* presence that fills you with awe and fear, the while it warms and draws you . . . (3) You will know an inexpressible *loneliness*; for in the presence of Love you will still be far from Love, agonizingly aware that to find yourself you must lose yourself . . . (4) Even with sorrow you will sense a profound *joy* . . . that refuses to be imprisoned, must burst forth to be shared with others. (1983, pp. 34–35; cf. Forsyth 1909, chap. 7)

This is no strict recipe of results, because some of these features of experience may be hindered or delayed in humans. In addition, the presence of holiness may be just God's righteous goodness that brings awe to suitably receptive humans.

God's moral perfection, as indicated, would require God's perfectly loving all other persons, and the New Testament endorses this requirement in various ways, for God and for humans who cooperate with God (see, for instance, Matt. 5:43–48, Luke 6:32–36, Rom. 12:9–10, 20–21, Col. 3:13). God's self-manifesting would include "the presence of [redemptive] Love," as suggested, but a human still could perceive his or her own inadequacy relative to this powerful *agapē*. This inadequacy would be an important antidote to misplaced human pride and self-righteousness relative to God's redemption of humans. It could counter the kind of religious pride that would undermine the efforts of a redemptive God.

Redemptive companionship toward others requires unselfish caring toward others and hence *agapē* toward others. Such *agapē* depends on God rather than mere humans as its ultimate base and sustainer. Mere humans are evidently morally too weak and conflicted to produce and sustain such *agapē* on their own in any consistent way, particularly toward harmful enemies. So, the author of 1 John links the human fulfilling of the divine love command to human faith in God's representative Son and to "abiding" in God (1 John 3:23–24).

It is one thing to offer companionship and care toward those who return the favor. It is quite another thing, and a rare thing, to offer the same to one's destructive enemies. The kind of *agapē* in question is not limited to those who repay the favor. It is incompatible with selfishness in companionship, because, as Chapter 3 noted, it requires self-sacrifice for the good of others. Mere humans are notorious for being selfish at times, especially in circumstances of fear and moral weakness. So, we have no straightforward example of a mere human who is free of selfishness. This is significant for any case regarding the divine basis of unselfish love.

Characterizing the "enabling power" of divine *agapē*, Alan Richardson remarks: "The power [of *agapē*] makes us able to be what we could not have been by our own efforts. 'The grace of the Lord Jesus Christ' has been an historical fact, attested again and again by men and women who have changed the course of history, and who have all asserted that it was not their own strength which enabled them to be what they became and to do what they did" (1966, p. 115). *Agapē*, we might say, is God's perfect, self-sacrificial love, and humans share in it, if imperfectly, when they cooperatively receive it and conform to it. This claim gains credibility when we consider that divine *agapē* requires a genuine offer of forgiveness and reconciliation to all offending agents, even to one's resolute enemies. Given merely human power, we lack the moral strength needed to sustain such a high-risk offer, at least consistently in actual practice. Humans thus are far from exemplary in forgiving their enemies, as our history of destructive strife and warfare shows.

Various New Testament writers affirm the divine base of *agapē*, and they are on the right track here. The writer of 1 John, as noted, affirms that "love [*agapē*] is from God" (1 John 4:7). The same writer adds that "we love because [God] first loved us" (1 John 4:19; cf. 1 John 4:10), thus suggesting that God's love is a causal precondition for unselfish human love. Paul proposes that *agapē* is a fruit of God's Spirit (Gal. 5:22), and hence not a merely human product. Likewise, the author of John's Gospel suggests that abiding in God's love is the means for humans to obey God's command to love others (John 15:9–12). Here, again, we confront the idea that *agapē* has its ultimate base in God, and not in mere humans. Given that redemptive companionship of the kind mentioned in John 15:14–15 requires *agapē*, the immediate lesson is that such companionship depends on God as its ultimate base (even if one's awareness of God is at best dim). In the absence of God, we humans would have no stable redemptive companionship, because we would have no stable unselfish *agapē*. (We shall return below to the topic of experiencing divine *agapē*.)

We have considered that a distinctive self-manifesting of divine *agapē* will occur among suitably cooperative humans in the manner suggested in Romans 5:5: "Hope [in God] does not disappoint us, because God's love [*agapē*] has been poured into our hearts through the Holy Spirit that has been given to us." Paul has in mind, as suggested, disappointment at least in an evidential or cognitive sense, and therefore is suggesting that humanly experienced *agapē*, inwardly as a source of motivation ("in our hearts"), is a salient evidential basis for hope and faith in God. When one cooperatively receives God's *agapē* inwardly, one receives distinctive evidence and thus a cognitive basis for one's hope and faith in God. A similar view emerges from the writer of 1 John, who identifies God as the ultimate base of *agapē* (as indicated), and remarks: "Everyone who loves is born of God and knows God" (1 John 4:8; cf. 1 John 3:14).

Humanly experienced perfect *agapē*, as a manifestation of God's moral character, would be an adequate basis for knowing God and thereby for faith in God (assuming that one's evidence is free of undefeated defeaters). This evidential basis, although widely neglected by philosophers and others, can save one from seeking refuge in either the evidential arbitrariness left by fideism or the highly suspect arguments offered by traditional natural theology. The divine self-manifesting in question, as Chapter 4 indicated, would not depend for conferring evidence of God's reality on speculative philosophical arguments of any sort.

In this book's perspective, God, as a causal agent, authenticates God's own reality and character for humans by self-manifesting God's unique character to them. As a self-manifesting agent, God can be self-evidencing and self-authenticating toward humans, in the manner noted in Chapter 3. The idea of divine self-authentication, as noted, figures in the biblical theme of *God's* confirming God's reality for humans, given that God inherently has a morally perfect character and cannot find anyone or anything else to serve this purpose of confirmation (see Gen. 22:16–17, Isa. 45:22–23, Heb. 6:13–14). God's own moral character, as self-manifested, would set the standard for adequate evidence for God's reality. So, nothing altogether subjective in humans or anything independent in them would need to set this standard, or, for that matter, could set this standard. This consideration can save belief in God from epistemic arbitrariness.

God, as suggested, would want the self-entrustment of a human agent to *God*, and not to a speculative philosophical argument. Donald Miller notes: "Our *ideas* grow wobbly under the weight of events and cannot hold up the structure of our faith when life tumbles in with too great force"

(1954, p. 29, italics added). This fits with the biblical theme that God, in self-manifesting and self-authenticating, is our cognitive foundation regarding God's reality (see Ps. 18:2, 31, 28:1, 31:3, Isa. 44:8; cf. 1 Cor. 2:9–13). As unique redeemer, *God*, in self-manifesting, would want to be one's evidential foundation for faith in God and for believing that God exists, and therefore would not want a philosophical argument or anything else to have this foundational role. This foundation would include divine *agapē*, and not just a report about it.

Emil Brunner has commented on redemptive fellowship and the place of reciprocity and *agapē* in human faith in God.

Fellowship with God is present only when the creature meets [God's] love with responding love, when the creature knows and appropriates his freely giving love. . . . God communicates himself in love: and this happens in the fullest sense only when his love is known in responding love. Unless this happening takes place, self-communication cannot consummate itself. . . . Because God's will is both will to Lordship and will to fellowship, he wills to have a creature face-to-face with himself, who in freedom gives back to him what he first gives to the creature. (1964, pp. 100, 101; cf. Brunner 1962, pp. 286–87)

The "responding" in question is the reciprocity of giving oneself, including the direction of one's will, in love back to the God who first intervenes in one's life with self-giving *agapē*. As a free agent, one can respond otherwise, with either rejection or indifference, which amounts to a kind of rejection. Human motives for rejection or indifference toward God are legion, and some of them stem from a preference for human autonomy that includes a desire not to have a universe governed by God (as noted previously, see, for example, Nagel 1997, p. 130). Whatever the motive, the rejection or indifference obstructs the kind of reciprocity under consideration and thereby blocks redemptive fellowship with God. It blocks fellowship, communion, and companionship in divine *agapē.*

Brunner's talk of "fellowship" with God fits with the idea of communion with God suggested in Chapter 2, namely: intimate cooperative engagement of a spiritual nature. It seems narrower, however, than the proposed idea of companionship with God, which requires ongoing cooperation with God, including in action over time. Bernard Häring has characterized God's communion with humans as "the free self-bestowal through which God wants to be with us, to share with us his own freedom to love, to understand and to respond" (1978, p. 107; cf. Baillie 1929, pp. 112–14, George 1953, pp. 238–45). John V. Taylor sums up divine communion with humans in terms of "the in-between-ness" of God's Spirit (1972, p. 17). The interpersonal, I–Thou component in such communion is irreducible to anything merely intellectual.

Communion between God and humans would entail interpersonal sharing of love in mutual responsiveness. Brunner's talk of "fellowship" with God evidently agrees with this sense of "communion" with God. The kind of communion in question would be vital for a relationally curative God in relating to humans in a redemptive way. Such communion would bring humans into direct interpersonal relationship with God in a manner that enables them to be personally transformed and guided by God. It would provide a context for formative communication and power from God for alienated humans in their redemption by God.

Communion with God could become communion *in companionship* with God if it has a basis in the ongoing sympathetic cooperation of a human with God, in action over time. This position accommodates the familiar view that companionship is diachronic rather than merely synchronic or instantaneous. It typically does not occur just at an instant but is instead episodic, occurring over time.

In this respect, companionship is an ongoing relationship, and not just an event.

A diachronic feature can hold for divine self-manifesting to humans and thus for foundational evidence for God's reality and character. Like companionship, the latter two can take time and hence involve a person through a span of time. One thus might think of God as redeeming a span of time in a human life as a person cooperates with God over time. A perfectly redemptive God would not be satisfied with redemption or faith for just a moment, when a human life overall extends beyond a particular moment. This fits with this book's emphasis on the importance of the God *relationship*, beyond isolated experiences, thoughts, feelings, or actions.

We should expect divine *agapē* to include an offer of redemptive companionship that is intended to be morally corrective over time for humans alienated from (companionship with) God. Symptoms of alienation from God can include, among other things, the following actions and attitudes listed by Paul: idolatry, hatred toward others, murder, adultery, and drunkenness (Gal 5:19–21; cf. Col. 3:5–9). In contrast, symptoms of companionship with God would include the fruit of God's empowering Spirit: for instance, love, joy, peace, patience, gentleness, and meekness (Gal 5:22–23; cf. Col. 3:12–15). Seeking redemptive companionship with humans, God would promote the latter fruit of God's Spirit, but oppose the former traits of alienation from God. In opposing those traits, God would seek to be morally corrective, or curative, of humans toward those things that obstruct a good, cooperative relationship with God. We can think of the aforementioned fruit of God's Spirit as yielding reciprocating virtues, courtesy of God's redemptive gift-giving to cooperative humans. The main gift resides in the giving of *God*, as a personal agent, to humans, in a relationship of sharing God's moral character traits with cooperative humans.

Neither the law of Moses nor an alternative moral law could supply humans with good life in the way that redemptive companionship with God could. Neither of those former options could forgive and justify humans before God as part of reconciling them to God in a curative relationship for them (see Gal. 3:21). Only a personal God capable of redemptive companionship with cooperative humans could supply such life in person-to-person reconciliation. Laws, rules, and commandments (whatever their role in morality) are not candidates for personal companionship, because they are not intentional agents and hence are not either persons or personal companions with anyone. The same is true of any special information, truth, or wisdom, however profound, religious, or theological.

Without denying the value of propositional truths, we should acknowledge that they do not constitute redemptive companionship of the kind to be expected of a God worthy of worship. Personal agency resists any reduction to propositional information, given that such agency calls for extra-propositional agents and their intentions, feelings, and actions. This kind of agency underlies *agapē* relationships of companionship, including the God relationship and its offer of reconciliation.

Regarding gracious companionship, reconciliation, and forgiveness, we should distinguish between (a) their being *offered* by God to humans and (b) their being cooperatively *received* by humans from God. God could offer these to all humans without any human cooperatively receiving them, because God would not coerce any human to receive them. We should expect God to offer these benefits in seeking the redemption of humans, but we betray a serious misunderstanding if we expect God to coerce their realization in humans. The latter expectation would ignore or misunderstand the role of genuine human agency in such reciprocating virtues as redemptive companionship and reconciliation. Morally responsible agency allows for human rejection of these reciprocating virtues, even if God recommends against this rejection and uncoercively works against it. God, then, could try to enter in to redemptive companionship with humans even when they choose not to reciprocate.

Many humans reject or ignore the reciprocating virtues in question, owing to their rejecting or ignoring a God who actively seeks the uncoerced redemption of humans. We can identify some common obstacles to human companionship with such a God.

4. OBSTACLES AND RESPONSES

The first common obstacle to human companionship with God stems indirectly from the fact that a redemptive God would be a companion on the move, engaged in uncoercive redemptive *action*. God's aim would be to bring about change in persons toward God's perfect moral character. God's perfect *agapē* thus would be on the move, actively seeking humans willing to cooperate in redemptive companionship (1 John 4:10; cf. Luke 19:10). Humans would need to follow suit if they are to be in sympathetic cooperation with God's redemptive *agapē* and companionship (see 1 John 3:18). They would need to participate in God's redemptive character, purpose, and action, and this would go beyond positive thoughts, beliefs, and feelings.

The writer of 1 John asks rhetorically: "How does God's love abide in anyone who has the world's goods and sees a brother or sister in need and yet refuses help?" (1 John 3:17) The answer: God's *agapē* does not abide in such a person, even if such a person allows it in intermittently. This lesson leads to the following practical standard for knowing God: "Whoever does not love does not know God, for God is love" (1 John 4:8). People who know God must actively cooperate, in their attitudes, feelings, and conduct toward others, with divine *agapē* in action for the sake of others. This perspective includes the same lesson for divine righteousness: "the one not doing righteousness is not of God"

(1 John 3:10, my literal translation). Knowing God, then, has a profound ethical component that includes doing God's righteousness and love for the sake of others. Such knowing is thus not purely intellectual, but is actively and morally robust.

By failing to cooperate actively with God's redemptive action, one can obstruct, at least for oneself, God's power of companionship *and* the corresponding salient evidence of God's reality. The writer of 1 John suggests this point: "Whoever says, 'I am in the light', while hating a brother or sister is still in the darkness. Whoever loves a brother or sister lives in the light, and in such a person there is no cause for stumbling. But whoever hates [his or her brother or sister] is in the darkness, walks in the darkness, and does not know the way to go, because the darkness has brought on blindness" (1 John 2:9–11).

The writer of 1 John suggests that one's lack of (sharing in God's) *agapē* toward others leaves one in spiritual darkness, owing to a case of spiritual blindness regarding knowing the way to go, including the way to (knowing) God. One thus might be *agapē*–blinded owing to one's selfish ways. Here we find a definite evidential or cognitive consequence from a human practical failure to cooperate with divine *agapē* toward others. A person thus uncooperative misses out on salient evidence of God's reality, because that evidence would stem from the transformative power of divine *agapē* toward humans and be intended by God to be cooperatively received by humans. Inquirers rarely give due attention to this cognitive lesson about God's reality.

H.R. Mackintosh has proposed the following explanation of our missing out on salient evidence of God's reality:

It is because we are such strangers to sacrifice [motivated by *agapē*] that God's sacrifice leaves us bewildered. It is because we love so little that His love is mysterious. We have never forgiven anybody at such a cost as his... It is our unlikeness to God that hangs as an obscuring screen impeding our view. ...

And the one cure for that is just to let God's own Spirit of love . . . fill our hearts and clear our vision. As the lessons of love are mastered, we shall more and more have understanding of [God's] wonderful grace that gave Christ for [all humans]. (1938, p. 177; cf. Mackintosh 1929, chap. 7)

This lesson deserves attention in religious epistemology, but it rarely emerges in philosophical discussions of the evidence for God's existence.

Chapter 3 acknowledged the possibility of pre-cooperative evidence of God's reality, perhaps in human conscience. A person could have initial evidence from divine self-manifesting of *agapē* but not cooperate with God at all in conforming to the perfect will represented in it. This kind of evidence, as suggested, would be highly elusive and unstable, because God as perfectly redemptive would not want people to rest content with it, apart from cooperating with God. In failing to cooperate with God, one would block God from manifesting divine reality to a redemptive, volitionally transformative extent, where God's *agapē* is uncoercively poured out in one's heart and thereby yields not only salient evidence of God's reality but also character change toward God's moral character (see Rom. 5:5).

Perhaps God intends the human appropriation of evidence of God's reality to be volitional and practical in order to nudge humans out of relational alienation from God into cooperative reconciliation with God. The evidence of God's reality thus would be *purposively* available to humans, in keeping with God's redemptive purposes for humans (as proposed in Moser 2008, 2010). Perhaps humans need to direct themselves cooperatively toward God's moral character to be aware of it with suitable clarity, because otherwise God would be elusive and even hide at times. As Chapter 3 suggested, God could be elusive in such a manner in order to save alienated humans from (further) devaluing, trivializing, or dismissing God's unique moral character and its redemptive value for them. This could be a divine means to avoid a premature human rejection of God and God's redemptive purpose.

God's motive would include the divine desire to have humans reciprocate in *agapē* toward God, rather than simply to know that God exists. God's agenda would be redemptive in ongoing relationship toward humans, and not just cognitive. This would be a requirement for a morally perfect God who is worthy of worship; failing that requirement, God would be redemptively deficient and hence morally suspect. Our redemptively knowing God, then, would not be reducible to our knowing that God exists. (For discussion of this matter in connection with divine hiding, see Chapter 3; cf. Moser 2008.)

Philosophers sometimes proceed as if evidence of God would be available to humans in a merely reflective or contemplative manner, in keeping with the image of Aristotle's god (as thought thinking itself) in Book Lambda of the *Metaphysics*. Some philosophers, particularly in the tradition of natural theology, regard discursive thinking on the basis of specific philosophical arguments as the most effective means to knowledge of God. These philosophers miss the mark, as Chapter 3 contended, because they neglect the cognitive importance of human *willing* and *acting* in accordance with divine *agapē* on the move for the sake of others. If God seeks redemptive companionship with humans, the evidential or cognitive landscape regarding God will be significantly different from that regarding a lesser god. The pressing question for humans then will be not so much whether God is available to us as whether *we* are sincerely available to God in being willing to cooperate sympathetically with God's perfect will.

In this book's perspective, agapeic action, understood as faithful, responsive obedience to God, becomes at least as important as reflection about God in knowing God (cf. 1 John 2:4, 3:14, 18). This fits with the pointed questions of the prophet Jeremiah on knowing God: "Did not your father . . . do justice and righteousness? . . . He judged the cause of the poor and needy. . . . Is not this to know me?, says the Lord" (Jer. 22:15–16). In this Hebraic perspective echoed by the writer of 1 John, human reflection and even well-grounded belief, however sophisticated and accurate, fall short of what a redemptive God would seek. Such intellectual realities cannot replace the obedient, responsive action required by divine *agapē*; they lack the needed human action cooperative with God's redemptive action in righteous love. They thus neglect the need for the redemption of full human agency.

The proposed image of a God on the redemptive move is foreshadowed in the life of the patriarch Abraham, a wandering Aramean (cf. Deut. 26:5), and in the nomadic history of Israel on its adventurous way to the Promised Land. The redemption in divine companionship includes the deliverance of humans from their destructive ways, and hence is redemptively nomadic, on the move out of death toward lasting life in cooperation with God. Even nomads can leave some time to "be still and know that [God is] God" (Ps. 46:10), but only with limits, because the divine redemption of humans requires redemptive action. Ideally, intellectual and contemplative efforts contribute to such action, for the sake of others. Otherwise, they would fall short of the redemptive effort of a God who seeks companionship with humans.

The second common obstacle to human companionship with God includes a denial of the human need of forgiveness and reconciliation relative to God. The attitude in question is that we humans, at least many of us, are well positioned relative to God because we have done "our best" in our lives. The message offered by such people is: "I'm OK, and you're OK"; and, more to the point, "God is therefore OK with us." The alleged payoff is that forgiveness and reconciliation relative to God are beside the point, given the supposed position of our having done our best. One must inquire, however, about the actual moral accountability of humans before God on this convenient approach. We can bracket the implausibility of any controversial assumption that many actual humans always "do their best." Our evidence does not typically support that self-congratulating assumption.

A human doing his or her "best" can fall short of moral perfection, and can, as a result, be out of cooperation with God's perfect moral character. In addition, we should distinguish between humans doing their best by their own power and their doing their best with the aid of God's power. We should not assume that God would approve of humans operating solely out of their own power, without receiving the available aid of God's unique intentional power for human moral life. God may expect imperfect humans to depend (at least *de re*) on available divine power for the moral life, including the power of *agapē*. In that case, it would not be acceptable to God for humans to presume that they are OK with God owing to their "doing their best." Their best may not be good enough for a morally perfect God. So, the proposal at hand fails to convince. It does not remove the need of human forgiveness and reconciliation before God. The explanatory burden is still with the one who assumes otherwise.

The third common obstacle to human companionship with God stems from a demand for a certain kind of evidence of God's reality that seems to be unavailable to humans. One variation on this demand requires that any awareness of God's character that qualifies as evidence of God must yield one's having defensible answers to skeptical questions about God's existence. The latter requirement, however, is too demanding. As Chapter 3 suggested, one's *having* conclusive evidence of God does not entail one's having a *propositional answer* to a question about God or about any alternative to God. It would be a dubious kind of level-confusion to suggest otherwise, and this often includes a confusion of the conditions for one's *having* evidence and the conditions for one's *showing*, *giving*, or *presenting* evidence in answer to a question or challenge. The latter confusion makes one's having evidence overly intellectual by linking it to one's formulating a presentation of one's evidence. A theory easily falls prey to that kind of defect whenever the conditions for answering questions become necessary conditions for one's simply having evidence. Correspondingly, one could have a particular reciprocating virtue without one's having the intellectual resources to formulate, describe, or show that one has it.

Typically, answers to questions are propositional; evidence, however, need not be, and foundational evidence is not, as suggested previously. Issues about our "answering questions" typically concern our *showing*, *giving*, or *presenting* evidence, in addition to our offering true answers. The latter concern is more intellectual and reflective than the more basic conditions for one's having evidence (see Moser 1989). It would be a mistake to assume that mere doxastic diversity or disagreement, even among one's peers, yields a defeater for a proposed theistic belief. Mere disagreement is akin to mere belief in lacking the evidential status to generate an epistemic defeater. Otherwise, we could produce defeaters pretty much at will, but that would rob evidence of its distinctive status. Many philosophers neglect this basic point about defeaters.

Some inquirers might have misgivings about the proposed *de re* evidence in human experience of divine *agapē*, on the ground that we humans have abundant selfishness and pride. I have no brief against the reality of our moral defectiveness in this regard, but this defectiveness can be a distorting human overlay on God's gift of *agapē*, freely added by imperfect humans. Virtuous life in cooperation with God could include a human struggle to remove this defective overlay for the sake of revealing the underlying gift received from God. In addition, God could allow for human freedom not only to receive this gift but also to reject it, even after we receive it. Our defectiveness in receiving a divine gift, however, does not automatically preclude the reality of the gift.

A redemptive God ideally would seek to combine in humans *de re* and *de dicto* evidence of God, for the sake of human moral transformation toward divine *agapē* and forgiveness, even toward one's enemies. God would aim to combine at some time (in reality, but not conceptually) humans' *knowing God* with humans' knowing *that* God exists. Human reflection on God thus would serve ideally not as a spectator sport or an armchair pastime, but instead as a life-forming challenge from the morally authoritative presence of God. A redemptive God would offer a new, experienced dimension of redemptive companionship with God that could overcome the seemingly endless doubts about God's reality prompted by some philosophy of religion. We have noted that Paul thinks of this as God's "new creation," and contrasts it with "knowing according to flesh" (2 Cor. 5:16–17, my trans.). We might think of the relevant knowing of God as "knowing according to redemptive companionship," courtesy of God's gracious initiative in self-manifesting toward humans.

A second variation on the evidential demand under consideration requires a more compelling kind of evidence for God. Theorists unfriendly to God's existence, however, do not share an understanding of the kind of evidence needed. So, it is hard to identify what exactly is being demanded of reasonable belief in God. A demand for peer consensus will fail from the start if God seeks volitional redemption among humans whose volitional tendencies vary. John Baillie identifies the problem: "We ask for an unmistakable sign [of God], but I think we have difficulty in saying what would be such a sign. What sign would we accept? We do not know what to suggest" (1956, p. 139). So, skeptical challenges can be intolerably vague in what they actually demand.

Perhaps the problem is that we do not like or want the kind of agapeic sign offered by God's self-manifested character.

Maybe we prefer not to undergo the kind of self-surrender to God required by an offer of redemptive companionship with God. If, however, God's unique power includes *agapē*, as required by worthiness of worship and suggested by the author of 1 John (4:15), then humans should look for *that* distinctive power as evidence of God. In that case, people who cooperate with that power cooperate with God, at least *de re*. In effect, people who refuse to cooperate with the manifested power of *agapē* would refuse to cooperate with God, the personal base of that unique power.

I have been talking largely about what God *would* do, because a God who hides on occasion could withhold divine evidence from uncooperative people. We therefore should not assume that evidence of God is equally realized among humans, although this lesson is widely neglected. My talk of what God *would* do avoids begging a key question against skeptics, but it invites skeptics to undergo self-examination concerning their alleged lack of evidence regarding God that many other, seeming reasonable people have. A relevant question for them is: Why do they lack evidence regarding God that is had by many other reasonable people? Perhaps volitional considerations will, and should, emerge.

This chapter leaves room for the needed self-examination about one's volitions, but it does not assume that we have a recipe to produce divine self-manifesting to a person. God would engage in divine self-manifesting in God's good time, with sensitivity to the readiness of a person to respond to God's presence and purpose. Even so, one's willingness to cooperate with a morally perfect will can benefit one's being in a position to discern the presence of God. It can direct one's attention in a manner that helpfully relates one to any pertinent evidence on offer. If, however, one is unwilling to cooperate in companionship with a self-sacrificial redemptive God, one should not expect to know this God in any salient manner. God could intend this to be the case for the redemptive reasons sketched previously.

The virtue of human companionship with God is partly intellectual, owing to its involving human thinking, but it is also volitional, owing to its involving human willing, and affective, owing to its role for human feelings. It would bring distinctive power as well as good news to humans. As a redemptive companion, God would be on our side, working for what is morally and spiritually good for us, even when we resist or despair, or are altogether unaware of God's efforts. A morally perfect God could not be more of a redemptive companion for us, even though we do not merit this companionship and sometimes resist it.

A certain human struggle, as indicated, often would accompany redemptive companionship with God: a struggle to cooperate with and to manifest divine *agapē*, even toward enemies. This result prompts an important question for all humans: Are we *willing* to undertake an ongoing struggle to cooperate with and to manifest the kind of *agapē* and redemptive companionship that conflicts with our selfish tendencies and the opposing attitudes of our peers? The conflict is personal and social, and it persists as long as genuine *agapē* is a live option for us.

Our question is volitional, and not merely intellectual, because it concerns the direction of our wills, and not just our beliefs. Perhaps many humans prefer not to undertake the redemptive struggle in the divine companionship on offer. In that case, all of the sound arguments in the world will fail to move these humans. Something else would be needed, and it would require the cooperation of free agents toward redemptive companionship in divine *agapē*. Here, therefore, we would need to take leave of philosophy to face practical life, a life of active pursuit regarding the virtue of redemptive companionship and the prospect of actual evidence for it. Our inquiry thus will continue or end with our own life-forming intentions (which may or may not be redemptively virtuous), but, to be responsible, our inquiry should seek the relevant evidence.

Inquirers will demand a *defense* of the theological perspective under consideration, and rightly so. We need to turn, then, to that matter, beginning with some considerations from some biblical writers regarding a unique *witness* to God's reality. We need not, however, treat these biblical considerations as automatically authoritative; it will be enough that they introduce a perspective worthy of our assessment for explanatory value relative to our overall experience.

5. SOME BIBLICAL DATA ON WITNESS

Some writers of the Jewish and Christian scriptures speak of the "Spirit" (*ruach* in Hebrew, *pneuma* in Greek) of God and of this Spirit's interventions in human experience. They do not offer a detailed metaphysics of the Spirit, but they often characterize this Spirit functionally, as *God in action*, with distinctive intentional power. The kinds of power characteristic of the Spirit of God are diverse and sometimes subtle, but they share the feature of intentionally serving God's redemptive purposes in action. Some of these purposes include God's witnessing to humans regarding who God is and what God expects of humans.

Something is a witness only if it is a witness *to something*, that is, only if it indicates (perhaps fallibly) the reality of the thing in question. God's Spirit might witness *to* God's moral character by presenting divine *agapē* to a person, say via that person's conscience. This witness would not be reducible to the Spirit's witnessing *that* God manifests *agapē*. The latter witness would be *de dicto* in virtue of its having propositional content (namely, a *that* clause), whereas the former witness would be *de re* in virtue of its presenting *the reality* in question, with no *required* propositional content, even if a *that* clause happens to be present. Analogously, I could present you with the blue card in my pocket without presenting any propositional content, or, alternatively, I could witness to you *that* I have a blue card in my pocket. I also could do both, but this does not challenge the distinction at hand.

Witnessing *to* something need not be witnessing *that* something is the case. Otherwise, the familiar distinction between *showing* (or manifesting) and *telling* (or describing) would collapse, and simple experiential witnessing would be lost. Typically, talk of divine "testimony" includes a notion of divine "telling," but witnessing, including divine witnessing, does not reduce to telling. We shall return to this topic, but we need now to gather some relevant biblical considerations for the sake of a perspective worthy of assessment for explanatory significance.

The book of Job captures a recurring theme of the Jewish Bible about God's Spirit as the sustainer of human life: "If [God] should take back his spirit to himself, and gather to himself his breath, all flesh would perish together, and all mortals return to dust" (Job 34:14–15; cf. Ps. 104:29–30). The book of Job also represents the biblical theme that the Spirit of God gives understanding to humans: "Truly it is the spirit in a mortal, the breath of the Almighty, that makes for understanding" (Job 32:8; cf. Deut. 34:9). Combining these two themes, we may say that God's Spirit would sustain human life as a life of understanding, or wisdom. Insofar as understanding and wisdom have epistemic import, the writings in question from the Jewish Bible identify such import for God's Spirit. This theme is absent from many approaches to epistemic import in circulation, owing to an absence of theological concern.

The Jewish Bible's characterization of God's Spirit takes on profound moral and spiritual significance with the following prayer from the psalmist: "Create in me a clean heart, O God, and put a new and right spirit within me. Do not cast me away from your presence, and do not take your holy spirit from me" (Ps. 51:10–11). The psalmist also prays to God: "Restore to me the joy of your salvation, and sustain in me a willing spirit" (Ps. 51:12), thus suggesting an important connection between the presence of God's Spirit and a human spirit *willing to cooperate* with

God's redemption of humans. This indicates the redemptive importance of the presence of God's Spirit, beyond the
mere sustenance of human life and understanding. The
role of a *willing human spirit*, we shall see, is important in
the witness of God's Spirit to humans and thereby in the
epistemic significance of the Spirit for humans.

The book of Ezekiel offers a prophecy concerning the
Spirit of God and human spirits in Israel: "A new heart I will
give you, and a new spirit I will put within you; and I will
remove from your body the heart of stone and give you a
heart of flesh. I will put my spirit within you, and make you
follow my statutes and be careful to observe my ordinances"
(Ezek. 36:26–27). This promise links reception of the Spirit of
God with obedience to God's commands. It thus reiterates
the psalmist's connection between receiving God's Spirit
and having a "willing spirit" toward God. Given the role
of human obedience in redemption by God, the promise at
hand has significant value for the redemption of humans.

The Spirit-empowered obedience in question is part of
what Ezekiel anticipates in his vision of the valley of dry
bones, in which God promises to Israel: "I will put my spirit
within you, and you shall live, and I will place you on your
own soil; then you shall *know* that I, the Lord, have spoken
and will act" (Ezek. 37:14, italics added). God's Spirit thus
would bring new life with God to willing humans, even
life from the dead, whereby humans relate obediently to
God. In addition, the role of the Spirit would contribute to
human knowing that God has spoken and will act.

God's Spirit would not only bring new life with God
to humans, but also witness to the reality of such life for
humans. Various writers of the New Testament suggest
this view, and we can benefit from attention to their con-
tributions. According to the earliest Jesus movement, Jesus
Christ as God's risen representative is still present among
his human followers. His presence is no longer in his earthly
body, but is instead in his Spirit abiding in the hearts, the volitional and affective centers, of his disciples. This Spirit, the
"Holy Spirit," is the Spirit of Jesus and of his divine Father,

according to the New Testament. Many New Testament writers elucidate pneumatology with Christology, given that God's Spirit is to be understood in terms of the crucified and risen Christ. New Testament Christology, including the character of Christ, gives some definite contours to the understanding of God's Spirit and thereby saves it from obscure mysticism. (See Dunn 1998 and Thiselton 2013, pp. 70–81, for details.)

A recurring theme of the New Testament is that Jesus as God's unique representative would baptize his willing followers with the Spirit of God (see Mark 1:8, Luke 3:16, Matt. 3:11, John 1:33, Acts 1:4–5, 11:16). In doing so, Jesus would bring people into reconciliation, communion, and companionship with God, in God's kingdom family. Peter finds the prophecy of Joel 2:28 to be fulfilled in the Pentecost experience of Acts 2, and he credits the risen Jesus as the source of the fulfillment: "This Jesus God raised up, and of that all of us are witnesses. Being therefore exalted at the right hand of God, and having received from the Father the promise of the Holy Spirit, he has poured out this that you both see and hear" (Acts 2:32–33). According to the four canonical Gospels and Acts, the risen Jesus has the authority and the power to give receptive people the Spirit of God and thereby to make them renewed members of God's kingdom. The book of Acts clarifies, with due amazement from Jewish Christians, that this gift of the Spirit was not limited to Jewish believers but extended also to Gentiles who receive Christ (Acts 10:44–48, 11:15–18).

The Gospel of Luke (4:18–19) portrays Jesus as announcing the fulfillment of Isaiah 61:1–2 in his own ministry:

The Spirit of the Lord is upon me,
because he has anointed me
to bring good news to the poor.
He has sent me to proclaim release to the captives
and recovery of sight to the blind,
to let the oppressed go free,
to proclaim the year of the Lord's favor. (Luke 4:18–19)

God's Spirit anoints Jesus to bring not only good news to the poor but also the power of freedom to live cooperatively with God (see also Acts 10:38). In this way, God's Spirit witnesses to God's reality and character through Jesus as God's beloved son (see Mark 1:9–11, Luke 3:21–22, Matt. 3:16–17). This is a divine witness through a historical human being, and it thereby replaces abstract talk of "divine spirit" with concrete talk of a particular human life that exemplifies the Spirit of God. The contours for the witness of God's Spirit thus become more definite and identifiable in the person and life of Jesus. This witness thereby takes on a definite epistemic role, as a personal model, concerning the reality and the action of God. In addition, it includes historical considerations but is not reducible to them (see Forrest 1906, pp. 332–98, Mackintosh 1913, pp. 363–82).

We can clarify the nature of the Spirit's witness by attending to the relevant good news and power in connection with some remarks from Paul and John on God's Spirit. Paul uses the language of "the Spirit of God," "the Spirit of Christ," and "Christ" interchangeably at times. He writes to Christians in Rome:

You are in the Spirit, since the Spirit of God dwells in you. Anyone who does not have the Spirit of Christ does not belong to him. But if Christ is in you, though the body is dead because of sin, the Spirit is life because of righteousness. If the Spirit of him who raised Jesus from the dead dwells in you, he who raised Christ from the dead will give life to your mortal bodies also through his Spirit that dwells in you. (Rom. 8:9–11)

In keeping with this usage, Paul thinks of Jesus as having become at his resurrection a "life-giving Spirit" (1 Cor. 15:45). He also connects the life of God's Spirit with "righteousness," thereby linking it to God's moral character (see Rom. 8:2, 4, 10; cf. Rom. 5:18, 21). We shall see that this lesson has definite epistemic significance.

In agreement with some of Paul's remarks, John's Gospel represents the coming of God's Spirit as the coming of the risen Jesus. It also represents Jesus as being in an authoritative position to control the sending of God's Spirit to receptive humans. John's Jesus remarks to his disciples: "If you love me, you will keep my commandments. And I will ask the Father, and he will give you another Advocate, to be with you forever. This is the Spirit of truth, whom the world cannot receive, because it neither sees him nor knows him. You know him, because he abides with you, and he will be in you. I will not leave you orphaned; I am coming to you" (John 14:15–18). In the coming of God's Spirit to people, then, the risen Jesus himself comes.

The Spirit of God witnesses for John's Jesus in an epistemically significant manner: "When the Advocate comes, whom I will send to you from the Father, the Spirit of truth who comes from the Father, he will testify [that is, witness, *marturēsei*] on my behalf" (John 15:26; cf. 1 John 5:9, 11). The Spirit of God, according to John and Paul, is as much the Spirit of Jesus as the Spirit of his Father. This suggests that the power of God's Spirit is inherently the power of self-sacrificial *agapē* exemplified in the obedient crucified Jesus. Given this lesson, we should not separate the character of God's Spirit from the self-sacrificial character of the crucified Jesus, as Paul emphasizes in various contexts (see Gal. 3:10–14, 1 Cor. 2:2–5, 13:1–13). We shall see how these considerations illuminate an approach to divine witness to humans.

6. DIVINE WITNESS TO FILIAL *AGAPĒ*

Even if the risen Jesus assumed an authoritative role in manifesting and sending God's Spirit to humans, we should ask what the main point of the Spirit's witness is. A hint arises both from Jesus's filial use of the term "*Abba*" ("Father") for God and from the subsequent use of this Aramaic term in the Greek writings of Paul and in the Greek Gospel of Mark (Mark 14:36).

Paul introduces the filial theme to the Galatian Christians by using the Aramaic language of Jesus: "When the fullness of time had come, God sent his Son, born of a woman, born under the law, in order to redeem those who were under the law, so that we might receive adoption as children. And because you are children, God has sent the Spirit of his Son into our hearts, crying, 'Abba!, Father!'" (Gal. 4:4–6). The Spirit of the risen Jesus, then, epistemically confirms one's being a child of God with the cry "Abba!, Father!"

Paul makes a filial point to the Roman Christians: "You did not receive a spirit of slavery to fall back into fear, but you have received a spirit of adoption. When we cry, 'Abba!, Father!' it is that very Spirit bearing witness with [*summarturei*] our spirit that we are children of God" (Rom. 8:15–16). This filial language of Paul, in the wake of Jesus, indicates that the Spirit of God seeks to witness, in an epistemically important manner, not only to God's reality and faithfulness, but also to one's having become (or, at least, one's becoming) a cooperative child of God. This position is distinctive in giving God's Spirit a central role in epistemically confirming God's reality and work.

Paul thinks of the human reception of the Spirit of God as God's way of now providing a guarantee, or a down payment, for the future realization of God's redemptive promises. The guarantee is epistemic, courtesy of God's Spirit as a personal witness. Paul writes to the Corinthian Christians: "It is God who establishes us with you in Christ and has anointed us, by putting his seal on us and giving us his Spirit in our hearts as a first installment" (2 Cor. 1:21–22; see 2 Cor. 5:5, Eph. 1:13–14). This suggests that the witness of the Spirit is eschatological, because the presence of the Spirit, like the kingdom of God, has not fully arrived yet. So, the Spirit points to the fullness of God's future, for which one can hope on the basis of a distinctive ground of divine *agapē* in one's experience.

Although we do not apprehend the full perfection of God's presence among humans, one can experience, according to Paul, the "first fruits of the Spirit." He remarks: "We ourselves, who have the first fruits of the Spirit, groan inwardly while we wait for adoption, the redemption of our bodies" (Rom. 8:23). Paul expresses a related eschatological point: "Through the Spirit, by faith, we eagerly wait for the hope of righteousness" (Gal. 5:5). Paul holds that the disciples of Jesus have already received, as a gracious gift, righteousness from God, reconciliation with God, and adoption into God's family (see Rom. 3:21–26, 5:11, 8:14–16, Gal. 3:7, 4:4–7).

Paul acknowledges that redemption is *now realized in part* but *not yet fully realized*, owing in part to the future redemption of human bodies. Paul emphasizes eschatological hope in God that awaits the completion of God's redemption for humans (see Rom. 8:24–25). The witness of God's Spirit is thus partly eschatological, owing to its pointing to God's future completion of redemptive promises. So, the epistemic confirmation from God's Spirit awaits fullness in the future.

Paul and John portray the human reception of God's Spirit (and the accompanying witness of the Spirit to becoming God's child) as requiring a definite, cooperative human response to the intervention of the Spirit in human experience. Paul remarks to the Galatian Christians: "Did you receive the Spirit by doing the works of the law or [instead] by believing what you heard? Are you so foolish? Having started with the Spirit, are you now ending with the flesh? . . . [I]n Christ Jesus the blessing of Abraham [would] come to the Gentiles, so that we might receive the promise of the Spirit through faith" (Gal. 3:2–3, 14). Paul thus holds that one receives God's Spirit by responding in faith, including trust, toward God's redemptive intervention. Insofar as God's Spirit brings epistemic confirmation of God's reality and work, this confirmation can depend on human receptivity as cooperation toward God's Spirit.

It thus would be cooperative, in keeping with a suggestion of Chapter 3.

The writer of John's Gospel, in agreement with Paul, links faith in Christ directly with the reception of God's Spirit. John's Jesus announces: "As the scripture has said, 'Out of the believer's heart shall flow rivers of living water'. Now he said this about the Spirit, which believers in him were to receive" (John 7:38–39). John, like Paul, understands faith in God and Jesus to include obedience to God and Jesus. So, John makes a similar point about receiving God's Spirit in terms of obedience. As noted previously, he portrays Jesus as saying: "If you love me, you will keep my commandments. And I will ask the Father, and he will give you another Advocate, to be with you forever. This is the Spirit of truth, whom the world cannot receive, because it neither sees him nor knows him. You know him, because he abides with you, and he will be in you" (John 14:15–17). Like Paul, then, John understands the reception of God's Spirit to emerge from the human response of obedient faith in God and Christ. He also acknowledges the epistemic significance of this response.

We can isolate some distinctive features of the filial relation that emerge from the human reception of God's Spirit via faith in God. We may understand this relation in terms of a goal regarding moral and spiritual character: "like parent, like child." On the assumption that Christ is "the image of God" (2 Cor. 4:4, Col. 1:15), Paul identifies God's goal that humans "be conformed to the image of his Son, in order that he might be the firstborn within a large family" (Rom. 8:29). Writing to the Corinthian Christians, Paul makes a related point in terms of "the Lord, the Spirit": "All of us, with unveiled faces, seeing the glory of the Lord as though reflected in a mirror, are being transformed into the same image from one degree of glory to another; for this comes from the Lord, the Spirit" (2 Cor. 3:18). We need not digress to ontological questions about the exact relation between "the Lord" and "the Spirit" in Paul's thought.

The key point is that the work of God's Spirit includes the transformation of humans into the image of Christ, who is the "the image of God." This transformation, we shall see, has definite epistemic significance and requires human cooperation.

The image of God in Christ has distinctive moral and spiritual features. A central feature is exemplified in the self-sacrificial *agapē* of the crucified Jesus. Paul highlights this feature not only in his influential chapter on *agapē*, 1 Corinthians 13, but also in his letter to the Roman Christians. We have made considerable use of the following passage on the witness of God's Spirit: "We also boast in our sufferings, knowing that suffering produces endurance, and endurance produces character, and character produces hope, and hope does not disappoint us, because God's love has been poured into our hearts through the Holy Spirit that has been given to us" (Rom. 5:3–5; cf. 2 Cor. 5:14). This passage captures a central feature of the "inner witness" of God's Spirit, because it identifies the work of God's Spirit in relaying a central feature of God's moral character to the volitional and affective center of humans (their "hearts"). This is an "inner" work, but it is not a matter of merely subjective opinion; nor is it beyond describing (Paul just described it, to an extent). In addition, it has definite epistemic import in grounding hope and belief in God.

Paul does not relinquish in the previous passage a central role for God's witness through the crucified Christ. The passage is followed by this remark: "God proves his love for us in that while we still were sinners Christ died for us" (Rom. 5:8). God's witness to divine *agapē* for humans in the cross of Christ does not depend on any mere human receiving an inner witness from God. Even so, the inner witness manifests in a cooperative human's "heart" the kind of *agapē* that motivated Christ to obey God's call to the cross, in order to "prove" God's love for humans. (On the role of obedience in Christ's undergoing crucifixion, see Phil. 2:8.)

We might think of the cross of Christ as a divine witness that is "outer" or "public" as a spatiotemporal historical event, which is not itself relayed to a human heart. Historical events that are spatiotemporally finite or bounded are not themselves (as tokens) relayed, strictly speaking, to any other spatiotemporal situation, even if *descriptions* of them are. The witness of the historical cross of Christ, as a spatiotemporal historical event, was not inner to any mere human. Even so, the *message* of the cross and, more basically, the divine *agapē* conveyed by the cross can become inner, in virtue of being relayed to a human heart, particularly a heart willing to cooperate with divine *agapē*.

We can distinguish two kinds of inner witness of the Spirit in virtue of two kinds of "being relayed" for the message and the *agapē* of the cross of Christ. The message and the *agapē* of the cross can be *cooperatively* relayed, and they can be *uncooperatively* relayed. They are cooperatively relayed if and only if they are relayed to an intended recipient in a manner whereby that recipient cooperatively receives them. By contrast, they are uncooperatively relayed to an intended recipient if and only if they are relayed to an intended recipient in a manner whereby that recipient does not cooperatively receive them. So, an inner witness of the Spirit to an intended recipient need not be cooperatively received by that intended recipient. Humans could reject the Spirit's inner witness to the message and the *agapē* of the cross, and thereby exclude themselves from important evidence from God's Spirit. Even so, God would intend to have this witness cooperatively received by humans and would save this witness from being trivialized by humans, at times by hiding its fullness from uncooperative humans.

Humans could have varying degrees of cooperatively receiving the message and the *agapē* of the cross of Christ. Some people could cooperate more than others in receiving, for various reasons. This fact allows, however, for there being a definite threshold of volitional cooperation for one's cooperatively receiving the message and the *agapē* of the cross. The threshold would include one's committing oneself *as a supreme priority* to cooperation with God's message and *agapē*. So, people could be responsible to God for how they respond to the inner witness of the Spirit, and this fits with the remarks in Chapter 2 on the ethics for responsible inquiry about God. As agents, they could exercise their will to cooperate sympathetically with, reject, or withhold judgment on the inner witness. This allows for a volitional element and an affective element in one's receiving or not receiving evidence from the Spirit of God. So, as Chapter 3 suggested, one's epistemic position relative to God could involve volitional and affective tendencies beyond intellectual reflection.

As noted, Paul says concerning people who respond in faith to God that God's *agapē* is poured out into their hearts through the Spirit. Paul also says that hope in God does not disappoint these people because this *agapē* has been poured out into their hearts. Paul, as suggested, would say the same of *faith* in God, given that he began Romans 5 with the importance of faith in God, and he regards faith and hope as closely interconnected, so much so that he remarks that "in hope we were saved" (Rom. 8:24). He holds, then, that neither hope nor faith in God disappoints the Roman Christians, because they have received distinctive evidence in God's supporting *agapē* in their hearts, courtesy of the Spirit of God.

The experienced *agapē* is evidential regarding God in virtue of indicating the reality and unique character of God; it is therefore epistemically significant. Paul's idea in Romans 5:5 includes a notion of psychological disappointment, but not just of psychological disappointment. He is saying more than that the Roman Christians are not psychologically disappointed by their hope in God. Given their experience of God's powerful *agapē* in their hearts, as suggested, the Roman Christians had received inner *evidence* of God's reality, and therefore they are not cognitively, evidentially, or epistemically disappointed. This evidence is a distinctive kind of power that goes beyond talk.

G.C. Berkouwer acknowledges the general point regarding power:

Paul knows the question about authorization and is faced with it also in the Church: "you desire proof (*dokimēn zēteite*) that Christ is speaking in me" (2 Cor. 13:3). To this question he can only answer that "Christ is powerful in you." Neither in visions and revelations (cf. 2 Cor. 2:1) is there a proof that is sufficient for every critical or uncritical observer. But that does not mean defenselessness, since Paul knows of the empowerment and the power of Christ that works in and through him (Rom. 15:18). (1976, p. 243)

We need to specify, however, that Paul regards the unique power to be divine *agapē* offered to empower cooperative humans.

God's Spirit, as a personal agent, could give a *de re* personal manifestation of God's moral character. This Spirit could witness to God's reality and moral character via divinely self-manifested *agapē* poured into a cooperative human's heart, and this witness would include distinctive experiential evidence received by such a human. The directly experienced, self-manifested *agapē* from God, in Paul's view, saves one from cognitive or epistemic disappointment in hope and faith in God, because one thereby has a cognitive base, or epistemic foundation, from God for one's hope and faith in God. As noted, this also would avoid any kind of implausible fideism regarding hope and faith in God. In addition, it would set an epistemic standard for humans for God's reality and thereby save them from subjectivism. The self-manifestation in question would be God's effort to promote a good relationship of companionship in *koinonia* with humans, but the fulfillment of this effort would depend on human cooperation with God.

The divine *agapē* in question would be God's *compassionate will* to bring about what is morally and spiritually best, all things considered, for cooperative humans. Humans who refuse to cooperate would block the power (and the epistemic significance) of this *agapē* for themselves, because, by divine intention, this power would not be coercive of human wills but would be received cooperatively. When humans cooperatively receive divine *agapē*, they would be transformed toward the moral and spiritual character of God in Christ. In being thus transformed, humans would receive distinctive evidence of God's reality and character. In cooperatively responding to God's intervention, one would find God's will manifested within oneself (if imperfectly), particularly God's will to love others, even enemies. One could be surprised by this new reality of *agapē* within oneself, given that it could mark a discernible change from one's previous inclinations, especially toward one's enemies.

The evidence from the divine *agapē* in question would be *inner*, given its presentation directly to the will (or heart) of humans. It would not, however, be purely subjective, because it would not depend just on human desires, intentions, beliefs, hopes, or feelings. This *agapē*, when cooperatively received, would yield and support a distinctive life direction, a Godward or Christward direction, we might say. A human life with this direction would be a God-shaped or Christ-shaped life, owing to its being formed or shaped by the Spirit of God in Christ (see Gal. 4:19). Paul thinks of this formation as empowered by the Spirit of God and Christ.

One can see, from a perspective of cooperation with God, the salient reality of Christ-shaped lives in such disciples as Paul, Francis of Assisi, and Mother Teresa. It would be a mistake to call the morally distinctive reality of these lives purely subjective. The disciples in question have become life-sized evidence of the reality of God and God's empowering Spirit. The opportunity to become such living, personified evidence would be available to all disciples of God in Christ (cf. 2 Cor. 3:2–3), even if its realization demands considerable human resolve and obedience toward God.

The Johannine writings in the New Testament agree with Paul's emphasis on the role of *agapē* in the Spirit's witness. The writer of 1 John states: "No one has ever seen God; if we love one another, God lives in us, and his love is perfected in us. By this we know that we abide in him and he in us, because he has given us of his Spirit" (1 John 4:12–13). The idea is that God's *agapē* is being realized and perfected in humans who cooperate with this *agapē*, and the Spirit of God empowers such change and thereby supplies distinctive evidence of God's reality and character. The author of 1 John links this idea to knowing God: "Beloved, let us love one another, because love is from God; everyone who loves is born of God and knows God. Whoever does not love does not know God, for God is love" (1 John 4:7–8).

Agapē, according to 1 John, has its source in God, not in humans, and cooperative human participation in it is necessary for knowing God, given God's inherently loving character. Humans come to know God by knowing God's character of love, and cooperative human participation in God's love is the main avenue to knowing God's character. The writer of 1 John also sounds a note similar to Paul's on confident hope in God: "Love has been perfected among us in this: that we may have boldness on the day of judgment, because as he is, so are we in this world" (1 John 4:17). This remark agrees with Paul's idea, in Romans 5:5, that inner *agapē* from God epistemically grounds a disciple's confident hope in God.

An important theme in John's Gospel is that the witness of God's Spirit includes the convicting of humans regarding their waywardness from God's character of perfect *agapē*. John's Jesus says: "It is to your advantage that I go away, for if I do not go away, the Advocate will not come to you; but if I go, I will send him to you. And when he comes, he will prove [RSV margin: convict] the world wrong about sin and righteousness and judgment" (John 16:7–8). This convicting and convincing work aims to witness to God's character of *agapē* and to invite humans to cooperate with it, in faithful obedience. Because this *agapē* is inherently unselfish and servant-like, it is self-sacrificial and, in that regard, kenotic. By way of *de re* contrast, it can show a person's falling short of God's standard and needing to turn away, or repent, from selfishness. As Chapter 3 noted, 1 John 3:16 connects *agapē* with self-sacrifice directly: "We know love by this, that he [Jesus] laid down his life for us – and we ought to lay down our lives for one another." The Spirit's witness, then, points to and manifests divine *agapē* and thereby involves the kind of agapeic self-sacrifice found in the cross of Christ. In doing so, the Spirit of God would provide evidence of God's reality and unique character.

Paul concurs with the implication of the Johannine writings that God's Spirit empowers a robust moral life for cooperative humans (see Rom. 8:2–4). Paul thinks of "the Spirit of life in Christ" as the Spirit of righteous life in Christ. This life requires that people "walk . . . according to the Spirit," that is, in cooperation with the Spirit. Even so, Paul opposes any human means for supposedly earning, or meriting, God's approval or righteousness, such as by the Mosaic law or any other law (see Rom. 4:2, 9:31–32).

Paul holds that an aim of the cross of Christ and the guiding Spirit of God in Christ is that "the just [or, righteous] requirement of the law might be fulfilled in us" (Rom. 8:4). We may understand this as a challenge to be conformed to God's righteous moral character represented in the law *as "fulfilled"* by the obedient Christ. This reading fits not only with Paul's emphasis on human righteousness via Christ and his Spirit (see Rom. 5:21, 2 Cor. 5:21, 1 Cor. 3:16), but also with a central lesson on righteousness in the Gospel of Matthew (see Matt. 5:17–18, 20). It also fits with Paul's view that divine grace works "through righteousness" (Rom. 5:21). The witness of the Spirit, then, is inseparable from a witness to God's righteousness available to humans without their earning it. That is, it is inseparable from a witness to the gift of divine grace to humans. (On grace as a gift in Paul, see Barclay 2015.)

Paul thinks of the inner witness of the Spirit as including the inner intercession of the Spirit in prayer to God. He states: "Likewise the Spirit helps us in our weakness; for we do not know how to pray as we ought, but that very Spirit intercedes with sighs too deep for words. And God, who searches the heart, knows what is the mind of the Spirit, because the Spirit intercedes for the saints according to the will of God" (Rom. 8:26–27). Paul understands this intercession as experiential for cooperative humans, and not abstract or distant. The "sighs too deep for words" are within a person who has received God's Spirit, and are thus part of the inner witness of the Spirit. These sighs would witness, in an epistemic manner, to God's profound redemptive intervention in a person's experience, even if they are too deep for words. They would qualify as experiential evidence of God's intervention for a recipient, as they would not be produced by that recipient but indicate the presence of God's self-manifesting Spirit.

The sighs in question include eschatological groanings that originate from God's Spirit. As indicated, Paul remarks: "not only the creation, but we ourselves, who have the first fruits of the Spirit, groan inwardly while we wait for adoption, the redemption of our bodies" (Rom. 8:23). He regards this groaning as part of the "pains of childbirth" (Rom. 8:22; cf. Gal. 4:19). We may think of this inward groaning as co-groaning with the Spirit of God, who witnesses through the depth of this groaning for eschatological redemption, for the fullness of redemption. This inner witness would be to God's character of redemption toward humans. We now can clarify further the epistemic role of God's Spirit.

7. ABIDING IN *AGAPĒ*

One can come to know *that* the President of the United States
exists without coming to know the President of the United
States. Most people who come to know the former fact are
in that situation. Perhaps an analogy holds for knowing
God and knowing that God exists, but, in any case, knowing God may be the most secure and stable way to know
that God exists. A relevant concern is that without knowing God in an interpersonal I–Thou manner on the basis
of divine self-manifesting, one's supposed knowledge that
God exists will be unstable and existentially anemic. In that
case, the latter knowledge will be subject to easy dismissal
by the person, given the highly mixed character of his or
her evidence.

Many cases arise of one's avowing knowledge that God
exists but later coming to dismiss this supposed knowledge upon reconsidering one's evidence. The relevant
evidence would be significantly less mixed for a person
if he or she had evidence from knowing God on the basis
of divine self-manifesting, and not just from knowing that
God exists. Evidence from knowing God, as Chapter 3
indicated, would be interactive or responsive between
personal agents in a way that evidence from knowing that
God exists would not. It typically would develop over
time in a way that extends and deepens one's evidence
for God and even includes a new identity for oneself on
the basis of a morally transformative experience of divine
self-manifesting. A key feature of the relevant transformation would be a cooperative reordering of one's priorities toward the primacy of *agapē* toward others. It
would be difficult for a person with such a new identity
to dismiss it as illusory (see Forsyth 1909, pp. 195–205; cf.
Hubbard 2002).

Philosophers of religion have neglected a distinctive
approach to knowing God suggested in John's Gospel and
in the First Epistle of John. This approach is more durable

than the familiar alternatives and more suitable to a God worthy of worship. In addition, it fits with the role of companionship in the God relationship, particularly with continuing in companionship in an *agapē* relationship. John's Gospel suggests that a kind of human "abiding" figures in knowing God. Its initial suggestion is: "Jesus said to the Jews who had believed in him, 'If you [abide] in my word, you are truly my disciples; and you will know the truth, and the truth will make you free'" (John 8: 31–32). (I have replaced "continue" with "abide" in the NRSV translation of *meinēte* in this passage.)

Abiding in God's word, including in God's commandments, is more than intellectual, because it includes abiding in divine love: "As the Father has loved me, so I have loved you; abide in my love. If you keep my commandments, you will abide in my love, just as I have kept my Father's commandments and abide in his love" (John 15:9–10; cf. John 14:23, 1 John 4:16). Abiding in God's love thus includes cooperating with God's expressed will, ideally as Jesus did in Gethsemane. More to the point, it includes cooperating with the Spirit of God who extends God's love to humans, particularly in the self-manifesting of God's moral character to humans.

Abiding in God's Spirit would include sympathetically sharing in the moral character traits of God, otherwise known as the "fruit of God's Spirit": "love, joy, peace, patience, kindness, generosity, faithfulness, gentleness, and self-control" (Gal. 5:22–23). Such abiding calls for *supreme-priority* abiding, that is, *centering* oneself in the self-manifested character of God. This centering entails decentering toward one's own will and any other will contrary to God's. It requires the centering of one's whole life in God's sustaining Spirit: including one's affections, volitions, thoughts, and actions. It is to be wholehearted toward the authority of God as self-manifested in God's active Spirit. As Dietrich Bonhoeffer says: "The responsible [person before God] seeks to make his whole life a response to the question and call of God" (1953, p. 16). In addition, he identifies God's proper place at "the center of life" rather than as a "stop-gap" in connection with what we do not know (1953, pp. 142–43).

If God is to be at "the center of life," rather than just at its periphery, a question arises: How does one *put* God at the center of one's life? Once again, the response of Gethsemane is the key to the answer, because it would put obedience to God at the center of human life, in recommending to God, "Your will be done." Its obedience is the obedience of faith by which one learns to trust God in yielding one's own will to God's will. God would not be at the center of my life if I refused to follow Jesus in Gethsemane, because God's will would be at the center only if it had supreme priority in my life, that is, Gethsemane priority after the model of Jesus himself. So, the yielding prayer of Jesus in Gethsemane may be called "centering prayer," because it expresses the centering of his will and the rest of himself on God's will and life as his supreme priority. (For discussion, see Koenig 1992, pp. 53–65.)

A typical human life that aims to place God at its center will do so imperfectly. It will be at best a work in progress, characterized by frequent ups and downs in the struggle to center oneself on God's will and life. Even so, it will include an attitude of there being "one thing" that is necessary in relation to God (see Luke 10:38–42). The "one thing," as Chapter 1 noted, concerns a person's supreme love toward God, in contrast with a person's many lesser loves. A person's supreme love is the person's primary love and does not depend on his or her other, lesser loves. Instead, the lesser loves should be subsidiary to one's supreme love. Unless we agree with Jesus regarding the "one thing" necessary for humans in relation to God, we will be at risk (as Chapter 1 suggested) of finding God to be grudging, untrustworthy, and unworthy of worship. The risk then is that the frustration of our other loves will threaten to discredit God's love for us.

The centering in question will include sympathetic trust in God and thereby will enable God to self-manifest and self-authenticate to a person without that person's full resistance or distortion. The Spirit's self-manifesting witness would be God's way of authenticating God's reality and character for humans. This way would be *self*-authentication, because it would include God's *self*-manifesting the divine moral character to cooperative humans, perhaps in their conscience, via the intervening Spirit. It also would include God's producing traits of this divine character, such as divine *agapē*, in the experiences and lives of cooperative recipients.

As suggested, God could be self-evidencing and self-authenticating toward cooperative humans, given God's Spirit who self-manifests God's unique, morally perfect character. This view, as indicated, does not entail the implausible view that a subjective human experience is self-authenticating regarding God's existence. The key implication, instead, is that *God* would be an independent moral agent, with causal powers, who is the ultimate source of perfect *agapē* and hence of divine evidence and self-authentication in human lives.

According to various New Testament writers, as Chapter 3 noted, *God* ultimately testifies to God, including God's reality and moral character, via God's Spirit. We noted that Paul attributes the following statement to God: "I have shown myself to those who did not ask for me" (Rom. 10:20). Similarly, John's Gospel portrays Jesus as being self-manifesting: "Those who love me will be loved by my Father, and I will love them and reveal myself to them" (John 14:21). God's self-authenticating via self-manifesting would challenge humans to cooperate with enemy-love and forgiveness, in opposition to destructive selfishness and pride. It would set a high moral standard, by self-presented example, and humans would be challenged to respond cooperatively.

Cases of a *nondiscursive witness* to God in self-manifesting, as Chapter 3 noted, need not be accompanied by a judgment that something is the case regarding God. A dual witness, however, would include both a nondiscursive and a discursive witness, with the *discursive witness* interpreting the nondiscursive manifestation via a concept or a judgment. The inner witness of God's Spirit thus need not come with a propositional affirmation or even a concept that elucidates the Spirit's nondiscursive witness. The Spirit's manifesting of God's *agapē* to a person could be free of any discursive characterization, but still have salient *qualitative* content in one's experience: the qualitative content of divine love, which is different from a concept or a report of love. Even if such love calls for human discernment, its content could be distinctive and even unique, and hence different from other content found in one's experience. Nonetheless, God's Spirit could help in the ongoing interpretation of such content for humans, as they cooperate in its reception.

Contrary to some theologians, the witness of God's Spirit need not be limited to the propositional content of the Jewish Bible and the New Testament. It would be unduly restrictive to limit the Spirit's witness to the propositional content of the biblical writings. Paul had in mind the Spirit's nondiscursive witness when he remarked: "My speech and my proclamation were not with plausible words of wisdom, but with a demonstration of the Spirit and of *power*, so that your faith might rest not on human wisdom but on the power of God" (1 Cor. 2:4–5, italics added). This power would include at least the self-manifested *agapē* of God, courtesy of the Spirit's inner witness to receptive humans. It would seek the kind of human cooperation that is crucial to divine–human companionship.

The Spirit's inner witness of divine *agapē* aimed at divine–human companionship could bridge the historical chasm between the first-century life and death of Jesus

Christ (where God reportedly manifested divine love to humans) and contemporary humans. As suggested, it could do this by relaying not the historical, first-century event (token) of the life or death itself, but the divine *agapē* that motivated that life and death. This kind of witness would supply an alternative to the kind of historicism that limits evidence of God's redemptive work to past history. It would offer evidence regarding the historic Christ that is not itself evidence just from the past. The witness of the Spirit with *agapē*, we might say, would transcend the limitations of historical events and thereby provide a distinctive kind of evidence of God's reality and unique character. In this respect, not all evidence regarding God would be limited to past events, and some such evidence could be contemporary. History is important as evidence, but it does not exhaust the evidence potentially given by the witness of God's Spirit (see Mackintosh 1913, pp. 306–20, 363–82; cf. Berkouwer 1977, chap. 6). This should be expected if God is a living God, and not just a historical artifact.

The cooperative human reception of God's Spirit, as suggested, is no merely subjective matter, because it yields one's becoming loving and forgiving (to some discernible degree) as God is loving and forgiving. It yields salient fruit of God's Spirit, such as love, joy, peace, patience, kindness, goodness, faithfulness, humility, and self-control (see Gal. 5:22–23). These are not merely subjective phenomena. They are discernible by anyone attentive to them and open to the redemptive power of God in human experience. People nonetheless are free to ignore or to resist the relevant evidence, and they can do so with internally consistent beliefs. In the latter case, one's presentation of evidence for God's reality on the basis of explanatory considerations will fail to produce a non-question-begging argument for some people. This failure, however, does not challenge the existence of the relevant evidence of God's reality and character for the person who has it.

The writer of 1 John, as indicated, advises people to "test the spirits to see whether they are of God" rather than to believe every spirit (1 John 4:1). Otherwise, people can be led away from truth into serious error by false teachers. Jesus offers similar advice: "Beware of false prophets, who come to you in sheep's clothing but inwardly are ravenous wolves. You will know them by their fruits. . . . Every good tree bears good fruit, but the bad tree bears bad fruit" (Matt. 7:15–17). We could know the reality of the presence of God's Spirit by means of the fruits yielded by the Spirit, because God's Spirit, if cooperatively received, would make one loving (to some discernible degree) as God is loving. This would be the primary fruit of the Spirit, and it would be identifiable and testable in a person's life. The presence of God's Spirit thus would come with salient evidence observable by any suitably receptive person willing to be discerning about God's self-manifesting to humans.

The salience of the evidence for God's Spirit for some people at some times, as Chapter 3 suggested, does not exclude its elusiveness or even its hiddenness at times for some people. Paul remarks: "Those who are unspiritual do not receive the [things] of God's Spirit, for they are foolishness to them, and they are unable to understand them because they are spiritually discerned" (1 Cor. 2:14; cf. John 14:22–24). God could hide the witness of the Spirit from people who are unwilling to engage it with due seriousness and sincerity. Their unwillingness may be understood, at least in some cases, as a refusal to face a Gethsemane crisis with the obedient attitude of Jesus toward God. The divine hiding would save some people from self-harming by their treating as trivial something that is vital for them. In this respect, at least, the witness of God's Spirit would be elusive and even hidden at times.

If the overall evidence for God's reality is elusive, people should reconsider some of the main assumptions of traditional natural theology. In that case, as Chapter 3 suggested, we should not assume that the arguments of natural theology can make acknowledgment of God's reality reasonable for all intelligent people. We then would need a more qualified story of the evidence for divine reality and of the presentation of that evidence by way of a defense. We turn now to the latter matter.

8. I–THOU DEFENSE OF FAITH IN GOD

If God is self-authenticating via a self-manifesting witness in human experience, one might look to the use of abductive, or explanatory, considerations to present evidence for God's reality. *Presenting* evidence, in any case, goes beyond *having* evidence, and the two should not be confused, as Chapter 3 explained. One might argue that the intentional power of self-sacrificial love in a cooperative disciple of God is explained best, at least so far as our available evidence indicates, by the good news that God's Spirit has genuinely intervened with *agapē* in the disciple's life. This power could supply a salient kind of evidence for the reality and the moral character of God, at least for the recipient of this power. Even so, one's recognition of such divine power and evidence as being from God would depend on one's willingness to acknowledge these as not of one's own, human making. One would receive them as a gift from God, or one would fail to receive them for what they are intended to be: an unmerited gift from God, even if a gift that comes with expectations for recipients.

Witness and Reason

We have identified the suggestion of some biblical writers that the Spirit of God witnesses by self-manifesting moral character traits of God, particularly *agapē*. Now we should consider that humans could have an opportunity to witness similarly for the sake of a defense of faith in God, that is, a defense of its veracity or its evidential groundedness regarding God's actual involvement. This witness could be *de re* and in action, and it may (or may not) be joined by a *de dicto* witness, identifying God via conceptual content.

A human witness to God's moral character, via a human moral character reflective of divine *agapē*, could figure in a positive defense of faith in God. Such a positive witness-based defense could join with a negative defense that undermines arguments against the veracity or evidential groundedness of faith in God. A question, however, concerns how a witness-based defense relates to reason and the role of reason in a defense of faith in God. An adequate positive defense, I contend, must witness in the case of general faith in God to the self-manifestation of God in human experience. In the case of Christian faith in God, such a defense must witness to the self-manifestation of God in Christ in human experience.

The term "reason" is as ambiguous as the term "faith," and this factor has hindered inquiry about the relation between reason and faith in God. A prominent definition of "reason" offered by the *Oxford English Dictionary*, second edition, is: "A statement of some fact (real or alleged) used to justify or condemn an action, or to prove or disprove some assertion, idea, or belief." If a reason is a "statement used to justify" a claim or an action, then a reason has a crucial role in an argument. The *OED* thus offers the following subsidiary definition of "reason": "A premise of an argument." This is a widespread use of "reason," but it is too narrow for how we typically think of reasons, inside and outside of philosophy and theology. An experience is not a "statement" of any kind, let alone a statement used as a premise in an argument. Nonetheless, we typically think of an experience, including a perceptual experience, as capable of being a reason or evidence for a belief. My experience of an apparent computer screen, for instance, can be a reason or evidence for my belief that there is a computer screen before me, even in the absence of my using a statement to justify a belief within an argument.

The *OED* offers, in addition to the previous definition, the following definition of "reason": "The intellectual . . . capacity for rational thought. . . . The power of the mind to think and form valid judgements by a process of logic; the mental faculty which is used in adapting thought or action to some end." Here, too, the definition omits the important role of experience as a reason or evidence for beliefs. Instead, it focuses on a mind's ability "to form valid judgements by a process of logic." If the terms "valid" and "logic" concern inference, as is suggested, we again have a characterization of reason in terms of its role in an argument. Even if this is a prominent use of "reason," it does not exhaust our typical use of the term "reason," because it omits the important role of experience as a reason or evidence for belief. We gain nothing by omitting experience from the category of reason; in fact, we gain more explanatory benefit from the category by including it.

One important explanatory benefit concerns the long-standing issue of whether faith in God is somehow at odds with reason or evidence. A related issue concerns how such faith can be supported by reason, if it can be so supported. As Chapter 3 suggested, if divine *agapē* presented to a human is a divine self-manifestation to that human, it can be evidence of God's reality and moral character for that human. It can be such evidence, because it *indicates* the reality of God to a human by presenting, if only *de re*, the center of God's unique moral character in *agapē* to that human.

If God is *sui generis* at least in moral character, as monotheists typically hold, God's self-manifestation of the divine moral character to humans would be the most direct way to convey God's reality and goodness to humans. Everything else would fall short of directly indicating the real article, or, better, the real intentional *agent*. So, some of the biblical writers portray God as ratifying divine authority and reality by a divine appeal to God himself (see, e.g., Heb. 6:13). This fits with the idea of God as having a unique perfect moral character and as needing to invoke it for direct authentication of divine reality and goodness. It also fits with the idea that God would want the ultimate source of authentication of divine reality to be a personal agent with a perfect moral character, and not something less representative of God.

Some inquirers assume that a (good) reason for faith in God must involve an argument that would be compelling for all rational inquirers. This is a mistake, as Chapter 3 explained. The first consideration is that one's reason for belief in God can be evidence that does not involve one's having an argument at all for God's existence. Arguments for God's existence are much more intellectually complex than basic experiential evidence for God's existence. By analogy, there is a clear distinction between my basic experiential evidence of a black object before me and a more intellectually complex argument for the existence of that object. I could have the former without the latter, and the former could be a reason for me for my belief that there is a black object before me.

The second consideration is that a reason or evidence for belief in God can be had from a first-person perspective that is not shared by others, and hence an argument that generalizes on the evidence to apply to rational belief *for others* may fail, owing to a failure to capture the evidence of others. By analogy, some perceptual or sensory experiences vary among humans, and hence do not yield or serve an argument that generalizes on the evidence to rational belief for all inquirers. Arguments that fail to capture a person's evidence will fall short of rational cogency for that person, even if they capture the evidence of a different person.

We can imagine that God wants to anchor all divine self-revelation to humans in a first-person human perspective that includes a *de re* encounter with God. We seem not to be in a position to exclude this live option, and it is not clear why one would want to exclude it, given that it would be the most direct and accurate way to represent God's moral character and reality to humans. Many theistic and

Christian philosophers and apologists exclude it uncritically in their reasoning practices in favor of theism, when they assume that reasonable belief in God must be based on a supporting argument.

We cannot exclude that *God* rightly would want to be the ultimate convincer or persuader of people believing in God, by means of the self-manifestation of God's unique moral character to them, and not by means of an argument. The approach to reason and faith in God offered here allows for this divine option, and this lends credibility to the approach. It removes the pretensions of those approaches to theistic or Christian apologetics presuming that human uses of arguments are crucial to reasonable belief in God. The present approach recommends apologetic modesty regarding the evidence for God.

Exaggeration of the importance of reasons as arguments for faith in God typically stems in part from a failure to distinguish between one's *having* reasons and one's *showing* or *presenting* reasons for such faith. As noted, one can have (good) reasons for faith in God without one's showing one's reasons to others or oneself in an argument, and even without one's *being able* to show one's reasons to others or oneself in an argument. The intellectually complex process of showing one's reasons in an argument is not required for one's having (good) reasons for faith in God. A contrary view shows confusion about the nature of reasons.

God could build up to intersubjective evidence of divine reality for humans on the basis of evidence in a first-person human perspective. People could have *in common* a *de re* encounter with God, and this could yield intersubjective evidence underlying mutuality in reasons for belief in God. Such evidence would be a kind of (limited) public evidence in virtue of being shared by a number of people. It would not, however, necessarily be had by all rational inquirers or be an argument. So, its evidential cogency would have limits, being relative to the people who have that actual evidence. In any case, we should not expect the ultimate evidence or reasons for faith in God to be a source of persuasion for all people; nor, more basically, should we expect divine self-manifestation to be public or shared in all cases. This lesson bears directly on *de dicto* faith that God exists and its defense.

Faith that God exists, as noted, is *de dicto* in virtue of its propositional and conceptual content: that God exists. Related content (such as faith *about* God that God exists) can be interpretive *de re* when coupled with faith *in God*, because the latter content would interpret or classify the *de re* component as the divine object (and as the divine subject) of an encounter with God. The interpretation would characterize the encounter as including the *reality of God*. In doing so, it would affirm that something is real, thereby implying that a claim is *made true*, with the reality in question being the truth-maker, namely, *God's* reality.

An interpretation of a human experience can be wrong or incorrect (at least typically), and therefore we can ask whether *de dicto* faith that God exists is correct in its interpretation. Correctness here would entail the kind of fact-based truth identified by Aristotle in his *Metaphysics*, Book IV: To say of what is that it is, or of what is not that it is not, is true. A correct or true interpretation, in other words, must match the relevant facts. The consequences of departing from such a realist approach to truth are philosophically devastating (see Moser 1989, 1993), and nobody has improved on Aristotle's basic characterization of truth. Faith that God exists cannot be properly understood apart from the question of whether it is true that God exists. Responsibly answering the latter question, however, need not be, and is not, quick and easy.

Abduction and Agapē

The most promising approach to the question of whether faith that God exists is correct or true is a variation on a broader approach to epistemic reasonableness, the kind of reasonableness suited to factual knowledge. This approach invokes *abduction*, an inference to a best available explanation of the relevant evidence for a person, as a key factor in epistemically reasonable belief (for details, see Moser 1989, 2008, chap. 2). The main idea is not that a person must always draw an inference to a best available explanation to have epistemically reasonable belief. Instead, it is that the epistemic reasonableness of a belief for a person depends on there being *available* an inference to a best available explanation from the person's evidence to the belief in question. Large areas of the sciences rely on such reasonableness based on abduction, but in connection with faith in God, an explanation depending on a superhuman personal agent merits consideration.

The *foundational* evidence will be the person's overall base of (non-propositional) experience, and the *non-foundational* evidence will be the person's beliefs (or at least those propositions) made epistemically reasonable (for that person) on the basis of the foundational evidence. The epistemic connection between the two tiers is an available inference to a best available explanation. A person's belief, or faith, that God exists will be fully grounded when it is suitably based on the evidence in question and on the epistemic connection between the evidence and the belief. Even so, the *proposition* (not to be confused with a belief) that God exists could be epistemically supported for a person, on the basis of experience, although that person does not base a belief that God exists on the supporting evidence or epistemic connection.

My abductive approach to epistemic reasonableness gives a central role to explanation-seeking why-questions about foundational evidence in one's (non-propositional) experience. A typical question of that sort is: Why am I now having *this* experience, rather than none at all or, alternatively, some other experience? This question calls for an answer, and there are better and worse answers relative to a person's overall experience and evidence. For instance, my current experience of an apparent computer screen prompts the question of why I am now having *this* experience rather than none at all or some other experience. A bad answer, from an abductive point of view, would be: I am now perceiving a brown Bengal cat. The latter claim would not explain why I am having the actual experience in question. That claim's propositional content does not correspond to or elucidate my actual experience. I am *not* now having an experience of a brown Bengal cat (my Bengal is elsewhere now).

We can extend the abductive lesson to skeptical worries. A skeptic may suggest that my present experience could be but a dream or an illusion, and therefore recommend that I withhold judgment on the matter. If "could" connotes logical possibility, we have no reason to dissent, because neither epistemic reasonableness nor knowledge rules out the *logical* possibility of being mistaken. Knowledge, given its truth condition, does rule out the *actuality* of being mistaken, but that leaves the logical possibility of error intact. Epistemic reasonableness does not require truth; there can be epistemically reasonable belief that is false. So, any skeptic using a modal notion of "possible mistake" owes us clarification of the relevant domain of modality.

My overall evidence does not give me any indication that I am now undergoing a dream or an illusion. I have had dreams and illusory experiences, and, so far as my evidence goes, they always have been accompanied by indicators of being dreams or illusory experiences. So, I do not find myself wondering now, in genuine doubt, whether any of my actual experiences is a dream or an illusion. I am able to tell, so far as my evidence goes, which experiences of mine were dreams or illusions, because dreams and illusions have had telltale indicators in my actual experience. Some of the familiar indicators are: inconstancy, abruptness, indistinctness, and incongruity. We all have been aware of such indicators in connection with (what we know to be) dreams and illusions. These considerations bear on my evidence regarding whether I *actually* am undergoing a dream or an illusion, not on the *possibility* of my undergoing a dream or an illusion.

My present experience of an apparent computer screen does not include any of the telltale indicators. This entails that my present experience does not include any evidence (or indicator) of its being a dream or an illusion. Again, I *logically could* be undergoing a dream or an illusion, but that *modal* truth is not to the *epistemic* point now. Epistemic reasonableness is determined by *actual* truth-indicators, and I do not have an actual truth-indicator in my evidence of a dream or an illusion in the present case. The burden is on the skeptic, then, to provide an actual indicator of a dream or an illusion, and a mere modal claim will not discharge this burden. Without an actual truth-indicator, the skeptic will not be able to discharge the burden. The skeptic then will be neutralized. (For further discussion of neutralizing skepticism, see Moser 2004, 2008, pp. 60–70, 138–40, 265–78.)

We now can identify an important lesson about a foundational reason or evidence for faith that God exists. When I confront a certain kind of *agapē* in my experience, I (at least from an epistemic point of view) should ask: Why am I having *this agapē* experience rather than no experience or a different experience? My answer calls for close attention to my experience, and I may need to put myself in a position to give a responsible answer. For instance, I may need to set aside any bias I have against the value of unselfish love, including such love directed toward me. In addition, I may need to be willing to cooperate with such love in order to comply with what God intends it to be and do.

A perfectly good God would intend divine love to inaugurate or sustain a divine–human relationship of *koinonia* that is in the best interest of a human. If a person is oppositional or indifferent to divine love, God may hide from that person to avoid a kind of rejection that hardens opposition or indifference to God. After all, if God seeks human cooperation with divine love, God's self-manifestation of such love to a person would not be satisfied with human responses that encourage further alienation from God. (On divine hiding, see Chapter 3; cf. Moser 2008, 2013.)

The phenomenology of general human experience of divine love is complex and subtle, as we should expect. We need not, and should not, assume that all humans would experience divine love in exactly the same way. We should expect a certain amount of variability, owing to distinctiveness in persons and their circumstances. A key question is whether the relevant experience of divine love includes an experience of *personal*, agent-centered traits suited to a God worthy of worship. Such traits would include the perfect love's being *intentional*, directed, and nudging (without coercion) toward a recipient's cooperation with it and conformation to it. So, we need to ask whether a superhuman agent manifests such intentionality, directedness, and nudging in any human experience. Is the manifestation of unselfish love in some human experience a *personal* disclosure or *self*-manifestation that transcends humans? This leads to the question of whether such love is *intentionally directed* toward me, and thus is not haphazard. In addition, it prompts the question of whether it is directed by a mere human. We thus may ask whether it is demanding of love of one's enemies in a manner foreign to typical human love.

The experience of my being presented with and directed toward divine love could be diachronic rather than just synchronic. That is, it could take place over time, and not just at an instant. So, I could assess it over time for its source, without a snap judgment at a moment. In addition, the experience could include my conscience being bothered, and perhaps even convicted, by the standard of experienced love over time, including my experienced failure to conform to that standard. In experiencing an attempt to rouse me and lead me away from my selfishness, I could experience my falling short of the love directed toward me.

This could create dissonance in my experience (including in my conscience) and in my self-understanding. It thus could create a morally relevant crisis in my life. (For relevant discussion, see Farmer 1936, chaps. 1, 11, Niebuhr 1941, vol. 1, chap. 9, and Moser 2018c and 2018d.) Part of this crisis could include my cooperatively receiving a reordering of my moral priorities and a new moral identity whereby *agapē* toward others, even enemies, takes first place in my commitments.

My experience could show signs of my being *intentionally* challenged, and perhaps even my willingly being convicted, by God to let go of my selfishness for the sake of unselfish love toward others, even my enemies. The apparently intentional challenge could go against my own preferences and intentions, and it could come to me via my conscience without input from another human. So, I could lack any indicator that the love presented to me, including its apparently intentional challenge to me, comes from me or another human. In that case, nothing in my experience would oppose that my experience of the challenge of love to me arises from a personal source independent of me and other humans. In this experience, I would seem to be intentionally guided or led, via conscience without coercion, toward unselfish love for others and away from unselfishness. As it happens, this is true of my own experience and conscience, and it indicates the involvement of a personal agent other than a human agent.

The self-manifestation of God would be intentional with a unique goal: having persons willingly being convicted by God and thereby being led by God toward (increasing) reconciliation and fellowship with God and others. This kind of "being convicted" is suggested by John 16:8, as previously noted, and it emerges in Revelation 3:19: "As many as I love, I convict and instruct" (my trans.). This talk of "conviction" suggests an intentional power at work in human experience. One can be convicted by God either against disobedience or toward righteous love for God and others. One's being thus convicted would have a passive component but would not coerce a human will. So, one still would need to decide in favor of God's will, perhaps repeatedly. Cooperative conviction would figure in God's initiated process of reconciliation and fellowship among humans. The ideal Christian model is Jesus in Gethsemane, and thus the cooperative yielding is, ideally, filial in spirit. (On the relevant sense of "filial" and its relation to knowing, see Moser 2008.)

The self-presentation of God's moral character can convict by way of sharp contrast with one's present character and will. It could occur in one's conscience when one has one's attention attracted by a contrast between divine love toward oneself (perhaps as a kind of opponent or enemy of God) and one's lack of love for one's own enemies. If one is cooperative and does not suppress the divine pressure toward conviction, this self-manifestation would create a conflict of conscience and an existential dissonance for one, and thus call for a resolution, either in favor of enemy love or against it. God would self-manifest the standard in morally perfect personality to a human, and this indicative state for one could ground an imperative for one to be conformed to God's moral reality. A vital moral duty thus could arise from divine self-manifestation by which one is cooperatively convicted.

As direct evidence for God's reality and character, one's being convicted toward perfect goodness would be inherently purposive. The purposive component in being convicted by God could emerge saliently in experience, with human cooperation toward it, as the goal-directedness of being convicted emerges. If God seeks the perfecting of divine love in humans over time and they cooperate with divine conviction toward that end, their experience will feature an intentional increase in loving others, in depth and in scope. This increase would rest on one's increasingly being convicted by God toward perfect moral goodness, including the love of one's enemies. It also would make salient the role of a morally perfect intentional agent in my moral transformation, and thus indicate that the process is uniquely personal. By including love of my enemies, it would counter a suggestion that the process results just from my ordinary desires or imagination, and would go against my natural desires. God would want our cooperatively being led, while being convicted, toward a life of reconciliation and fellowship with God and others, even our enemies. (For more on the pertinent role of conviction, see Moser 2018c and 2018d.)

Over time I could reasonably decide, on the basis of my overall evidence, that an intervention from a perfectly good God figures in a best available explanation (for me) of the challenging, convicting, and guiding love that troubles my conscience and reorders my priorities. I thus could lack the availability of a better or even an equally good alternative explanation of this love presented to me. Somebody could propose, however, a purely natural explanation as an underminer or defeater of a theological explanation of my experience. For instance, a critic could propose that I myself somehow am creating for myself my experience of the challenging and guiding love in question. We can grant the logical possibility of my creating this, even without our specifying a mechanism, but actual evidence, as we noted, requires an actual truth-indicator, beyond mere possibility. So, a critic needs somehow to base the critical proposal in my actual evidence; otherwise, the proposal will not get *epistemic* traction, at least for me. Without a basis in my evidence, the critical proposal of self-creation will not figure in a best available explanation for me, relative to my actual evidence. It thus will have an inadequate epistemic status for me, given my evidence.

My experience of the challenging, convicting, and guiding love presented to me could benefit, epistemically, from well-grounded reports from others. Such reports could come from well-grounded parts of a written religious tradition, such as relevant well-grounded parts of the Bible, or from well-grounded testimony from my contemporaries. The explanatory coherence of such well-grounded reports, in a manner fitting with my own experience, would add to the positive epistemic status of the best available explanation for me. In contrast, *mere* reports or testimonies, like mere beliefs, do not add to positive epistemic status. They are epistemically arbitrary in a way that well-grounded reports are not. Evidential support is the key difference here, and such support can vary among people.

Defeaters are underminers of epistemically reasonable belief for one, and they can come from any relevant aspect or area of one's experience. (They do not arise from mere belief or mere disagreement.) Likewise, added explanatory coherence for a belief relative to any aspect or area of one's experience can add to the positive epistemic status of that belief for one. My epistemic abductivism is thus evidentially holistic for a person, in terms of its attention to one's *overall* positive evidence and defeaters. The ultimate status of evidence for a person depends on *all* of that person's evidence and potential defeaters. Epistemic reasonableness, as suggested, is relative to persons and their evidence in this way, and it thus differs from truth and factuality. Such reasonableness does not entail or otherwise guarantee truth, but it is the responsible, non-arbitrary way to aim at acquiring truth and avoiding error. It is responsible to one's overall indicators (or evidence) of what is true, even if those indicators are fallible and defeasible.

Epistemic abductivism accommodates the truth that basic, foundational evidence in experience is not an argument or even a belief. The fact that the explanatory value of a belief relative to one's experience confers epistemic status on that belief allows that the basic evidence in experience is free of an argument or a belief. So, evidence from divine *agapē* in experience need not include an argument or a belief. Even so, it can figure in the epistemic reasonableness of a belief that serves in the best available explanation of that experiential evidence for a person. One's ultimate evidence for God's existence, then, need not be an argument or a belief. Philosophers and theologians have given inadequate attention to this important lesson, and the discussion of the relation between reason and faith in God has suffered accordingly.

De dicto faith, as suggested, can offer an interpretation of basic experiential evidence (for instance, by specifying what it is), and that interpretation can figure crucially in a best available explanation of one's experience. When it does figure thus, in the absence of defeaters, such faith can be well-grounded and hence epistemically reasonable for a person. Even when offering an interpretation and a best available explanation of experience, however, *de dicto* faith in God will allow for incompleteness, perplexity, and mystery. We should expect these when the object of faith is a God who cannot be fully comprehended by humans. After all, the God in question would transcend the created order and any understanding its members enjoy.

As Chapter 1 suggested, we should not expect to have a theodicy that fully explains God's purposes in allowing evil or in divine self-manifestation. For such a theodicy, God would need to reveal divine purposes in a way that bears on all cases of allowed evil, but our evidence does not indicate the reality of such revealing, and we should not expect it to do so. Even so, the human limitations in question could serve a divine redemptive purpose, because they could encourage a felt need for dependence on God (rather than just on a theory), thereby countering human pride and presumed self-sufficiency. (For elaboration on the relevant values of incompleteness, perplexity, and mystery, see Niebuhr 1949 and Rahner 1991.)

A *de re* factor from the divine self-manifestation of *agapē* can give *de dicto* faith the basic, foundational evidence it needs. It can give a person a firsthand acquaintance or direct encounter with divine reality and goodness. On the human side, faith in God would include a cooperative commitment to the divine love presented in experience. This commitment would include one's committing to turn away from selfishness for the sake of being committed to cooperate with such love, even if one fails (in action) to love unselfishly at times. This would include a significant reordering of one's priorities in life, and it could include an ongoing struggle for consistency in one's commitments.

We might wonder why we should not simply replace the role of faith with the role of active *agapē*. One consideration is that faith in God, being a disposition-oriented state, can be more constant for humans than concrete actions of loving God and others. Unselfish love in action toward God and others tends to waver more significantly among humans than does faith in God, at least among humans having faith in God. So, faith in God can serve as a means to loving God and others when such active loving is in short supply. When such faith is in place, it is a state rather than an episode, and hence can endure through times of human frailty in action, such as in failing to love in action. This fits with the consideration that a perfectly good God would seek an ongoing *relationship* with willing humans, beyond mere experiences, thoughts, feelings, or actions. An account of faith in God should accommodate the latter consideration in presenting the importance of the God relationship.

Witness and Defense

Many Christian apologists take their inspiration from the following remark in 1 Peter 3:15: "In your hearts sanctify Christ as Lord. Always be ready to make your defense (*apologia*) to anyone who demands from you an accounting (*logos*) for the hope that is in you; yet do it with gentleness and reverence." The author of 1 Peter calls for readiness in offering a *defense* of one's hope in God, but he insists that any defense should be offered with gentleness and respect toward inquirers. I cannot pursue the important issue of whether Christian apologists are known for their gentleness and respect toward their critics. I suspect that the evidence on this matter is mixed, but that is a separate topic.

The author of 1 Peter is not using the term *"apologia"* in the way often used by contemporary Christian apologists. He is not using the term to connote or to denote any argument of natural theology. As Chapter 3 noted, we find an absence of arguments of natural theology not only in 1 Peter but also in the rest of the New Testament writings. Paul is not using an argument of natural theology in his early speech at Athens (Acts 17:16–31) or, as noted, in the opening chapter of his later Epistle to the Romans, contrary to some apologists. Romans 1 does not offer a natural theological argument from nature to God, or from anything to God. As suggested previously, the key claim of Romans 1:19–20 is that *"God* has shown" things about God to humans, if through nature. There is no suggestion here that an *argument* from nature (or from any of its features) alone delivers a cogent argument for God's reality.

The New Testament writers, I have suggested, could have used philosophical arguments of natural theology, but chose not to do so. This is an important fact about the New Testament writers. Why did they forgo arguments of natural theology? They were not fideists or opponents of the use of either evidence or arguments. Instead, they sought evidence that was not speculative in a way that is vulnerable to quick doubt and easy rejection without existential challenge. They sought a kind of resilient evidence that was not supplied by the traditional arguments of natural theology.

Another relevant passage for many Christian apologists is 2 Corinthians 10:4–5: "We destroy arguments [*logismoi*] and every proud obstacle raised up against the knowledge of God, and we take every thought captive to obey Christ." Paul has in mind the refuting (*kathaireō*) of reasoning against the Christian message that God can be known in Christ. He does not have in mind, or in any way endorse, the use of the arguments of natural theology. Instead, he recommends considerations that refute various bad arguments against knowing God in Christ. We may call this "negative apologetics" and contrast it with the "positive apologetics" that presents evidence in favor of faith in God or Christ.

At Corinth, in a church he founded, Paul faced philosophical "wisdom" and "arguments" that interfered with the good news of knowing God in Christ. So, he offered the Christians at Corinth a portrait of God's wisdom in Christ, as an alternative to the wisdom and arguments influential at Corinth. After quoting the book of Isaiah, "I [God] will destroy the wisdom of the wise, and the discernment of the discerning I will thwart" (1 Cor. 1:19; cf. Isa. 29:14), Paul raises some rhetorical questions and offers a comment: "Where is the one who is wise [*sophos*]? Where is the scribe? Where is the debater of this age? Has not God made foolish the wisdom of the world? For since, in the wisdom of God, the world did not know God through [its] wisdom, God decided, through the foolishness of our proclamation, to save those who believe" (1 Cor. 1:20–21).

Paul, as Chapter 4 noted, assumes a sharp distinction between the wisdom of God and the wisdom of the world that humans formulate on their own and take pride in, without acknowledgment of God's redemptive work. The wisdom of God involved in Paul's apologetics, unlike the kind of wisdom promoted by many Christian apologists, does not underwrite philosophical boasting over others; instead, it deflates human pride or boasting toward others (1 Cor. 1:28–31). The widespread neglect of Paul's account in 1 Corinthians had led to neglect of this lesson, especially among Christian apologists.

Paul affirms that "in the wisdom of God, the world did not know God through [its] wisdom," and he would add that "the world did not know God" through its arguments of natural theology. He makes his concern clear in a remark already noted, 1 Corinthians 2:4–5: "My speech and my proclamation were not with plausible words of wisdom, but with a demonstration of the Spirit and of power, so that your faith might rest not on human wisdom but on the power of God." As suggested, human wisdom does not acknowledge God's role in wisdom, but it sometimes includes the premises of arguments of natural theology, which are intended to stand without acknowledgment of God's role. Paul seeks not to have faith in God rest on such human wisdom, including the "wisdom" of natural theology. His reason is clear: Such wisdom is an inadequate substitute for "the power of God," which is to be the causal and epistemic basis of faith in God. Paul leaves no room for a "both–and" approach that combines natural theology and the power of God. Divine power has no need for such a combination, and combining the two would only detract from the singular role of God's power. Many apologists miss this important lesson, and thereby offer an inadequate basis for faith in God.

The central, singular role for "the power of God" as the epistemic basis of faith in God displaces any need for the arguments of natural theology. The arguments of natural theology lack a needed role even as a preliminary to the preached gospel, where one might be concerned with mere theistic belief that God exists. No such preliminary is needed or is epistemically helpful, and, in any case, the arguments fail to yield a God worthy of worship. So, the arguments of natural theology play no role in the writings of the New Testament or in the work of the earliest Christians with preaching or teaching ministries. Those arguments emerged later in Christian thinking, after Paul's key notion of the "power of God" had been forgotten and neglected. Neglect of that notion accounts for the centrality of natural theology in later Christian apologetics. It also accounts for the absence of a resilient epistemology in much so-called "Christian philosophy." Some Christians look to the natural theology of Aquinas rather than to the epistemology of

Paul, in a way that eclipses Paul's important contribution. This is a serious mistake for Christian apologetics.

It would be misleading to infer that Paul does not argue for the good news of God in Christ. Paul argues vigorously, but he does not argue on the basis of natural theology or speculative philosophy, and thus he differs from many Christian apologists. Paul argues on the basis of distinctive religious experience, without relying on any argument of natural theology or speculative philosophy. He attributes the key experience to the Spirit of God, and thus we may call the relevant experience and evidence "pneumatic." We see his emphasis on pneumatic experience in 1 Corinthians 2:10, 12: "These things God has revealed to us through the Spirit; for the Spirit searches everything, even the depths of God. . . . Now we have received not the spirit of the world, but the Spirit that is from God, so that we may understand the gifts bestowed on us by God." Paul would regard human knowledge of God as a gift, courtesy of divine cognitive grace.

Paul speaks of "God, who has given us the Spirit as a guarantee" (2 Cor. 5:5; see also 2 Cor. 1:22; cf. Eph. 1:13–14, Rom. 8:16). God's giving of the Spirit is intended to be a guarantee at least in an epistemic or evidential sense. This is confirmed in an important remark from Paul we have emphasized in the previous discussion: "Hope [in God] does not disappoint us, because God's love [agapē] has been poured into our hearts through the Holy Spirit that has been given to us" (Rom. 5:5). Here we have the experiential and evidential foundation of hope and faith in God for Paul's pneumatic epistemology. This is the kind of "power of God" that Paul identifies as the singular epistemic basis for faith in God (1 Cor. 2:4–5).

There is no argument of natural theology in Paul, but there is an appeal to a direct experience of God's intervening Spirit, in the experience of divine love in one's heart, or volitional center. This kind of life-changing and priority reordering experience, according to Paul, saves one from being cognitively or epistemically disappointed regarding hope and faith in God. It adequately grounds such hope and faith, and thereby saves them from being a leap in the dark or any other kind of guesswork. Paul does not allow for the dilution of this unique evidence from God by any argument from natural theology. So, he cannot be co-opted by the apologetics movement that relies on arguments from natural theology.

The foundational evidence in "the power of God" is not static in the way the evidence in the arguments of natural theology is. Coming directly from a personal God, this foundational evidence shows features of personal awareness and discernment. So, it can vary at times and among persons, in the ways that the interventions of a personal agent can and often do. This is important, because it allows the foundational evidence for God to be elusive and even hidden at times in the ways the biblical God is, for redemptive purposes.

What is the fate of apologetics in the light of the avoidance of natural theology by the New Testament writers? The answer depends on what one builds into apologetics. If one weds apologetics to the arguments of natural theology, as many apologists do, then one will face at best an uneasy alliance with the seminal writings of the Jesus movement, namely, the writings of the New Testament. One then will promote a questionable add-on to the good news message of those writings and its defense by their authors. I have contended, in keeping with Paul's First Epistle to the Corinthians, that this add-on is unnecessary and potentially obscuring to the suitable epistemic basis for Christian faith in God and to a resilient defense of the veracity or the evidential groundedness of such faith.

It is, as suggested, one thing to have evidence for faith in God, and it is another thing to have a presentable *defense* of faith in God. Having the former evidence does not require having the latter defense. It is a serious category mistake to confuse the two. So, we should resist any assumption that adequate evidence for faith in God necessarily includes a public argument cogent for all inquirers. It would be misleading at best to rely on such an assumption in a defense of faith in God. One consideration is that God may have no reason to supply the kind of public defense in question. It is not clear, in any case, that such a defense would have redemptive value if God seeks volitional cooperation from humans, beyond assent to propositions. In fact, that kind of defense could interfere with a divine challenge to human wills alienated from God's will. It could reduce the question of God's existence to a merely intellectual question that fails to challenge the direction of human wills in relation to God. In any case, I should not automatically attribute my own religious experience or evidence to others, who may not have it. Otherwise, I risk a kind of cognitive bullying that will fail to convince others and may actually alienate them.

If the experience of divine love varies among humans, with some humans lacking the experience, we should not expect an argument from experienced love to God's reality to be cogent for all inquirers. People lacking the relevant experience will not have the evidence needed to make an argument convincing for their own situations. A related lesson bears on universal atheism or agnosticism. An atheist, for instance, can lack crucial foundational evidence from an experience of divine love. Such a person thus could lack the needed basis for epistemically reasonable belief that God exists.

It would be premature at best for an atheist to generalize his or her epistemic situation to all people. Other people still could have the needed experience of divine love, and this experience could figure in their epistemically reasonable belief that God exists. So, generalization of evidence regarding God's existence needs to be sensitive to a person's actual evidence and to the potential variability of relevant evidence among people. Attention to this lesson will put arguments regarding God's existence in their proper place regarding their cogency or lack of cogency among people. It also will save people from exaggerated expectations for a reasoned defense of faith in God.

In the perspective offered here, a defense of faith in God is, *ultimately*, God's *self*-defense; and God's self-defense is, *ultimately*, God's *self*-manifestation via divine *agapē* in human experience. Any non-ultimate defense, such as one relying on arguments, must derive from and point to the aforementioned facts of the ultimate defense. The current lesson, however, is that faith in God admits of a defense, but it is not the kind of defense typically considered by philosophers, theologians, apologists, and others.

The relevant defense will prompt the question of why some people report an experience of divine love whereas others do not. In doing so, it will raise the issue of whether some people oppose or are indifferent to such an experience for themselves. That issue can invite us to consider whether the matter of having divine evidence has as much to do with a human as with God, owing to a crucial redemptive role for human cooperation with God and divine evidence. A related inquiry would concern the identification of impediments to having divine evidence and alternatives to such impediments. In any case, there does seem to be variability among humans in perceiving a self-manifestation of God's character in *agapē*. Theologians and philosophers of religion, among others, would do well to attend to such considerations in a religious epistemology that considers the reality of a God worthy of worship.

9. CONCLUSION

According to the New Testament, the Spirit of God is the Spirit of Christ and thus is seen most clearly in his life, death, and resurrection. The witness of this Spirit, in the New Testament story, relays God's redemptive love and the message thereof to cooperative people. Humans will apprehend this Spirit's reality only if they are willing, in the words of Jesus, to have "eyes to see and ears to hear" what God intends for humans. The intended recipients of the witness must open themselves to be attuned to the perfect moral character of God, including divine *agapē*. In the case of humans knowing God, God would seek to move their wills toward obedience to God's perfect will, just as Jesus obeyed in Gethsemane. Being perfectly loving, God would seek to have humans learn to love and to obey as Jesus loves and obeys. So, the witness of God's Spirit would aim for the reconciliation of humans to God.

The final issue is: Will we humans cooperatively receive the challenging witness on offer? Whatever our ultimate answer, the role for sincere human decision in response is now clear and vital. In addition, we now have a sense of the kind of relevant evidence to be expected of a God who self-manifests and self-authenticates to cooperative humans. This leaves us with an important practical matter of decision regarding the question of God's reality. Each willing person will have to face this matter for his or her own experience and life, relative to his or her own overall evidence. We should expect this if God makes an effort to redeem humans as *individual persons* with distinctive experiences and lives.

We should expect God to seek, at the opportune time, a God relationship with humans of the kind outlined here. Given the nature of this relationship, we should expect there to be an ethics of responsible human inquiry about God. We have seen that this ethics may call for a reordering of one's priorities for life. Anything less than this would fall short of the moral perfection of a God worthy of worship. In the matters of such a God, even in inquiry about such a God, ethics will loom large, always. We humans would need to follow suit, regardless of the difficulties for us. The value of the God relationship in question merits our responsible attention and pursuit, perhaps even above all else.

References

Aristotle. *Metaphysics*, trans. Hugh Lawson-Tancred. London: Penguin, 1999.

Aristotle. *Nicomachean Ethics*, 2nd ed., trans. Roger Crisp. Cambridge: Cambridge University Press, 2014.

Aristotle. *Posterior Analytics*, 2nd ed., trans. Jonathan Barnes. Oxford: Clarendon Press, 1994.

Augustine. 402/2011. *Homilies on the First Letter of John*, trans. Boniface Ramsey. New York: New City Press.

Baillie, John. 1929. *The Place of Jesus Christ in Modern Christianity*. New York: Charles Scribner's Sons.

1956. *The Idea of Revelation in Recent Thought*. New York: Columbia University Press.

1962. *The Sense of the Presence of God*. New York: Charles Scribner's Sons.

Balentine, Samuel. 1983. *The Hidden God*. Oxford: Oxford University Press.

Barclay, John. 2015. *Paul and the Gift*. Grand Rapids, MI: Eerdmans.

Barr, James. 1981. *Fundamentalism*, 2nd ed. London: SCM Press.

Berkouwer, G.C. 1976. *Studies in Dogmatics: The Church*, trans. J.E. Davison. Grand Rapids, MI: Eerdmans.

1977. *A Half Century of Theology*, trans. L.B. Smedes. Grand Rapids, MI: Eerdmans.

Bonhoeffer, Dietrich. 1953. *Letters and Papers from Prison*, trans. R.H. Fuller. London: Macmillan.

Bradley, Ian. 1995. *The Power of Sacrifice*. London: Darton, Longman, and Todd.

Brown, Alexandra R. 1995. *The Cross and Human Transformation*. Minneapolis: Fortress Press.

1996. "Apocalyptic Transformation in Paul's Discourse on the Cross." *Word & World* 16: 427–36.

1998. "The Gospel Takes Place: Paul's Theology of Power-in-Weakness in 2 Corinthians." *Interpretation* 52: 271–85.

Brunner, Emil. 1962. *Dogmatics, vol. III: The Christian Doctrine of the Church, Faith, and the Consummation*, trans. David Cairns and T.H.L. Parker. Philadelphia: Westminster Press.

1964. *Truth as Encounter*, rev. ed., trans. David Cairns. Philadelph ia: Westminster Press.

Buber, Martin. 1923. *I and Thou*, trans. R.G. Smith. New York: Charles Scribner's Sons, 1958.

Buckley, Michael J. 1987. *At the Origins of Modern Atheism*. New Haven, CT: Yale University Press.

Burghardt, Walter. 1983. "From Study to Proclamation." In *A New Look at Preaching*, ed. John Burke, 25–42. Wilmington, DE: Michael Glazier.

Cosgrove, Charles H. 1988. *The Cross and the Spirit*. Macon, GA: Mercer University Press.

Craig, William Lane. 2014. "Is Faith in God Reasonable?" In *Is Faith in God Reasonable?*, eds. Corey Miller and Paul Gould, 13–19, 24–29, 32–34. New York: Routledge.

Crump, David. 2013. *Encountering Jesus, Encountering Scripture*. Grand Rapids, MI: Eerdmans.

Daly, Robert J. 2009. *Sacrifice Unveiled*. London: T&T Clark.

Dawkins, Richard. 2006. *The God Delusion*. New York: Houghton Mifflin.

Dodd, C.H. 1936. *The Apostolic Preaching and its Developments*. London: Hodder and Stoughton.

1960. *The Authority of the Bible*, rev. ed. Glasgow: Collins.

Dunn, James D.G. 1998. *The Christ and the Spirit: Pneumatology*. Grand Rapids, MI: Eerdmans.

Eichrodt, Walter. 1967. "The Forms of God's Self-Manifestation." In Eichrodt, *Theology of the Old Testament*, trans. J.A. Baker, Vol. 2, 15–45. London: SCM Press.

Farmer, Herbert H. 1927. *Things Not Seen*. London: Nisbet.

1936. *The World and God*, rev. ed. London: Nisbet.

1942. *The Servant of the Word*. New York: Charles Scribner's Sons.

1943. *Towards Belief in God*. New York: Macmillan.

1954. *Revelation and Religion*. London: Nisbet.

Fee, Gordon D. 1994. *God's Empowering Presence*. Peabody, MA: Hendrickson Publishers.

Ferré, Nels. 1961. "The Nature and Power of Christian Experience." In Ferré, *Searchlights on Contemporary Theology*, 184–95. New York: Harper.

Fiddes, Paul S. 1988. *The Creative Suffering of God*. Oxford: Clarendon Press.

1989. *Past Event and Present Salvation*. London: Darton, Longman, and Todd.

Fitzgerald, John T. 1988. *Cracks in an Earthen Vessel*. Atlanta: Scholars Press.

Fitzmyer, Joseph. 1993. *Romans: The Anchor Bible*. New York: Doubleday.

2008. *First Corinthians: The Anchor Yale Bible*. New Haven, CT: Yale University Press.

Forrest, David W. 1906. *The Authority of Christ*, 2nd ed. Edinburgh: T&T Clark.

1914. *The Christ of History and of Experience*, 7th ed. Edinburgh: T&T Clark.

Forsyth, P.T. 1909. *The Person and Place of Jesus Christ*. London: Independent Press.

Furnish, Victor Paul. 1972. *The Love Command in the New Testament*. Nashville: Abingdon Press.

George, A. Raymond. 1953. *Communion with God in the New Testament*. London: Epworth Press.

Gilson, Etienne. 1955. *History of Christian Philosophy in the Middle Ages*. New York: Random House.

Gorman, Michael J. 2001. *Cruciformity*. Grand Rapids, MI: Eerdmans.

2009. *Inhabiting the Cruciform God*. Grand Rapids, MI: Eerdmans.

Häring, Bernard. 1978. *Free and Faithful in Christ, Vol.1: General Moral Theology*. New York: Seabury Press.

Harrisville, Roy A. 2006. *Fracture: The Cross as Irreconcilable in the Language and Thought of the Biblical Writers*. Grand Rapids, MI: Eerdmans.

Heim, Karl. 1936. *God Transcendent*, trans. E.P. Dickie. New York: Charles Scribner's Sons.

Hengel, Martin. 1977. *Crucifixion*, trans. John Bowden. London: SCM Press.

Heschel, Abraham. 1955. *God in Search of Man: A Philosophy of Judaism*. New York: Jewish Publication Society of America.

1962. *The Prophets*. New York: Jewish Publication Society.

Hick, John. 1964. "Sceptics and Believers." In *Faith and the Philosophers*, ed. John Hick, 235–50. New York: St. Martin's Press.

1971. "Rational Theistic Belief without Proofs." In *Arguments for the Existence of God*, ed. John Hick, 101–20. New York: Herder.

1978. *The Center of Christianity*. New York: Harper and Row.

2010. *Evil and the God of Love*, 2nd ed. London: Macmillan.

Holland, H.S. 1923. *The Fourth Gospel*. London: John Murray.

Hooker, Morna. 1979. *Pauline Pieces*. London: Epworth Press.

Hubbard, Moyer V. 2002. *New Creation in Paul's Letters and Thought*. Cambridge: Cambridge University Press.

Käsemann, Ernst. 1969. "'The Righteousness of God' in Paul." In Käsemann, *New Testament Questions of Today*, trans. W.J. Montague, 168–82. London: SCM Press.

1980. *Commentary on Romans*, trans. G.W. Bromiley. Grand Rapids, MI: Eerdmans.

2010. "The Righteousness of God in Paul." In Käsemann, *On Being a Disciple of the Crucified Nazarene*, trans. R.A. Harrisville, 15–26. Grand Rapids, MI: Eerdmans.

Keck, Leander. 1983. "Biblical Preaching as Divine Wisdom." In *A New Look at Preaching*, ed. John Burke, 137–56. Wilmington, DE: Michael Glazier.

1988. *Paul and His Letters*, 2nd ed. Philadelphia: Fortress Press.

1993. "Paul as Thinker." *Interpretation* 47: 27–38.

1996. "God the Other Who Acts Otherwise: An Exegetical Essay on 1 Cor 1:26–31." *Word & World* 16: 437–43.

2005. *Romans*. Nashville: Abingdon Press.

Kierkegaard, Søren. 1846. *Concluding Unscientific Postscript to Philosophical Fragments*, trans. H.V. and E.H. Hong. Princeton: Princeton University Press, 1992.

1847. *Works of Love*, trans. H.V. and E.H. Hong. Princeton: Princeton University Press, 1995.

Knight, George A.F. 1959. *A Christian Theology of the Old Testament*. London: SCM Press.

Koenig, John. 1992. *Rediscovering New Testament Prayer*. New York: Harper.

Lemcio, Eugene E. 1991. *The Past of Jesus in the Gospels*. Cambridge: Cambridge University Press.

Levenson, Jon D. 2015. *The Love of God*. Princeton: Princeton University Press.

Mackintosh, H.R. 1913. *The Doctrine of the Person of Jesus Christ*, 2nd ed. Edinburgh: T&T Clark.

1921. *The Divine Initiative*. London: SCM Press.

1927. *The Christian Experience of Forgiveness*. New York: Harper & Brothers.

1929. *The Christian Apprehension of God*. London: SCM Press.

1938. "An Indisputable Argument." In Mackintosh, *Sermons*, 171–79. Edinburgh: T&T Clark.

Martin, Michael, ed. 2007. *Cambridge Companion to Atheism*. Cambridge: Cambridge University Press.

Martin, Ralph P. 1981. *Reconciliation: A Study of Paul's Theology*. Atlanta: John Knox.

Martyn, J. Louis. 1967/1997. "Epistemology at the Turn of the Ages." In Martyn, *Theological Issues in the Letters of Paul*, 89–110. Edinburgh: T&T Clark.

1997. *Galatians: The Anchor Bible*. New York: Doubleday.

Matthews, W.R. 1936. "Who is God?" *The Modern Churchman* 26: 176–82.

1939. *God in Christian Thought and Experience*, rev. ed. London: Nisbet.

Mavrodes, George. 1970. *Belief in God*. New York: Random House.

1983. "Jerusalem and Athens Revisited." In *Faith and Rationality*, eds. Alvin Plantinga and Nicholas Wolterstorff, 192–218. Notre Dame, IN: University of Notre Dame Press.

Miller, Donald G. 1954. *Fire in Thy Mouth*. New York: Abingdon Press.

Minear, Paul S. 1966. *Eyes of Faith*, rev. ed. St. Louis: Abbott Books.

1994. *Christians and the New Creation*. Philadelphia: Westminster.

Moltmann, Jürgen. 1981. *The Trinity and the Kingdom*. San Francisco: Harper and Row.

Moser, Paul K. 1989. *Knowledge and Evidence*. Cambridge: Cambridge University Press.

1993. *Philosophy after Objectivity*. New York: Oxford University Press.

2004. "Skepticism Undone?" In *Ernest Sosa and His Critics*, ed. John Greco, 135–44. Oxford: Blackwell.

2008. *The Elusive God: Reorienting Religious Epistemology*. Cambridge: Cambridge University Press.

2010. *The Evidence for God: Religious Knowledge Reexamined*. Cambridge: Cambridge University Press.

2012. "Natural Theology and the Evidence for God." *Philosophia Christi* 14: 305–11.

2013. *The Severity of God: Religion and Philosophy Reconceived*. Cambridge: Cambridge University Press.

2017. "How Not to Defend Positive Evidential Atheism." *Religious Studies* 53: 1–7 (online version).

2018a. "Pascal's Wager and the Ethics for Inquiry about God." In *Pascal's Wager*, eds. Paul Bartha and Lawrence Pasternack. Cambridge: Cambridge University Press, forthcoming.

2018b. "Attributes of God: Goodness, Hiddenness, Everlastingness." In *Macmillan Interdisciplinary Handbooks: Philosophy, Vol. 8: Philosophy of Religion*, ed. Donald Borchert, 17–31. New York: Macmillan, forthcoming.

2018c. "Convictional Knowledge, Science, and the Spirit of Christ." In *Christ and the Created Order*, eds. Andrew Torrance and Tom McCall. Grand Rapids, MI: Zondervan Academic/Harper, forthcoming.

2018d. "Divine Hiddenness, *Agapē* Conviction, and Spiritual Discernment." In *Discernment for Things Divine: Towards a Constructive Account of Spiritual Perception*, eds. Paul Gavrilyuk and Frederick Aquino. Oxford: Oxford University Press, forthcoming.

Nagel, Thomas. 1997. *The Last Word*. New York: Oxford University Press.

Niebuhr, Reinhold. 1937. *Beyond Tragedy*. New York: Charles Scribner's Sons.

1941. *The Nature and Destiny of Man, Vol. 1: Human Nature*. New York: Charles Scribner's Sons.

1949. *Faith and History*. New York: Charles Scribner's Sons.

Niebuhr, H. Richard. 1963. *The Responsible Self*. New York: Harper & Row.

Otto, Rudolf. 1923. *The Idea of the Holy*, trans. J.W. Harvey. London: Oxford University Press.

Pascal, Blaise. 1662. *Pensées*, trans. A.J. Krailsheimer. London: Penguin, 1966.

Piper, Otto A. 1959. "The Origin of the Gospel Pattern." *Journal of Biblical Literature* 78: 115–24.

Plato. *Apology*. In *The Last Days of Socrates: Euthyphro, Apology, Crito, Phaedo*, trans. Hugh Tredennick. London: Penguin, 1970.

    The Laws, trans. A.E. Taylor. London: Dent, 1934.

    Meno. In *Meno and Other Dialogues*, trans. Robin Waterfield. Oxford: Oxford University Press, 2005.

    Phaedo. In *The Last Days of Socrates: Euthyphro, Apology, Crito, Phaedo*, trans. Hugh Tredennick. London: Penguin, 1970.

    Phaedrus, trans. Robin Waterfield. Oxford: Oxford University Press, 2009.

Rahner, Karl. 1960. *Encounters with Silence*, trans. J.M. Demske. Westminster, MD: Newman.

    1964. "God is Far from Us." In *The Content of Faith*, eds. Karl Lehmann, Albert Raffelt, and Harvey Egan, 216–20. New York: Crossroad, 1993.

    1973. "Images of God." In *The Content of Faith*, eds. Karl Lehmann, Albert Raffelt, and Harvey Egan, 211–12. New York: Crossroad, 1993.

    1978. *Foundations of Christian Faith*, trans. W.V. Dych. New York: Seabury Press.

    1991. "Christian Pessimism." In Rahner, *Theological Investigations XXII*, 155–62, trans. Joseph Donceel. New York: Crossroad.

Ramsey, Paul. 1943. "The Great Commandment." *Christianity and Society* 8: 29–35.

    1950. *Basic Christian Ethics*. New York: Charles Scribner's Sons.

Rescher, Nicholas. 2010. *Axiogenesis*. Lanham, MD: Lexington Books.

Richardson, Alan. 1956. "Gnosis and Revelation in the Bible and in Contemporary Thought." *Scottish Journal of Theology* 9: 31–45.

    1957. *Science and Existence: Two Ways of Knowing*. London: SCM Press.

    1958. *An Introduction to the Theology of the New Testament*. London: SCM Press.

    1961. *The Bible in the Age of Science*. London: SCM Press.

    1966. "The Death of God: A Report Exaggerated." In Richardson, *Religion in Contemporary Debate*, 102–19. Philadelphia: Westminster Press.

Robinson, H. Wheeler. 1942. *Redemption and Revelation*. London: Nisbet.

Rosenberg, Alex. 2014. "Is Faith in God Reasonable?" In *Is Faith in God Reasonable?*, eds. Corey Miller and Paul Gould, 19–24, 29–31, 34–36. New York: Routledge.

Rossé, Gérard. 1987. *The Cry of Jesus on the Cross*, trans. S.W. Arndt. New York: Paulist Press.

Russell, Bertrand. 1903. "A Free Man's Worship." In Russell, *Mysticism and Logic*, 44–54. New York: Doubleday, 1957.

1970. "The Talk of the Town." *The New Yorker* (February 21, 1970): 29. Cited in *Bertrand Russell on God and Religion*, ed. Al Seckel, 11. Buffalo: Prometheus, 1986.

Savage, Timothy B. 1996. *Power through Weakness: Paul's Understanding of the Christian Ministry in 2 Corinthians.* Cambridge: Cambridge University Press.

Schellenberg, J.L. 2006. *Divine Hiddenness and Human Reason.* Ithaca: Cornell University Press.

Schillebeeckx, Edward. 1980. *Christ: The Experience of Jesus as Lord,* trans. John Bowden. New York: Seabury Press.

Schweitzer, Albert. 1933. *Out of My Life and Thought.* New York: Henry Holt.

Shope, Robert K. 2002. "Conditions and Analyses of Knowing." In *The Oxford Handbook of Epistemology,* ed. Paul K. Moser, 25–70. New York: Oxford University Press.

Speak, Daniel. 2014. *The Problem of Evil.* Cambridge: Polity Press.

Stauffer, Ethelbert. 1955. *New Testament Theology,* trans. John Marsh. New York: Macmillan.

Stewart, James S. 1940. "Who is this Jesus? (2)." In Stewart, *The Strong Name,* 80–89. Edinburgh: T&T Clark.

Taylor, John V. 1972. *The Go-Between God.* London: SCM Press.

1992. *The Christlike God.* London: SCM Press.

Taylor, Vincent. 1937. *Jesus and his Sacrifice.* London: Macmillan.

Terrien, Samuel. 1978. *The Elusive Presence.* San Francisco: Harper & Row.

Thielicke, Helmut. 1961. *How the World Began,* trans. J.W. Doberstein. Philadelphia: Muhlenberg.

1962. *Out of the Depths,* trans. G.W. Bromiley. Grand Rapids, MI: Eerdmans.

Thiselton, Anthony C. 2013. *The Holy Spirit.* Grand Rapids, MI: Eerdmans.

Torrance, Andrew B. 2016. *The Freedom to Become a Christian.* London: Bloomsbury.

Wahlberg, Mats. 2014. *Revelation as Testimony.* Grand Rapids, MI: Eerdmans.

Walsh, Sylvia. 2009. *Kierkegaard.* Oxford: Oxford University Press.

Westermann, Claus. 1979. *What does the Old Testament Say about God?,* trans. F.W. Golka. Atlanta: John Knox.

1982. *Elements of Old Testament Theology,* trans. D.W. Scott. Atlanta: John Knox Press.

Wright, G. Ernest. 1950. *The Old Testament against its Environment.* London: SCM Press.

1952. *God Who Acts.* London: SCM Press.

Index

Abraham, 73, 93–95, 96, 100, 120–22, 132, 161, 167, 199, 218, 291; allows his evidence regarding God to prevail over his fears and doubts regarding God, 94; and his faith in God, 95; and his monotheistic faith, 94, 99, 102, 110, 119–20, 128, 161; becomes the recipient of God's reckoned righteousness, 94

Acts of the Apostles, 244, 288, 324

agapē, 24–25, 72–74, 79–82, 130–34, 166–69, 266–70, 274–77, 280–83, 293–301, 304–6; abduction, 314–18; actions as responsive obedience to God, 277; active, 323; compassionate, 246; figures, 151; humanly experienced, 268–69, 295, 316; inner, 298; mutual relationships, 7, 273, 302; perfect, 149, 246, 298; redemptive, 176, 274; sacrificial, 220; self-giving, 175, 202, 270; self-manifested, 296, 305; self-sacrificial, 176, 289, 293, 299; stable unselfish, 268; the power of, 219, 279

agnostic philosophers, 120

agnosticism, 71, 90, 135, 143, 162–64, 239, 329

anti-God, 43, 50, 216

apologetic modesty, 312

apologetics, 46, 55, 328; Christian, 312, 324, 326–27; movement, 328; negative, 325; Paul's, 325; positive, 325

apologia, 323–24

apologists, 312, 323–27, 328

apostles, 14, 16, 51, 214; John, 14, 85–86, 167, 168–69, 267–69, 274–75, 288–89, 292, 298–99, 301–2; Luke, 8, 31, 42, 130, 174, 200, 237–38, 266, 274, 287–88; Mark, 15, 200; Matthew, 8, 43, 229, 252, 299; Paul, 73–74, 77–80, 92–96, 99–104, 200–10, 213–20, 223–26, 288–93, 295–300, 324–28; Simon Peter, 14–15, 175, 287, 323–24

Aquinas, Thomas, 159, 326

"argumentism about God", 49, 120

Aristotle, 28, 66, 116, 135, 156, 196–97, 258, 277, 313

atheism, 71, 135, 138–39, 161, 162–64, 239; evidence-based, 148; universal, 329

atheists, 118, 120, 128, 138–39, 143, 145, 159, 248, 329

attentiveness, ethics of, 15, 239

Augustine, 83, 102

Baillie, John, 83, 129, 205, 271, 281

Barth, Karl, 56

Bonhoeffer, Dietrich, 102, 302

Brown, Alexandra R., 214

Brunner, Emil, 12, 270–71

Buber, Martin, 12, 56, 221

Bultmann, Rudolf, 56
Burghardt, Walter, 266

Carroll, Lewis, 117
Carson, Tom, xii
charis, 33, 74, 169
Christ Jesus *see* Jesus, 82
Christian apologetics, 312, 324, 326–27
Christian belief, 186–87, 233
Christian faith, 96, 105, 193–94, 309, 328
Christian Good News *see* Good News, 92
Christian message, 173–74, 324
Christian philosophy, 198, 200, 228–30, 312, 326
Christianity, xii, 119, 198–99;
    Christians, 8, 62, 92, 99, 198–99, 220–21, 229, 288, 325–26;
    Corinthian, 200–3, 209, 214, 217, 223, 230, 290, 292–93, 324–26, 327–28; earliest, 326; Galatian, 290, 291; Jewish, 287; Roman, 80, 175, 290, 293, 295
churches, 175, 229, 296, 325
Climacus, Johannes, 8, 56
cognitive modesty, 140, 165, 249–50
communion, 36, 38, 41, 43–44, 53, 108–10, 122, 257, 271, 287; Biblical notion of, 109; ceremonies, 242; divine, 271
conscience *see also* human conscience, 15, 54, 125, 131–32, 134, 151–52, 154–56, 240, 243–45, 318–20
conviction, 122, 125, 138, 318–20; in conscience to forgive and to love my enemies, 243; of trust, 94; previously acknowledged, 138; uncoerced, 155
cooperation, 15, 37–39, 155–56, 164–65, 185–86, 191, 239, 260, 261–63, 278–79; harmonious, 238; human, 15, 20, 25, 155, 177, 182, 263–65, 293, 296, 305; interpersonal, 5; obedient, 219;

rejecting, 71; volitional, 5, 58, 86, 128, 294, 329; willing, 154
Corinthian Christians, 200–3, 209, 214, 217, 223, 230, 290, 292–93, 324–26, 327–28
Corinthians, First Epistle of, 133, 200–3, 209, 214, 217, 223, 230, 293, 324–26, 327–28
Cosgrove, Charles, 216, 218
cosmic authority problem, 161
curative, 33, 36–37, 43, 44, 47, 49, 51, 56–57, 117, 188–90; endeavors, 41; knowledge, 38–39; *koinonia*, 53; love, 84; power, 54, 113–14; process, 44, 48, 67, 75, 77, 108; purposes, 41, 51, 67, 152; relationships, 33, 45, 54–56, 96, 273; renewal, 80–81, 82; strength, 114

Dawkins, Richard, 145, 191
defense of faith, 46–47, 53–54, 212, 244, 250, 256, 308–9, 328–30
direct evidence, 91, 128, 243
disciples, 136, 174, 214, 216, 286, 289, 291, 297–98, 302, 308
distinctive evidence, 268, 295–97, 298
divine evidence, 29, 45, 47–49, 112, 131, 150, 213, 282, 304, 330
divine forgiveness, 108, 119, 213, 239, 262
divine grace, 33, 79, 99–102, 174, 197, 201, 211, 218, 261, 300
divine reconciliation, 66, 238
divine redemption, 38–39, 52, 108, 130, 217, 236, 250–51, 259, 262–64, 278
divine self-manifesting, 134–35, 150–51, 172, 177, 179–80, 183–84, 190–91, 204, 263, 301
divine wisdom, 51–52, 194, 197, 203, 215, 220, 228

epistemic, 136, 241, 290, 296, 327; abductivism, 321; arbitrariness, 269; basis of faith in God, 326; coherentism, 135; confirmation

from God's Spirit, 291; import, 285, 293; reasonableness, 314–16, 321; standards, 10, 136, 183, 241, 296; status, 321
epistemically significant, 289, 295
epistemology, xii, 137, 161, 192, 211, 215, 326; pneumatic, 327; religious, 117, 132, 143, 161, 181, 191, 276, 330; resilient, 326; theological, 178
ethics, x–xi, 1–2, 3, 15, 18–19, 22, 83, 87–90, 158, 331; and empowerment, 15; for inquiry, ix–x, 1–3, 19–20, 34, 36–37, 39, 47–53, 87, 116–17, 255–56; for theological inquiry, 19; "of belief", xi; principles of, 2
evidence, 15–18, 44–50, 87–92, 124–31, 143–53, 155–64, 188–94, 279–83, 306–13, 320–25; and the confusion with argument, 117, 135; direct, 91, 128, 243; distinctive, 268, 295–97, 298; divine, 29, 45, 47–49, 112, 131, 150, 213, 282, 304, 330; empirical, 163; experiential, 103, 135, 144, 146, 245, 300, 322; human, 18, 53, 90, 136, 161, 208, 243; interpersonal, 49, 88; intersubjective, 312; New Testament, 174; pre-cooperative, 156, 184, 276; transformative, 156; ultimate, 10, 313, 322; volition-sensitive, 211; withholding of, 149, 190
evil, 3, 8, 66, 67, 74–75, 106–8, 111, 144, 247, 322
existence of God, 116–18, 119–21, 138–40, 142–46, 157–59, 161, 162, 241–42, 279, 329
expectations, xi, 22, 47, 58, 108–9, 177, 194, 249, 273, 308; false, 118; good, 19; meeting divine, 23; moral, 9; redemptive, 40, 108, 153, 159
experience of God, x, 12, 18, 81, 123–25, 161, 184, 239, 242, 245
experiential evidence, 103, 135, 144,

146, 245, 300, 322; basic, 311, 322; direct, 128; distinctive, 296
Ezekiel, 286

faith in God, 68–76, 82–84, 92–96, 98–103, 113–15, 244–45, 268–70, 295–96, 312–14, 322–28; account of, 84, 323; defense of, 46–47, 53–54, 212, 244, 250, 256, 308–9, 328–30; neutral mode of, 69; obedience of, 179, 181; opponents of, 84; Paul's understanding of, 175; reasons for, 311–13; understanding of, 57, 256
Farmer, Herbert H., 12, 132, 138, 146, 239, 318
fideism, 84, 269, 296
filial, 289, 292; language, 290; relationship, 81, 212; theme, 290
forgiveness, 101, 133, 166, 188, 237–38, 243, 261–62, 263, 273, 281; and reconciliation, 122, 129, 213, 254, 262, 267, 278; human, 279; offered by God to humans, 122; see also divine forgiveness, 101
Francis of Assisi, 297
freedom, ix, 16–18, 106, 163, 214–15, 260–61, 270–71, 288; and the response to the problem of divine hiddenness, 163; human, 16–18, 37, 163, 171, 260, 280; value of, x; see also human freedom, ix

Galatian Christians, 290, 291
Gethsemane, 57, 75–83, 85–86, 99, 114–15, 154–55, 179, 182, 188–89, 302–3; and the story of the synoptic gospels, 85; and the weakness of yielding one's own will, 77; approach to God, 154; challenge of, 77; crisis of, 104, 155, 182, 191, 307; experience of, 182; faith, 115; prayer, 104–5; resolution, 232; trial for compassion with God, 105; weakness, 77, 114
Gettier-style problems, 146
Gilson, Etienne, 198–99

God, ix–3, 5–60, 62–147, 149–257, 258–314, 316–17, 322–31; and human life, x, 244, 248–49, 251; and moral character, 7–8, 10–15, 24–25, 30, 90–92, 132–33, 150–52, 157–60, 176–77, 310–11; apprehending in the cross of Christ, 217, 240; "argumentism about", 49, 120; as an elusive personal agent, 119, 143, 157, 191; authoritative power of, 75; belief in, 93, 125, 139, 269, 293, 311–12; betraying of, 14; caring of, 21–24, 27, 149; children of, 106, 212, 290; compassionate, 23, 28, 29–31, 72, 97, 102, 254; curative, 36–37, 39–40, 43, 44–58, 62, 67–68, 83, 117, 188–90, 271–72; empowered, 16, 95, 207; encountering of, 73, 124; enhancing of, 222; existence of, 116–18, 119–21, 138–40, 142–46, 157–59, 161, 162, 241–42, 279, 329; experience of, x, 12, 18, 81, 123–25, 161, 184, 239, 242, 245; grace of, 201; honoring, 18, 98, 101; hope of sharing the glory of, 102; loving of, 81, 110, 112, 162, 164, 323; neglecting of, 30; obeying of, 153, 236, 261; obligating, 95, 100, 264; obligating to approve of a person, 95; perfect, 9, 19–21, 23, 72–74, 87, 91, 259, 261–62, 277, 279; personal, 51, 95–96, 273, 328; receiving of, 175, 247, 263, 286, 292; seeking of, 43, 111, 186; sharing in, 265, 272; Spirit of, 210, 212, 213, 217, 221, 284–90, 295, 298–300, 302, 327; trust in, 11, 56–57, 70–71, 72, 78, 92, 94, 96, 98, 101; understanding of, 247; wisdom of, 201–2, 208–9, 219, 325
God in Christ, 35, 37, 187, 194, 200–1, 203, 212–13, 216, 223, 227–28; portrays philosophy of, 227; self-manifesting of, 187, 210; supreme authority of, 194; the image of, 99, 177, 187, 194, 210, 221–22, 228–30, 293, 297–98, 299
God relationship, 6–9, 55–56, 64, 77–78, 115–16, 192–95, 201–4, 230–32, 245–48, 254–56; and evidence, 49, 116; and faith, 56; of *koinonia*, 86; well-founded, 6
good news, 92, 95, 173, 229, 236, 253, 283, 287–88, 308; and the message of the New Testament writers, 328; and the philosophy of Paul, 251; of God in Christ (*kerygma*), 177, 221–22, 327; of knowing God in Christ, 325
goodness, 15–16, 54, 60, 61–62, 66, 88–90, 107, 109, 261, 266
Gorman, Michael, 216–18
grace, 73–74, 79, 100, 102, 203–4, 211, 214–15, 218, 262, 267; cheap, 159; cognitive, 211, 226, 327; interpersonal, 33; perfect, 262; *see also* divine grace, 33

Heschel, Abraham, 27, 81, 98, 187, 197, 199–200, 232
Hick, John, 18, 78, 127, 138, 163, 187, 226
hiddenness, 162–66, 170, 185, 189–91, 307
history, 27, 92, 113, 140–41, 145, 171, 233, 236, 267–68, 306; human, 132, 171; nomadic, 278; troubled, 61
Holy Spirit, 74, 79, 102, 189, 210, 213, 268, 285–87, 293, 327
human conscience, 52, 109, 154–55, 192, 240, 276
human cooperation, 15, 20, 25, 155, 177, 182, 263–65, 293, 296, 305
human earning, 74, 100, 175, 192
human evidence, 18, 53, 90, 136, 161, 208, 243
human freedom, 16–18, 37, 163, 171, 260, 280
human pride, 39, 50, 100, 161, 203, 235, 266, 322, 325

human reconciliation, 38, 66, 97, 106, 109–10, 117, 176, 188, 238, 245
human willingness, 41, 45, 48, 53, 75, 262

idolatry, 75, 171, 272
imitatio Dei, 7–8, 9, 15, 22, 53, 57, 101, 115, 179
inquiry, x–xi, 1–2, 4–7, 9–15, 19–24, 26–27, 48–50, 86–90, 108–9, 116–18; empirical mode of, 4–5; existential, 10; interpersonal mode of, 3–6, 10, 14–15, 87, 89; irresponsible, 2; scientific mode of, 5, 10, 15; theological, 19
intellectualism, 49, 117, 145, 155–56, 158–60, 183, 192
interpersonal, 4, 87, 110, 211, 217, 257–58, 271, 301; assurance, 51; conduct, 28; evidence, 49, 88; exchange, 257; features, 7; interaction, 5, 15, 257; relationships, 2, 16–17, 19, 22, 26, 28–29, 87, 120–22, 238, 241
intersubjective evidence, 312
Isaac, 121–22, 161, 167
Isaiah, 17, 119, 151, 201, 205, 287, 325
Islam, 7, 62, 119
I-Thou relation in faith in God, 12

Jansenism, 102
Jeremiah, 150, 184, 277
Jesus, 75–77, 79–82, 85–86, 92–93, 102–5, 198–210, 212–17, 219–30, 236–39, 286–94; and the commitment to die to his own will, 77; and the congruence between demeanor and God's character, 204; and the filial use of the term "Abba" ("Father") for God, 289; and the seminal writings of the apologists, 328; and the Spirit of God portrayed by John, 289, 292, 298; as a revelation of God's righteousness, 204; body of, 96, 229; character of,

133, 287; commands "Have faith in God", 92; cross of, 79, 200–3, 207–8, 216, 217, 293–94, 299; crucified, 202, 205, 215, 251, 293; lordship of, 214–15; message of, 202, 209, 223–24; mind of, 178–79; obeys God to the point of death, 104; portrayed by John that his disciples will be known by their *agapē* for others, 136; portrayed by Luke as having come to offer God's forgiveness to humans, 238; portrayed by Luke as linking wisdom to his ministry, 200; portrayed by Mark as being open to changing the redemptive plan, 85; resurrected, 216–17; risen, 180, 201, 209, 211, 213–14, 215–17, 287–90; sets the standard for faith in God, 76; sinners, 104, 203, 251, 293; supplies the representative human self-sacrifice on behalf of humans, 174; the living person of, 198; the mind of, 179, 185; the Spirit of, 220, 288, 299, 330
Jesus Christ *see* Jesus
Jewish Bible, 7, 27, 70, 129, 137, 171, 173, 181, 187, 285
Jewish Christians, 287
Joel, 287
John, 14, 85–86, 167, 168–69, 267–69, 274–75, 288–89, 292, 298–99, 301–2

Käsemann, Ernst, 210
Keck, Leander, 203–4, 206–7, 208–10
Kierkegaard, ix, 8–9, 12, 28, 46, 56
knowing God, 179–80, 197, 201, 223–24, 226–27, 274–75, 277, 298, 301–2, 325; and the consequences for, 179; and the existence of, 125, 179, 226–27, 277, 281, 301; and the implications for, 124; and the opportunities presented to humans for self-sacrifice, 129

koinonia, 15–16, 44–45, 50–58, 73, 77–78, 81–82, 86–88, 105–11, 166–69, 255–56; and God with humans, 82; divine-human, 49, 51, 316; enduring, 84; personal, 7; redemptive, 260; the God, 82, 231

Luke, 8, 31, 42, 130, 174, 200, 237–38, 266, 274, 287–88
Luther, Martin, 28

Mark, 15, 200
Martyn, Louis, 202, 215–16, 251
Matthew, 8, 229, 252, 299
Matthews, W.R., 186–87
Mavrodes, George, 126, 138, 140
Minear, Paul, 151, 156, 165, 170, 251
mode of inquiry, 3–6, 10, 14–15, 87, 89
modesty, 65, 140, 158, 165, 248, 249–50, 312; apologetic, 312; cognitive, 140, 165, 249–50
morally implicated in inquiry about God, 9
morally overwhelming, 48, 57–62, 64, 68, 74, 80, 84, 86, 91, 98
Moser, Paul, 131–33, 135–37, 144, 146–48, 159–60, 242, 243–45, 276–77, 313–14, 316–17
Mother Teresa, 297

Nagel, Thomas, 161, 270
natural theology, 131, 137–39, 142, 144, 159–60, 205–6, 223, 225–27, 241–42, 324–28; arguments over, 131, 137, 144, 159, 225–26, 242, 307, 324–28; philosophical arguments concernng, 137–38, 324; speculative human arguments in, 205; traditional arguments about, 51, 159, 180, 223–26, 269, 307, 324
neo-Platonism, 137
New Testament, 129–32, 136–37, 179–81, 224–26, 250–51, 266–68, 286–87, 304–5, 324, 328; and Christology, 287; and the Greek term for "grace", 33; category of "witness" (*marturia*), 135; evidence for the needed sharing in redemptive self-sacrifice, 174; Greek term for "love", 7; love commandment, 8; scholars, 217; writings, 324
Nicomachean Ethics, 116
Niebuhr, Richard, 2, 68, 103, 203, 318, 322
normative principles, 49, 88

obedience, 95, 104, 175, 178, 182, 220, 292, 293, 298–99, 303; grudging, 220; human, 53, 286; humble, 220; of faith, 95, 98, 175, 303; of Jesus, 154; redemptive, 174, 179; resolute, 94; responsive, 277; spirit-empowered, 286, 292; sympathetic, 41; willing, 179
Old Testament, 203

Pascal, Blaise, 39, 101–2, 162, 163, 235
Paul, 73–74, 77–80, 92–96, 99–104, 200–10, 213–20, 223–26, 288–93, 295–300, 324–28; anchors spiritual wisdom, 219; and his understanding of faith in God, 175; and the First Epistle to the Corinthians, 328; and writings of, 217; attributes to God a claim to self-manifesting suggested in Isaiah, 205, 304; christology of, 203; concurs with the implication of the Johannine writings, 299; doctrine of the Spirit, 214; epistemology for knowing God, 181, 224; highlights the lesson of "weakness (of Jesus) without end", 77, 293; idea of hope from God "not disappointing us", 103; likens Christian life to the Passover sacrifice, 179; links "being empowered in faith" with "giving honor to God", 95, 106, 215; notes "If anyone is in

Christ; there is a new creation: everything old has passed away", 220; perspective on allowing God to supply redemption by divine grace, 78, 211, 214, 217; reports that God has shown God's reality to people, 225; statement of the divine purpose for human weakness, 78

Pensées, 39, 101

Peter, Simon, 14–15, 175, 287, 323–24

1 Peter, 175, 323

Philippians, 293

philosophers, 17–20, 120, 123–26, 137, 193–94, 195–99, 220, 231, 257–59, 277; agnostic, 120; ancient Greek, 193; professional, 228; theistic, 135; traditional, 199; *see also* philosophers of religion, x

philosophers of religion, 44, 162, 167, 194, 301, 330

philosophical theists, 128, 137, 140–41, 144

Plato, 27, 156, 193, 196–97

Platonic Form, 219

Platonism, 137

power of God, 77, 80, 172, 201–2, 205, 207–9, 219, 305, 326, 328

pre-cooperative evidence, 156, 184, 276

pride, 50, 113, 133, 163, 181–82, 204–6, 235, 280, 304, 325; human, 39, 50, 100, 161, 203, 235, 266, 322, 325; intellectual, 160; misplaced, 206; religious, 266; self-exalting, 39; selfish, 50

principle, 2, 19, 49, 56, 88–91, 157, 182, 209, 219; ethical, 2; normative, 49, 88; speculative, 219

probing, 40–44, 141

problems, 49, 106, 112–13, 118, 159–60, 162–66, 171–73, 227, 251, 281; cosmic authority, 161; epistemic, 223; epistemic regress, 135, 223; Gettier-style, 146;

human, 237; intellectual, 165; logical, 144; volitional, 236

proofs, 169, 183, 191, 199, 211–12, 296

propositional content, 72, 94, 284, 305, 315

question-begging, 2, 143–44, 306

Quine, W.V.O., 26

Rahner, Karl, 65, 68, 77, 82, 129, 131, 322

rational, 11, 39, 41, 46, 128, 139–43, 144, 155, 310–12; belief, 39, 311; cogency, 311; credibility, 11; defense, 46; inquirers, 144, 311–12; thought, 310

rationality, 141–43, 155

reasonable doubt, 162

reconciliation, 35, 66, 121–22, 150, 166–68, 235–36, 238–41, 261–62, 273, 278–79; cooperative, 276; deepened, 221; divine, 66, 238; empowered, 229; human, 38, 66, 97, 106, 109–10, 117, 176, 188, 238, 245; interpersonal, 35; personal, 168; person-to-person, 273

redemption, 100–1, 109–10, 150–51, 173–75, 189, 218–19, 262–64, 286, 291, 300; divine, 38–39, 52, 108, 130, 217, 236, 250–51, 259, 262–64, 278; eschatological, 300; gracious, 263; human, 35, 95, 119, 170, 173–74, 179, 202, 212, 241, 262; meriting, 264; personal, 53, 264; plan of, 154, 229; uncoerced, 97, 274; volitional, 281; willing, 170

rejection, 37, 185, 270, 274, 316, 324; final, 99, 233; human, 273, 277

"relationally curative", 36–40, 43, 44–57, 62, 65, 67, 80–84, 108, 164–66, 188–90

relationship theism, 55, 115, 255

responsible inquiry, 2–3, 20–21, 48–50, 51–53, 88–89, 108–9, 116, 143–44, 147–48, 192–94

resurrection, 77, 80, 86, 93, 143–44,
    179, 204, 206, 215–16, 251; bodily,
    217; Christ's, 206, 214; power of
    the, 78; spiritual, 217
Richardson, Alan, 131, 135, 175,
    177–78, 212
Roman Christians, 80, 175, 290,
    293, 295
Rosenberg, Alex, 139, 141, 144
Russell, Bertrand, 145, 158–59,
    168, 252

sacrifice, 22, 161, 171–75, 181–82,
    275; bad, 171–72; destructive,
    171; exemplary, 182; human,
    173; ideal, 173; living, 175, 181;
    perfect, 173, 181; spiritual, 175
salient evidence, ix–x, 2–3, 17–18,
    36–37, 45–50, 90–91, 115–16,
    127–28, 254–55, 275–76; and
    forcing of divine reality on
    humans, 226; and knowledge
    of God's reality, 127; direct, 15;
    firsthand, 47; lacking for God's
    existence, 162; of God, ix, 16,
    20, 42, 87, 90, 191; overlooking
    of, 108, 177; responsible
    appropriation of, 90–91;
    withholding of, 23
Savage, Timothy, 79, 80–81, 83, 218
Schweitzer, Albert, 25
Seachris, Joshua, xii
self-authenticating, 10, 13, 129,
    131–33, 136, 180, 269–70, 304, 308
self-entrustment, 70–71, 95–96,
    218, 263–65, 269; cooperative, 69,
    94–95; human, 74; sympathetic,
    263
self-identifying, 35, 38, 185, 263
self-interest, 31
selfishness, 7, 10, 54, 60, 112–13,
    176, 181–82, 267, 317–18, 323;
    destructive, 133, 304; habitual,
    59–60; human, 50, 168
self-manifesting, 129–33, 151–52,
    179–81, 186–87, 190–92, 203–5,

213–14, 223–25, 265–66, 304–5;
    direct, 51, 179; distinctive, 268;
    divine, 134–35, 150–51, 172, 177,
    179–80, 183–84, 190–91, 204,
    263, 301; divine love, 236; God,
    114, 131, 160, 180, 197, 226, 269;
    human's, 180; interventions,
    134–36; irreplaceable, 224;
    redemptive, 138; Spirit, 217, 226,
    300, 304; unique, 205
self-offering (divine), 167
self-sacrifice, 50, 170, 172, 176;
    activity of, 129, 169; agapeic,
    299; intentional, 173; mutual,
    167; perfect, 173–74; power of,
    130, 175
semantic, 89, 117–18
Socrates, 193, 195–96, 197–98, 201
speculative principles, 219
Spirit's witnessing, 212, 284, 288–89,
    298, 299, 305
Stewart, James S., 131–32
submission, 77, 208, 244
sufferings, 28, 37–38, 79–80, 86, 102,
    106, 108, 213, 215, 293
sympathetic cooperation see also
    cooperation, 41, 44, 98, 100,
    167, 168–69, 235–36, 240–41,
    261, 264
sympathetic meaning, 52

Taylor, A.E., 196
Taylor, John, 175, 271
Taylor, Vincent, 172–73
Teresa, Mother, 297
theists, 120, 137–39, 141–45, 248–49
theodicy, 25, 65, 108, 144, 247, 322
Thielicke, Helmut, 169, 190
transformation, 54, 90, 99, 181–82,
    293, 301; inward, 221; moral-
    character, 77, 149, 281; personal,
    x–xi, 26; redemptive, 98
transformative, 11, 39, 87, 156,
    228, 275–76, 301; evidence, 156;
    experience, 301; extent, 276;
    power, 275

trial, xi, 26–29, 31, 33–34, 36, 38, 44–48, 52–53, 106, 108–9; faith's, x, 75; self-imposed, 28–29; shared, 112; twofold, 28
truth-indicator, 125, 316, 320

unbelief, 16
unselfish love, 10–12, 24, 42, 58, 102–3, 107, 110–13, 170, 316–18, 323

volitional cooperation, 5, 58, 86, 128, 294, 329
volitional dissonance, 11
volitional pressure, 12, 15

wisdom, x, 51–53, 192–206, 208–9, 215–16, 217–20, 222, 228, 230, 325–26; and the power, 205, 218; eloquent, 202, 204; evaluative, 195; love and pursuit of, 197–98, 228; of God, 201–2, 208–9, 219, 325; plausible words of, 201, 305, 326; practical, 195; real, 195; spiritual, 218–19; true, 201, 205; worldly, 206–8, 224
worthy of worship, 11–12, 43–44, 62, 87–88, 116–17, 193–94, 225–26, 242, 259–63, 330–31
Wright, G. Ernest, 64, 121, 129, 143–44
Wright, N.T., 143
writers, 169, 246–47, 268–69, 274–75, 278, 284, 285–86, 298, 326, 328; biblical, 41, 45, 54, 137, 150, 171, 284, 308, 310; Christian, 198; Plato, 201; theological, 28

CPSIA information can be obtained
at www.ICGtesting.com
Printed in the USA
LVHW111754230820
663954LV00001B/19